HOW TO CU

ERADI

HOW TO CULTIVATE VIRTUES AND ERADICATE VICES

Sri Swami Sivananda

Published by

THE DIVINE LIFE SOCIETY

P.O. SHIVANANDANAGAR—249 192

Distt. Tehri-Garhwal, Uttarakhand, Himalayas, India

www.sivanandaonline.org, www.dlshq.org

First Edition: 1952
Eleventh Edition: 2020

(1,000 Copies)

ISBN 81-7052-059-2

ES 64

PRICE: ₹ 180/-

Published by Swami Padmanabhananda for The Divine Life
Society, Shivanandanagar, and printed by him at the Yoga-Vedanta
Forest Academy Press, P.O. Shivanandanagar,
Distt. Tehri-Garhwal, Uttarakhand, Himalayas, India
For online orders and Catalogue visit : dlsbooks.org

Om
Dedicated to
Parents and Teachers
Leaders and Preachers
Who mould the characters
Of men and women

PUBLISHERS' NOTE

This volume would rank foremost among the works of H.H. Sri Swami Sivanandaji Maharaj. In this he has presented to the men and women of the present-day world a theme that is dearest to his heart and that would transform men into gods and nations into paradise on earth.

The keynote of Sri Swamiji's teachings is Righteousness in thought, word and deed, the cultivation of a sterling character, and the practice of the Religion of the Heart. In this respect, he is like Lord Buddha. But, like Lord Krishna, Sri Swamiji explicitly declares that righteousness is a means to an end, i.e., Jnana or Self-knowledge. This has a direct appeal to the soul of man.

Every one of Swamiji's books has uniformly stressed this aspect of Sadhana—Cultivation of Virtues and Eradication of Vices. Whenever Swamiji has spoken, at mass meetings or individual conversations, he has thundered: "It is only through Righteousness that you can attain the Supreme Reality."

In this volume Sri Swamiji Maharaj has given us a sweet garland of all the virtues that should adorn every earnest Sadhaka; and we offer it to the readers with our sincere prayer that it might ennoble them and divinise them, make them better and more successful men and women who would make the world they live in a vast home of peace and brotherhood.

8th September, 1952.   —THE DIVINE LIFE SOCIETY

INTRODUCTION

ETHICS AND MORALITY

Ethical culture will result in ethical perfection. An ethical man is more powerful than an intellectual man. Ethical culture brings in various sorts of occult powers.

Morality goes hand in hand with spirituality. Morality co-exists with spirituality. Ethical culture prepares you for Vedantic realisation of 'Sarvam Khalvidam Brahma'—all indeed is Brahman. There is no such thing as diversity.

All aspirants commit the mistakes in jumping to Samadhi and meditation all at once as soon as they leave their houses without caring a bit for ethical purification.

The essentials of moral life are: straightforwardness, honesty, mercy, humility, respect for life, tender regard for every creature that breathes, absolute unselfishness, truthfulness, celibacy, non-injury, non-covetousness, absence of vanity and hypocrisy, and cosmic love.

A man of right conduct has ideal principles and mottoes. He strictly follows them, removes his weaknesses and defects, develops good conduct and becomes a Sattvic man.

Righteousness is eternal. Do not leave the path of righteousness even if your life is in danger. A righteous, virtuous life and a clear conscience give great deal of comfort to man while living and at the time of his death also. Sound character is the only diamond you must crave to wear. Virtues are conducive to Self-knowledge.

Immortality can be attained only by performing acts of kindness constantly and sticking to ethical principles.

Practice of charitable acts, compassion and kind services purify and soften the heart, turn the heart-lotus upwards and prepare the aspirant for the reception of divine light.

The practice of truth, austerities, celibacy and self-restraint are all auxiliaries in the attainment of the knowledge of the Eternal.

Humility is the highest of all virtues. God helps you only when you feel utterly humble. Therefore develop this virtue to a considerable degree. Virtue will develop and survive only when practised positively and actively.

The law of non-injury is as much exact and precise as the law of gravitation. If you can be fully established in the practice of non-violence in thought, word and deed, you are God.

The path of Ahimsa is narrow, but if you practise Ahimsa in right earnest, you can easily travel the path, since you cannot but get the divine grace at every step.

A holy man with piety is far superior to the mighty kings of countries. God is much pleased with a pious man.

A man who keeps up his promise creates a very good impression on the minds of others and merges in Divinity.

Cultivate sympathy, love, mercy and sincerity and other divine virtues described in the Gita. Lead a well-regulated life. Moral strength is the backbone of spiritual progress. Ethical culture is part and parcel of spiritual Sadhana.

RELIGION: THE BASIS OF MORALITY

Morality is the quality of being moral. Morality is that in an action which renders it right or wrong. It is the practice of moral duties apart from religion.

Morality is the doctrine of the right and wrong in human conduct. It is virtuous life. Sometimes in a limited sense it means sexual purity.

Morality is virtue. Morality is ethics. It is the doctrine which treats of actions being right or wrong.

Morality is everywhere the same, because it comes from God.

Morality is religion in practice; religion is morality in principle.

What you ought to do, that you should do and that you must do, though it brings pain and loss. Why? Because, it is right.

You must do what is right at whatever cost of pain and loss.

All successful actions stand on the foundation of morality.

Morality without religion has no roots. It becomes a thing of custom, changeable, transient and optional.

There can be no high civility, no courtesy, no politeness, no elegant manners without a profound morality.

There is no true and abiding morality that is not founded on religion.

There can be no divorse of religion from morality. Morality is the basis of religion. Morality and religion are inseparable like heat and fire, coolness and ice, fragrance and flower.

Morality without religion is a tree without roots, a house built on the sand, a stream without any spring to feed it.

Discourses on morality are the best means to improve the character of man and recover him out of his vices and ignorance.

Morality must not be without religion. If so, it may change as you see inconveniences. Religion must govern it.

The morality of an action depends upon the motive from which you act. First have righteous principles and then you will not fail to do virtuous actions.

National morality cannot prevail in an exclusion of religious principle.

Without religion, morality will die. Religion is the very root of morality.

Put morality on its proper and right basis, viz., the fear and love of God.

Morals without religion will wither and die like a seed sown upon stony ground.

Morality is the doctrine of moral duties in life or of men in their social character.

Morality without God is bottomless impiety.

MORALITY AND ETHICS

The moral principles are not absolute in the sense that there is a state which transcends moral restrictions. But it does not mean that the moral laws can be neglected. Morality is the adherence to the inherent sense of the right which is voiced by the conscience that is not bound by selfishness and its several expressions or effects. Morality is the soul-sense, the truth-sense, which refuses to be restricted by the autocracy of the passions that disregard the universality of what is good, and which is free from the agony of imperfection. The purpose of the moral sense is to point out the way to perfection, and morality, therefore, can be judged from how far it directs the consciousness to unrestricted happiness which is not confined to one or some individuals or even to a part of the universe or merely to an aspect of existence. The wider the scope of the selfless consciousness and the joy consequent upon it, the

more moral is the method with which such selflessness is practised or the act by which such selflessness is expressed. All
selfish actions are immoral. What, then, is selfish action? It is
an action which is intended to bring satisfaction to the senses
and the ego of one's own individual being, without any intention to overcome the desires of the senses and the ego. In
addition to those positive indulgences, immoral action includes other acts like causing harm, practising falsehood
and committing theft, either in thought or word or deed. Passion, anger, greed, pride and jealousy are immoral qualities.
Even benevolence cannot justify the violation of moral rules.
Morality is "a great vow which is universal, not restricted either by conditions, states, places, times or circumstances."
(Yoga-Sutras)

CONTENTS

PART 1

HOW TO CULTIVATE VIRTUES

PART II

HOW TO ERADICATE VICES

PART I
How to Cultivate Virtues

ABSTINENCE

Abstinence is abstaining or refraining especially from some indulgence. Abstinence is temperance.

Abstinence is the act, practice or state of abstaining from
something or some act or practice especially a total abstaining
from the use of intoxicating drinks; self-denial, self-restraint as
abstinence from the pleasure of the table, abstinence from
alcoholic beverages, sexual indulgence.

Abstinence is refraining from an indulgence of appetite or
from customary gratifications of animal propensities. We speak
of abstinence from meat, abstinence from whisky, abstinence
from food or sexual indulgence.

Total abstinence is the specific name for the act and
practice of refraining from the use of intoxicating liquors.

Abstinence is continued temperance which gives longevity,
good health, and keeps the body free from diseases.

Abstinence is a discipline which gives Vairagya or
dispassion and helps the aspirant to march forward in the path
of Yoga. Abstinence is the practice of Yama or self-restraint. It
is the ground-work of virtue.

Abstinence is the strongest fence against diseases. It is the
defensive virtue against ailments. It is the bestower of radiant
health, vim, vigour and vitality.

Give up tea or coffee or smoking for a week. This will give
you strength or will-power for the next abstinence. The third abstinence will be more easy.

The aim of abstinence is to set the mind above the lower appetites. It is indeed an aid for self-improvement.

Abstemiousness, continence, fasting, moderation,
self-control, self-denial, self-restraint, sobriety, temperance are
synonymous with abstinence.

Drunkenness, excess, gluttony, greed, intemperance,
intoxication, revelling, revelry, self-indulgence, sensuality, wan-
tonness are the opposites of abstinence.

Abstinence from food commonly signifies going without it.
Abstemiousness is partaking moderately. Abstinence may be
for a single occasion. Abstemiousness is habitual moderation.

Self-denial is giving up what one wishes. Abstinence may be refraining from what one does not desire. Fasting is abstinence from food for a limited time and generally for religious reasons. Sobriety and temperance signify maintaining a quiet, even temper by moderate indulgence in something, complete abstinence from others. We speak of temperance in eating, but of abstinence from vice.

ADAPTABILITY

Adaptability is a virtue or noble quality by which one adapts or fits himself to others, whatever their nature may be. A man of adaptability accommodates himself with others, whatever their temperaments may be. This is a most desirable habit or quality for success in life. This has to be developed slowly. The vast majority of persons do not know how to adjust themselves with others. Adaptability is a peculiar knack or pluck to win the hearts of others and ultimately the battle of life by a little bit of bending.

The wife does not know how to adapt herself to her husband. She displeases her husband always and makes room for quarrels in the house and gets a divorce. The clerk does not know how to adapt himself to his boss or superior. He quarrels with him and gets an immediate sack. The disciple does not know how to adapt himself to his Guru. The business man does not know how to adapt himself to the customers and therefore loses his customers and business! The Dewan does not know how to adapt himself to the Maharajah. He has to leave the state service. The world runs on adaptability. He who knows the art or science of adaptability pulls on quite well in this world and is always happy under all conditions of life.

The man must be pliable if he wants to adapt himself. It does need much wisdom and ingenuity for developing adaptability. If the clerk understands well the ways, habits and temperament of his superior and accordingly adjust himself nicely to suit his ways, his superior becomes a slave of the clerk. You will have to use some kind words and castoroil. A little lubricant to soften his heart is all that is needed. That is all. Speak gently and sweetly. Carry out his orders to the very letter. Never retort him. Remember the maxim: "Obedience is greater than service." The superior wants a little respect. Say "Hanji-Hanji, Ji-huzur, very well Sir." It costs you nothing. Then your superior becomes your slave. He has for you a soft corner in his heart. You become his pet. He will do whatever you want. He will excuse your mistakes. Humility and obedience are necessary for developing adaptability. That egoistic, proud man finds it very difficult to adapt himself. He is always in trouble. He always fails in his attempts. Egoism and pride are two important and insurmountable obstacles in the way of developing adaptability.

When one student does not know how to adapt himself to his fellow students who are living in the same room, friction comes and their friendship is at stake. Adaptability makes friendship last for a long time. Students fight for little things. One student says: "I gave Mr. X tea for several days. I took him to the cinema on my own account for many days. I asked him to lend me the book 'Boswell's Life of Johnson' for reading. He has bluntly refused now. What sort of friend he is! I do not like him at all." Thus the friendship is broken now. A simple thing upsets the mind. Adaptability is a strong catgut ligature that links people in bonds of unbroken love and friendship. A man of adaptability can pull on with anybody in any part of the world. People unconsciously love a man of adaptability. Adaptability gives immense strength and profound joy. Adaptability develops will.

A man of adaptability has to make some sacrifice. Adaptability develops the spirit of sacrifice. It kills selfishness. A man of adaptability has to share what he has with others. He has to bear insult and hard words. A man of adaptability develops the feeling of unity or oneness of life. For Vedantic Sadhana it is of invaluable help.

He who practises adaptability has to destroy the feelings of Ghrina, contempt and the idea of superiority. He has to mix with all. He has to embrace all. Adaptability develops universal love and kills the feeling of hatred.

A man of adaptability has to put up with the unkind words of his fellowmen. He has to develop patience and endurance. These virtues develop by themselves when he tries to adapt himself with others. A man of adaptability can live in any environment. He can bear the heat of Benares or Africa. He can live in a hut. He can live in a cool place. He develops balance of mind. He can bear extreme heat and cold. Adaptability brings eventually Atma-Jnana. He who has this noble virtue is a great man in all the three worlds. He is always happy and successful.

ADVERSITY

I

Adversity is adverse circumstance. It is affliction or misfortune or calamity.

Adversity is a state or condition characterised by untoward, harassing circumstances, severe trial or affliction. It is opposed to prosperity. Adversity is an event or series of events which oppose success or desires. It is a state of unhappiness.

Adversity is a blessing in disguise. Sweet are the uses of adversity. It strengthens the will power and the power of endurance and turns the mind more and more towards God. It instils dispassion or Vairagya in the heart. It is the first path to truth.

Adversity is a virtue. It makes the idle industrious. It draws out the faculties of the wise. It puts a man to the necessity of trying his skill. It has the effect of eliciting talents, capacities which in prosperous circumstances have remained dormant.

It is easy to bask in the sunshine of prosperity. The crucial test is your conduct under hardship and adversity.

Do not put on a sad countenance when you are in adverse circumstances. Smile. Laugh. Rejoice. Draw power and strength from within. Sing Ram, Ram, Ram. Chant Om, Om, Om. There is a magazine of power and knowledge and bliss within in your own Soul or Atman. Feel this. Realise this.

A smooth ocean never made one a dexterous Captain of a ship or an Admiral. The storms of adversity rouse the faculties and talents of an individual and generate prudence, skill, fortitude, courage, patience and perseverance. Adversity makes one think, invent and discover.

When you are in a prosperous condition, you will have countless friends, but when you are in adversity, they will leave you. Adversity is the only balance to weigh friends; prosperity is no just scale.

You will learn many lessons during adversity. Adversity will mould you properly. It is your great teacher. It is the best and severe instructor.

Great persons and saints have been tried, smelted, polished and glorified through the furnace of adversity.

Adversity is highly beneficial. Do not weep when you are in adverse conditions. Adversity strengthens your nerves and sharpens your skill.

Bereavement, calamity, disaster, distress, hardship, ill-fortune, misfortune are synonymous with adversity.

Any considerable disappointment, failure, misfortune, such as loss of fortune, position and the like constitutes adversity.

For the loss of friends or relations by death we commonly use the term bereavement.

Calamity and disaster are used for sudden and severe misfortunes, often overwhelming; ill-fortune and ill-luck of lighter troubles and failures.

We speak of the misery of the poor, the hardship of the soldier.

Blessing, boon, happiness, prosperity, success are the opposites of adversity.

II

You will find in the writings of Shakespeare, "Sweet are the uses of adversity which, like the toad, ugly and venomous, wears yet on its head a precious jewel." The best thing in this world is pain or adversity. During pain only man remembers God. Pain is the eye-opener. The quest of God begins from pain. The starting point of philosophy is from pain. Had there not been pain in this world, man would never have attempted to get freedom (Moksha). He would have been satisfied with mundane life only. In trying to get rid of pain, he comes across Truth or the abode of Peace, Parama-Dhama. He starts prayer, Japa, charity, selfless service, study of religious books, etc. Bhaktas always pray to God, "O Lord! Give us sufferings always so that we shall ever remember Thee." Kunti Devi prayed to Lord Krishna, "Hae Prabhu, let me always have adversity, so that my mind shall be ever fixed at Thy lotus feet." Adversity develops power of endurance and will-force. Adversity develops fortitude and forbearance. Adversity melts a stony heart and infuses devotion to God. Adversity is a divine blessing in disguise. Do not be afraid, therefore, when you are in adverse circumstances. Adversity has got its own virtues. People have risen to power and position from adverse conditions of life. Adversity makes a man to struggle hard. The late Sir T. Muthuswami Iyer, Chief Justice, High Court, Madras, was in adverse circumstances.

He used to study at night under a municipal street lantern. Many Prime Ministers of England had risen high from adverse conditions of life. All the prophets, saints, Fakirs, Bhaktas, Yogins of yore had to struggle hard in adverse circumstances. Sankara, Jnana Deva, Rama Tirtha and Tukaram were all highly benefitted by adversity. They would never have achieved greatness and glorious spiritual heights had they been placed in luxurious conditions.

AHIMSA

(1) Let not anyone injure life, but be as assiduous in cherishing the life of another as his own. For Ahimsa is the highest religion.
—*Tirthankara Mahavira.*

(2) So let us for all creatures, great or small, develop such a boundless heart and mind. Aye, let us practise love for all the world.
—*Goutama Buddha.*

(3) Thou shalt not kill.
—*Jesus Christ.*

(4) He who saveth a life, shall be as though he had saved all mankind alive. (For) there is no beast on earth nor bird which flieth with its wings but the same is a people like unto you.
—*Mohammed (Koran, VI-38).*

(5) A man should prefer good to harm, good deeds to sins, virtue to vice, light to darkness.
—*Zoroaster.*

(6) One Self dwells in all. All are manifestations of the One God. By injuring another you injure your own self. By serving another you serve your own self. Love all. Serve all. Hate none. Insult none. Injure none, in thought, word or deed.
—*Swami Sivananda.*

ALERTNESS

Alertness is watchfulness. It is briskness. It is sprightliness.

Alertness is an attitude of vigilance. It is used principally in the phrase 'on the alert' as 'the watchman stood on the alert.'

A captain of a ship is ever alert. A fisherman is ever alert. A surgeon in the operation theatre is ever alert. Even so a thirsting, hungry aspirant, should be ever alert. Then alone can he curb and subdue this mischievous, turbulent and formidable mind. Alertness is an important qualification of a student in the path of Yoga.

Be on the alert. Have an alert attitude. Be on the lookout. Be ever ready. Be circumspect. Be watchful. Be vigilant. You will always attain success in all undertakings and spiritual Sadhana.

A man of alertness is keenly watchful. He is ready to act at a short notice. He is nimble like the squirrel. He is characterised by briskness.

An alert man is lively. He is prompt and ever prepared. He is wide awake.

'Alert', 'ready' and 'wide awake' refer to a watchful promptness for action.

'Ready' suggests thoughtful preparation. The wandering Indian is alert; the trained soldier is ready.

'Ready' expresses more life and vigour than 'prepared.' The gun is prepared. The man is ready.

'Prompt' expresses readiness for appointment or demand at the required moment. The good General is ready for emergencies, alert to perceive opportunity or peril, prompt to seize the occasion.

The sense of brisk 'nimble' is the secondary and now less common signification of alertness.

Drowsy, dull, heavy, inactive, sluggish, stupid are the opposites of 'alert'.

Let a pastor live in a state of alertness toward all resources of oratorical knowledge. Let magistrates alertly perform their parts.

The French are alert rather than spontaneous.

AMIABILITY

Amiability is the quality of being amiable or of exciting love.

A man of amiability is of sweet disposition. He radiates so much of mental sunshine, love and joy that he is reflected in all appreciative hearts.

Amiability is the constant desire to please and love others.

Amiability is kindness or sweetness of disposition. It is loveableness.

A man of amiability possesses the agreeable mood or social qualities that please and make friends. He is friendly or pleasing in disposition. He is kind-hearted, gracious, genial. He has good nature. He is free from irritation. He possesses sweetness of temper, kind-heartedness, excellent lovable disposition.

Kind smiles and courteousness pay high dividends.

The man of amiable character has ready affection and kindliness for others, with the qualities that are adapted to win their love. Amiable is a higher and stronger word than good-natured or agreeable.

'Amiable' denotes a disposition desirous to cheer, please and make happy. The really amiable man avoids harsh words and rudeness. He has an easy disposition to get along comfortably with every one in all circumstances.

Kind, good-natured people may be coarse and rude.

Abominable, churlish, cruel, disagreeable, hateful, ill-tempered, unlovely, unamiable are the opposites of "amiable."

Cultivate amiability. Let it become part and parcel of your nature.

APPLICATION

Application comes from the root *applicatio*, a binding on, or joining to; from *applicatus*, to join or fasten to. It is the art of fixing the mind. There is intensity of thought in application. It is close study.

Application is diligence. Application is close thought and attention. Assiduity is application.

Application is the testing or carrying into effect of a general law, truth or precept by bringing it into relation with practical affairs or applying it to a particular cause. It is also the capacity of being thus used or means of result of such action as the application of the Sermon on the Mount or the Yogic Yama-Niyama in daily life.

Application is the fixing of the attention closely on that upon which one is engaged; also the habit or capability of so fixing it.

Steady application to work is the healthiest training for every individual.

In common parlance we say: "Mr. John injured his health by application to study." We also say: "Had his application been equal to his talents, his progress might have been greater."

A man who is endowed with the virtue of application gets success in all his undertakings. Prosperity is his attendant.

A man of application rises up early and goes to bed at the proper time. He never wastes even a single second. He is ever watchful, vigilant and diligent. He is ever active. He never loses opportunities. He is like the surgeon in the operation theatre. He is like the captain in a ship.

He is healthy. His mind is light and cheerful. His thoughts are clear. His room is in order. He is methodical in his work. He has resolution and determination. He never repents nor regrets.

He is wealthy. He is free from want. He rises to power and eminence. He attains fame. He is honoured and respected.

Whatever you resolve to do, do it now, do it quickly. Tarry not a second. Defer not till the evening what you can accomplish in the morning.

This moment is yours. The next second is in the womb of the future. You know not what it may bring forth.

Do not depend much upon the future. Do not regret for the past. Live in the living, solid present. Act, act, act now. Strive, strive, strive now. Exert, exert, exert. Apply all your vigour, strength and energy. You are bound to succeed. You will surmount easily all sorts of temptations and obstacles. Failure is unknown to a man of intense application.

Without intense application you cannot enter into deep meditation and Samadhi.

Sloth, inertia, idleness, carelessness, recklessness, procrastination are the opposites of application.

O Ram! Cultivate application and attain success, plenty, peace and prosperity and Kaivalya now and here.

ASPIRATION

Aspiration is burning desire to attain God-realisation.

To aspire is to desire eagerly or to aim at high things.

God is the one true aim of all right human aspirations.

Aspiration is earnest longing or an earnest wish for that which is above one's present reach or attainment, especially for what is noble, pure and spiritual.

To aspire is to rise or reach upward. To aspire is to have an earnest desire, wish or longing as for something high and good, not yet attained usually accompanied by endeavour to attain it.

ATTENTION

Attention is steady application of the mind.

Attention is the direction of the mental powers to a specific object with vigour and concentration.

Attention strengthens the will. It is at the base of the will. Attention develops concentration.

Attention leads to sure success. It is for want of attention that man meets with failures.

Attention makes the genius. The power of applying attention, steady and undissipated to a single object is the sure mark of a superior genius.

All learning, science and skill depend upon attention. Attention opens new worlds, heals diseases.

Attention is the source of poetic genius and of the genius of discovery and success.

It was attention that led Newton to the discovery of gravitation, Hervey to find out the circulation of the blood, and Davy to those views which laid the foundation of modern chemistry.

Attention is a form of psychical energy which necessarily enters into the determination of the character of every field of consciousness.

It is the act or process of giving especial clearness to one or more particulars in the complex content of consciousness.

It is the form of mental functioning or faculty which makes possible the selection of certain of the contents of consciousness, for the purpose of giving to them an increasing clearness.

The general fact of experience from which the conception and doctrine of attention in modern psychology take their rise is that some objects or parts of objects in the field of consciousness are more clearly and vividly impressed than others or are apperceived and recognised, while others are only dimly or scarcely at all apprehended. This difference in clearness often seems to be dependent on a selective act or process of the subject. In reflex or non-voluntary attention the object seems to force itself upon the mind either through the intensity of the stimulus or the advantage of special interest. In voluntary attention, the subject in order to gratify curiosity or carry out some other purpose seems to choose the object which shall be more clearly apprehended.

A man hears with attention. Then we say: "He has an attentive ear." He sees with attention. Then we say: "He has an attentive eye." In contemplation one has application of the mind. When a man is attentive to the words of a speaker and to the manner and matter of his speech at the same time, he has application of the mind and the senses, too.

BEHAVIOUR

Behaviour is conduct, manners or deportment, especially good manners.

To behave well is to conduct well with others.

You can know the nature of a man and the nature of his mind from his behaviour.

Behaviour is a mirror in which every one shows his image.

Good behaviour is a passport for friendship and favourable reception in society.

Knowledge gives confidence to the outward behaviour.

Levity of behaviour or lightness of conduct is the bane of life.

Oddities and singularities of behaviour, whimsical peculiarities are blemishes of a man. He should correct himself and remove these defects. He who wants to improve himself must be ashamed of these defects.

To observe propriety in personal conduct is good behaviour. To conduct in a fitting or proper manner is good behaviour.

Behaviour is an expression of knowledge and taste and feeling in combination.

Behaviour is our action in the presence of others. Conduct implies personality and moral responsibility.

Carriage expresses simply the manner of holding the body, especially in sitting or walking as when it is said of lady "She has a fain carriage."

Bearing refers to the bodily expression of feeling or disposition, as a haughty bearing, a noble bearing.

Demeanour is the bodily expression, not only of feelings, but of moral states, as a devout demeanour.

Breeding denotes that manner or conduct which result from good birth and training.

Deportment is behaviour as related to a set of rules as "the students' deportment was faultless."

A person's manner may be that of a moment or toward a single person; his manners are his habitual style or behaviour toward or before others, especially in matters of etiquette and politeness, as 'good manners are always pleasing.'

Behaviour is the manner of our behaving ourselves towards others.

Conduct is the manner of our conducting ourselves and involves the general tenor of our actions. The former, like deportment, is shaped chiefly by circumstances; the latter is a development of the individual.

Behaviourism is the study of the individual based on objective analysis and personal behaviour. The theory that all investigation of behaviour must be objective and introspection is invalid.

BENEVOLENCE

Benevolence. Latin: *Benevolentia*, good feeling; *bene*—well, and *volens*—to wish.

Benevolence is disposition to do good. It is gift of money, especially for support of the poor. It is an act of kindness. It is generosity.

Benevolence is the disposition to seek the well-being or comfort of others. It is the desire to alleviate suffering or promote happiness. It is love of mankind or kindliness of heart or charitableness.

Benevolence is the all-inclusive virtue. In order to attain the perfection of benevolence itself the moral judgment of men requires all the other most cardinal virtues both of will and of judgment. All these other cardinal virtues qualify benevolence, as benevolence employs, consecrates and qualifies them.

Benevolence is the natural organ or propensity that prompts to kindness and liberality.

Benevolence is the minister of God. It is a rare virtue.

To feel much for others and little for ourselves, to restrain our selfish and excercise our benevolent affections, constitutes the perfection of human nature.

No one in this world is perfectly independent. He is in need of the assistance of others. Man is placed in society to receive and confer reciprocal helps and mutual obligations.

Your food, your clothes, your health, your protection from injuries, your enjoyment of the comforts and pleasures of life—all these you owe to the assistance of others. Therefore, be benevolent to others. Be a cosmic benefactor. Be a friend to mankind.

The conqueror is regarded with awe; the wise man commands our respect, but it is only the benevolent man who wins our affection.

A benevolent man enjoys peace, joy and tranquillity. He rejoices in the happiness and prosperity of his neighbour and all other people.

He who employs his wealth, his thought, his speech, to advance the good of others is a glorious man. He is a veritable god on this earth.

He always searches out occasions for doing good to others in a variety of ways.

The laws of social benevolence require that every man should endeavour to assist others.

Barbarity, brutality, churlishness, greediness, harshness, ill-liberality, illwill, inhumanity, malevolence, malignity, niggardliness, selfishness, stinginess, unkindness are the opposites of benevolence.

Alms-giving, beneficence, benignity, bounty, charity, generosity, goodwill, humanity, kind-heartedness, kindliness, kindness, liberality, munificence, philanthropy, sympathy, tenderness, are all synonymous with benevolence.

Kindness and tenderness are personal. Benevolence and charity are general. Kindness extends to all sentient beings whether men or animals, in prosperity or in distress. Tenderness especially goes out towards the young, feeble and needy. Humanity is kindness and tenderness toward man or beast. Generosity is self-forgetful kindness in disposition or action. It includes much besides giving.

Bounty applies to ample-giving, which on a larger scale is expressed by munificence.

Liberality indicates broad, genial, kindly views, whether manifested in gifts or otherwise.

We speak of the bounty of a generous host, the liberality of the founder of a college, or of the liberality of a theologian toward the holders of conflicting beliefs.

Philanthropy applies to wide schemes for human welfare often, but not always, involving large expenditure in charity or benevolence:

Do not wait for extraordinary circumstances to do good actions. Try to utilise ordinary situations.

CHARACTER

Character is the aggregate of peculiar qualities which constitute an individuality.

Character is the combination of qualities distinguishing any person or class of persons. It is any distinctive mark or trait of a person.

Character is power. Character is everything. Character is real property. It is the noblest of all possessions.

Character is perfectly educated will. It is higher than intelligence.

Every man is the architect of his own character. You sow an action, and reap a habit. You sow a habit and reap a character.

Actions, looks, words, steps, form the alphabet by which you may spell characters.

A man is known by what he loves—friends, places, books, dress, food, thoughts, actions, speech; from these his character is told.

Determination to build definite character in life is needed. This must be followed up with persistent striving.

All that is lasting is your character. You can take nothing else with you save your character when you leave the world.

Character is not born. It is formed.

The noblest contribution which any man can make for the benefit of posterity is that of a good character.

Character is a diamond that scratches any other stone.

Character lives and abides.

Good nature, benevolence, truthfulness, tolerance, temperance, justice, etc. lie at the foundation of character.

Character is the end and aim of all your intellectual discipline.

Character is the produce of self-discipline. The grand aim of man's creation is the development of a grand character.

Character is more worthy of attainment than anything else in this world.

The richest bequest which any man can leave to the world is that of a shining, spotless example.

The essential factors in character building are morality, truthfulness, justice, temperance, wisdom, nobility, nonviolence, purity and benevolence.

Nothing in this world—wealth, name, fame, victory—is worth a fig or a straw without character. Character must stand behind and back up everything.

It is not wealth or power nor is it mere intellect that governs the world. It is moral character associated with moral excellence that really rules the entire universe.

Character is not developed in a day. It is created bit by bit and day by day.

Wealth comes and goes. Fame evaporates. Power dwindles. Only one thing endures. That is Character.

Strong character is formed by strong and noble thinking.

A man's true estate of power and wealth lies in his own essential character.

Take care of your character. Your reputation will take care of itself.

A good character is the fruition of personal exertion. It is the result of one's own endeavours.

Truthfulness is a corner-stone in character.

Not education, but character, is man's greatest need and greatest safeguard.

There is no single royal road to build your character. A variety of routes will always need to be used.

Build your character; you can shape your life.

Character is power. Character is influence. It makes friends. It draws patronage and support. It creates friends and funds. It opens a sure and easy way to wealth, honour, success and happiness.

Character is the determining factor in victory and defeat, success and failure and in all the issues of life. A man of good character enjoys life herein and hereafter.

Man is not a creature of circumstances. He is really the architect of circumstances. A man of character builds an existence out of circumstances. He steadily perseveres and plods.

He does not look back. He marches forward bravely. He is not afraid of obstacles. He never frets and fumes. He never gets discouraged and disappointed. He is full of vigour, energy, vim and vitality. He is ever zealous and enthusiastic.

Small kind acts, small courtesies, small consideration, small benevolence, habitually practised in your social intercourse give a greater charm to your character than great platform lectures, discourses, oration, exhibition of talents, etc.

Character is like an inward and spiritual grace of which reputation is the outward and visible sign.

Character is what one is: reputation, what he is thought to be. His record is the total of his actions. A man's record will substantially express his character. His reputation may be higher or lower than his character or record will justify. One's nature includes all his original endowments or propensities; character includes both natural and acquired traits.

Character is the peculiar quality impressed by nature or habit on a person which distinguishes him from others.

Dominant characters are, in heredity, the predominant characteristics which are transmitted by either parent to the offspring with little or no variations and which form the prevailing characters.

Recessive characters are characters found in the offspring which may be referred to one or the other of the parental forms, but which are not the prevailing characters. In subsequent generations, the recessive characters never predominates.

CHARITY

I

Charity is alms-giving. It is the disposition to think favourably of others and do them good. Charity is universal love. It is liberality to the poor. It is benevolence. That which is given to relieve the needy is charity.

In a general sense, charity means love, benevolence and goodwill. In a theological sense it is universal goodwill to men and supreme love of God. In a more particular sense, it means love, kindness, affection, tenderness, springing from natural relations as the charities of father, son and brother.

True charity is the desire to be useful to others without thought of recompense or reward.

He who is least unjust is the most charitable in his judgement.

The deeds of charity you have done will stay for ever with you.

Give cheerfully, quickly and without hesitation.

Give one-tenth of your income or one anna per rupee in charity.

Charity covereth multitude of sins. Charity is a great purifier of the heart.

Prayer takes you halfway to God, fasting to the door of His Supreme Abode and charity procures you admission.

Charity is love in action.

Charity begins at home, but it should go abroad. The whole world is your home. You are a citizen of the world. Cultivate a generous feeling for the welfare of the whole world.

That charity which advertises ceases to be charity. It is only pride and ostentation.

Every good act is charity. Giving water to the thirsty is charity. An encouraging word to a man in distress is charity. Giving a little medicine to the poor sick man is charity. Removing a thorn or a glass piece on the road is charity.

A little good thought and a little kindness are often worth more than giving a great deal of money.

Defer not charities till death. Do charity daily.

If you give food to a poor man, he again wants food when he becomes hungry. The best form of charity is Vidya-Dana, imparting wisdom. Wisdom removes ignorance, the cause for taking a body and destroys in toto all sorts of miseries and suffering, for ever.

The second best form of charity is giving medicine to the sick. The third best form of charity is Anna-dana or giving food to the hungry.

Do charity silently. Do not advertise; what your right hand does, the left hand should not know.

First daughter to the love of God is charity to the poor.

Do discriminate charity in the beginning. Later on practise indiscriminate charity. When you feel that every being is a manifestation of the Lord, it is difficult to discriminate. Who is good? Who is bad?

Charity given with an unwilling heart is not charity.

Charity is not confined to giving in term of dollars, rupees or shillings. Think well towards suffering people. Pray for their welfare. This will accomplish more good than much money.

II

Prof. XYZ, M.A., Ph.D., gave a blanket in charity to a poor man. He afterwards thought, "I ought not to have given him a blanket." His heart was in a state of agitation and agony. He wanted to get the blanket back from the poor man. If you do such a kind of charity, you will not derive any benefit. You will not get purity of heart. Many worldly-minded people perform charitable acts of this description only. This world abounds in such charitable persons.

Charity must be spontaneous and unrestrained. Giving must become habitual. You must experience extreme joy in giving. You must not think, "I have done a very charitable act. I will enjoy happiness in heaven. I will be born as a rich man in the next birth. The charitable act will wash away my sin. There is no charitable man like me in my town or district. People know that I am a very charitable man." Begging is mean and deplorable.

Some people do charity and are anxious to see their names published in the newspapers with their photos. This is a Tamasic form of charity. This is no charity at all.

Lord Jesus says: "The left hand should not know what the right hand is doing." You should not advertise about your charity and charitable nature. There must not be an exaltation in your heart, when people praise you for your charitable nature.

You should be thirsty to do charitable acts daily. You should create opportunities. There is no Yoga or Yajna greater than Sattvic charity of the spontaneous type. Karna and Raja Bhoja did countless charitable acts. So, they still live in our hearts.

Give to the poor, the sick, the helpless and the forlorn. Give to the orphans, the decrepit, the blind, the helpless widows. Give to the Sadhus, Sannyasins, religious and social institutions. Thank the man who gives you an opportunity to serve him by doing charity. Give with the right mental attitude, and realise God through charitable acts. Glory to those who do charity with the right spirit.

CHEERFULNESS

I.

Cheerfulness is the state or quality of being joyful, lively and of good spirits.

Cheerfulness lightens sickness and the burden of life, poverty and affliction, and gives wonderful strength and great power of endurance.

A cheerful man will do more work, in the same time, will do it better, and will persevere in it longer than a cheerless man.

Be cheerful always. Cheerfulness is the best tonic. It gives radiant health and peace.

A kind and sympathetic man will be over cheerful. Cheerfulness is health. It makes the mind serene. It bestows longevity. It strengthens the heart.

The light of a cheerful face diffuses itself. You are refreshed by the presence of a cheerful man.

A cheerful man is like a sunny day. He radiates brightness on all around.

Be cheerful, sweet, happy and smiling. You will become very healthy and you will radiate health in every direction.

Cheerfulness is an index of a happy mind and a pure, good heart. It is a passport and recommendation in society.

A cheerful man is a public benefactor. He gladdens the hearts of all.

There is no friend like cheer.

The contagion of cheer has a wonderful effect. It transforms depression into brightness, sicklessness and health. A cheery word spontaneously gives cheer to others.

Cheerfulness is a habit of mind. Gaiety is an occasional excitement of animal spirit. Mirth or merriment is noisy gaiety.

A cheerful man smiles; a merry man laughs; a sprigthly man dances; a gay man takes his pleasure.

II

Cheerfulness is joyful frame of mind.

A cheerful man is full of good spirits. He is lively. He radiates joy everywhere.

Cheerfulness is a potent mental tonic.

A cheerful mind strengthens the head and makes one steadfast in good conduct.

Be cheerful always. Cultivate cheerfulness. Wear a cheerful smile with a cheerful face.

A cheerful man is a public benefactor. He makes others happy and cheerful. There is no friend like cheer.

Cheer is contagious. It has a marvellous effect on others. It transforms darkness into light, depression into brightness and sickness into health.

The cheerful live a long life. They are healthy, radiant and vibrant.

Cheerfulness is the soul. It is offshoot of goodness. It is a beautifier.

A cheerful man creates friends quickly. He is attractive to all.

What sunshine is to flowers, cheerful, happy smiles are to humanity.

Cheerfulness is a solace in solitude and distress. It lightens sickness, poverty and affliction.

Wonderful is the strength of cheerfulness. Cheerfulness is a power. A cheerful man has great power of endurance. He will do more in the same time, will do it better, will presevere in it longer, than a cheerless man.

Cheerfulness is health; cheerlessness is disease.

A man whose heart is full of kindness, benevolence and sympathy will always be cheerful.

Mirth is an act. Cheerfulness is a habit of the mind. Mirth is short and transient. Mirth is like a flash of lightning. Cheerfulness is fixed and permanent.

Cheerfulness is a friend to grace. It puts the heart in tune to praise God. A cheerful man can meditate for a long time.

There are some persons who are born cheerful. This is due to their previous good, spiritual samskaras or impressions.

A cheering word spontaneously gives cheer to others.

A cheering word is more distinctly planned to cheer and encourage.

Gaiety, mirth, merriment, blithesomeness, gladness, jollity, liveliness, sprightliness, vivacity are synonymous terms.

COMPLACENCY

(MUDITHA)

Complacency is the state of being pleased with oneself or others. It is self-satisfaction. It is satisfaction with one's acts or surroundings. It is pleasant, good nature. It is the manifestation of tranquil satisfaction.

Complacency is inclination or disposition to please others. It is civility or amiability. A man of complacency adjusts, adapts and accommodates.

We say: "Purushottam's manners are so elegant, so gentle, so unassuming, that they at once engage esteem and diffuse complacence."

Chatterjee says: "Every moment of Bannerjee's life brings me fresh instances of his complacency to my inclinations."

Father loves his son with the love of complacency.

Disposition or wish to please or oblige others is complacency.

He who has complacency will not be jealous of those who are in a better position. He will have Chitta-prasada or peace of mind. Complacency eradicates jealousy and fills the heart with love.

People seldom improve when they have no other model but themselves to copy after.

The majority of people fail in their life, because they never learn to guard and strengthen their weak points.

Complacency makes a superior amiable, an equal agreeable and an inferior acceptable. It pleases all, prejudices none, strengthens friendship, redoubles love.

Complacency is a social virtue. It gives lustre and brilliance to every talent a man posseses.

When complacency is united with justice and generosity, it makes a man a centre of attraction, admiration, love, respect and honour.

Complacency sweetens conversation, smooths distinction and makes everyone in the company pleasant with himself. It is a leveller in society.

Complacency generates good nature and mutual benevolence, soothes the turbulent and humanises the fierce.

COMPASSION
(KARUNA)

Compassion is fellow-feeling or sorrow for the sufferings of another.

Compassion opens the door for Freedom and expands the heart. It melts the sin-hardened hearts of worldly people, and makes them as soft as butter.

The heart of a saint, sage or Yogi is filled with compassion.

Compassion leads to the attainment of peace or Chitta-prasada.

Compassion is sorrow or pity with a desire to help or to spare, excited by the suffering or distress of another or others. It is sympathy with pain or sorrow, that prompts one to relieve the pain and suffering of others.

The dew of compassion is a tear.

By compassion you make another's misery your own and so by relieving them, you relieve yourself, too.

Pity, commiseration, fellow-feeling, sympathy, kindness, tenderness, clemency are synonymous with compassion.

Most of the people are unsympathetic. They have no compassion. They are absolutely selfish. They may present a car worth Rs. 15,000/- to their daughter. They may spend Rs. 3,000/- for the petrol. But they will not spend even a rupee to relieve the sufferings of poor people. They have their eyes and ears closed. They do not hear the cry of distress of people in distress. They do not see the stream of tears flowing from their neighbours. They close their doors and eat Rasagulla, Kalakand and Parottas.

The whole world is one family. All are children of God. The whole world is your abode. Feel this. Open your heart to compassion. Share what you have with others. Wipe the tears of sufferers. God will bless you.

Cultivate compassion. Have a tender, soft heart. Know and understand the sufferings of others, and be ever ready to help them.

Compassion is strength. It gives strength and joy. It prepares your mind for the descent of divine Light.

May compassion arise in your heart!

CONSIDERATION

Consideration is indeed a beautiful virtue. A man of consideration always attains success in all undertakings.

Consideration is the soil in which wisdom grows. Therefore, cultivate this virtue, consideration, to a maximum degree.

Disregarding, ignoring, overlooking, neglecting, slighting and trifling are the opposite of consideration.

A thoughtless and talkative man who speaks at random entangles himself in the web of foolishness of his words.

In consideration there is mature thought, there is serious deliberation. You consider a matter well at first and then decide.

In consideration, you consider the matter well before deciding. You think about it, closely reflect upon it, you ponder over it, you give close attention to it, you cogitate, you study, you weigh it, you observe closely and carefully.

The art of taking into account and examining a thing is consideration.

Moral causes come into consideration in proportion as the progress of knowledge is advanced. Men of faith consider conscience of more importance than knowledge.

Take into consideration the consequences of your hasty decision.

Think with consideration.

Act with consideration.

Have consideration, respect or regard for the feelings of others. Consider the virtues of others.

Weigh your words before you utter them.

Consider well every step you take.

Do not plunge suddenly into action. Consider the consequences well and then act. Then alone will you not repent, you will not feel sorry.

A thoughtless man who has not controlled his organs of speech speaks at random without any consideration and weeps for his foolishness in the end. He is put to shame and disgrace. Therefore, be considerate at all times, on all occasions.

O man! Harken unto the voice of consideration and become wise. She will guide you and show you the path to safety, security, wisdom, truth, peace, immortality and bliss.

CONTENTMENT

I

I will now talk to you this most vital subject, contentment. You all know the maxim "A contented mind is a continual feast." The mind is always restless on account of greed. Greed is a kind of internal fire that consumes a man slowly. Contentment is a powerful antidote for the poison of greed. Just as a man who comes from a long walk in the sun is quite refreshed by taking a plunge in the Ganges, so also that greedy man who is burnt by the fire of Lobha finds immediate joy and relief by a dip in the ambrosial water of contentment. There are four sentinels who guard the domain of Moksha. They are Santi, Santosha, Satsanga and Vichara. If you can approach any one of these sentinels you can get hold of the other three. If you can get hold of Santosha or contentment, you can easily see the other three sentinels following you.

There is no greater gain than contentment. A man who is fully endowed with this important virtue is the richest man in all the three worlds. The peace that he enjoys cannot be adequately described in words. He is a mighty emperor on this earth. Tayumana Swami, the reputed sage of Southern India sings: "Even the richest man in this world who is equal to Kubera, who possesses Chintamani, Kamadhenu and Kalpataru, desires to have domain overseas. He tries to practise alchemy to have more wealth. That man who is living up to 150 years tries to prolong his longevity by taking Rasayanas and Siddha Kalpas. He who possesses one hundred crores of rupees tries his level best to make it two hundred crores of rupees. The mind grasps one thing and leaves it the next moment and tries to grasp another. Man moves restlessly in this world and says: "This is mine. That is mine. I will try to possess that also. O restless mind! Do not drag me in these impure desires and sensual objects. I know your ways pretty well. Keep quiet. O Supreme Being! Give me a desireless pure mind. Let my mind be ever fixed in the Truth. Let me be mindless. Let me rest in the Satchidananda Swarupa. O All-full Bliss! O Radiant Bliss! that permeates and pervades all these names and forms." Contentment is one of the important items in the Niyamas of the Raja Yoga philosophy. The Gita also says: "Be contented with whatever you get by chance and apply yourself to meditation with a dispassionate mind." Socrates speaks very highly of this virtue.

Although people know that contentment is a virtue that gives peace of mind, yet they do not try to develop this virtue. Why? Because they have lost the power of discrimination and the power of Atmic enquiry or Vichara Shakti on account of passion and greed. Greed is the Chief Officer of Passion. Wherever there is greed, there is passion and wherever there is passion there is greed almost invariably. The understanding gets clouded, the intellect gets perverted and the memory gets confused by passion and greed. Therefore people find it difficult to develop this virtue, contentment.

An objector says: "Well, Swamiji, what you say is quite correct. I quite realise that contentment gives peace. But I have a doubt. If I become contented, all my ambitions will die. I will become lethargic and lazy. On account of my various sorts of ambitions, I move about hither and tither, I exert and I am energetic. Kindly remove this doubt of mine. I am quite bewildered." My reply is simply this: "Contentment can never make you idle. It is a Sattvic virtue that propels man towards God. It gives strength of mind and peace. It checks unnecessary and selfish exertions. It opens the inner eye of man and moves his mind towards divine contemplation. It turns his energy in the inner, Sattvic Channels. It transmutes the gross energy viz., greed that is forcing man towards selfish exertions into spiritual energy, Ojas. That man who is contented is full of Sattva. He is more energetic now. He is inward. He has an inner life in the Atman. He is always peaceful. He turns out more work calmly and with one-pointed mind. All the dissipated rays of the mind are collected now. Do you understand the point now?" The objector replies: "Yes, Swamiji, the matter is quite clear now. I am fully satisfied."

It is on the strength of contentment that the sages and Rishis of yore, the Fakirs and Bhikshus move about in the world in a carefree manner by living on Bhiksha. It is contentment that gives strength to an aspirant to walk in the path of Self-realisation and emboldens him to march fearlessly in the rugged and thorny path of spirituality. It is contentment that makes an aspirant look upon the worthless, perishable things of this world as dung, poison, straw or dust. Contentment develops Vairagya, discrimination and Vichara.

Mira had perfect contentment. She never cared for the paltry things of the world. She lived on Bhiksha though she was a Rani of Chitore. She lived on bread that came by begging and took it to the banks of Jumna and was quite satisfied with this meagre food and plain water which served as drink. What gave her strength? It was contentment. Contentment opens the door of Moksha and the realms of eternal bliss and sunshine. Contentment is a divine virtue. He who has perfect contentment brings balance of mind and perfect poise.

Pattinattu Swami, a very great sage of Southern India was a very greedy man in his earlier life. He was very rich too. Yet he wanted to hoard up wealth. Lord Siva took the form of a small boy and presented a bundle of needles which had no eyes with a chit inside which contained the message: "What is the earthly use of the treasure of this world? Even this broken needle will not follow you when you die." This opened the eyes of the greedy merchant and infused Vairagya and contentment. He abandoned his home, wealth, wife and everything and lived upon alms, developed perfect contentment and realised his Self.

Contentment is Bliss. Contentment is nectar. Contentment gives immortality and infinite peace. Therefore develop this virtue. Lead a happy life. Rest in everlasting peace. Have a mental image of this virtue. Repeat mentally "OM CONTENTMENT." The mental habit of contentment will develop.

II

A contented mind is the greatest blessing a man can enjoy in this world. It has a beneficial influence on the soul of man. It destroys all inordinate ambitions, all murmuring, repining, and makes one serene, happy and rich. It is a pearl of inestimable value.

Contentment is the best tonic. It is the best medicine. It gives best health and peace of mind.

Happiness consists, not in possessing much but in being content with what you possess. He who wants little always has enough.

Wealth or power brings its peculiar inconveniences and troubles. A rich man is ever unhappy and discontented. Artha (wealth) is Anartha (an evil).

A poor man does not experience the vexations and anxieties of the rich, the difficulties and perplexities of power. A rich man and a man of power have their own secret griefs.

When your mind is troubled for want of shoes, think of the man who has no feet and be contented.

When you are discontented by looking at people who are superior to you, look at those who are inferior to you and be contented.

Want of desire is the greatest wealth. A desireless man is the most wealthy and contented man in this world. A contented man is never poor. The discontented man is never rich.

Be always contented with what happens. Know that what God chooses is better than what you choose.

If you are not contented with what you have, you will not be contented with what you like to have.

Contentment is natural wealth. Luxury is artificial poverty.

Abandon all desires. Desire only the will of God. Seek Him alone. You will find perfect contentment, peace and bliss.

If you increase your wealth, you increase your cares, worries and anxietes. But a contented mind is a hidden, supreme treasure. A man of contented mind knows not cares and anxieties.

A contented man is easy in mind. He does not repine. He is satisfied with things as they are. He never complains. He is resigned, satiated and satisfied.

Contentment is a celestial ambrosia or nectar. It cools the fire of greed.

O man! Lead a life of perfect contentment and be happy for ever. Live in God who is Nitya Tripti or Supreme Satisfaction or Contentment.

III

Contentment is the best virtue; contentment is called the true enjoyment; and the contented man gets the best repose. For a man of contentment sovereignty of the world is no better than chaff. Enjoyments of objects will appear to be poison to him. His mind is turned towards higher spiritual things and Atma Vichara. He derives happiness from within. He is never disturbed in adverse conditions. Contentment is the healer of all evils. It is a panacea for the cure of the dire disease—avarice or greed. The mind cooled by calm contentment is ever peaceful. Divine light can descend only on an aspirant who is endowed with contentment. A contented man though poor is the emperor of the whole world. A contented man is one who does not long after what he has not possessed; and enjoys what he has in right manner. He is quite satisfied with whatsoever he gets. He is magnanimous and graceful. Siddhis and Riddhis wait on him as if they are his servants. He is free from cares and anxieties. The sight of the calm countenance of a contented person gives delight to those who come in contact with him. Such a person is revered by the great Tapaswins and all great men.

COUNTER-THOUGHTS
(PRATIPAKSHA BHAVANA)

Thoughts of worry and thoughts of fear are fearful forces within us. They poison the very sources of life and destroy the harmony, the running efficiency, the vitality and vigour. While the opposite thoughts of cheerfulness, joy and courage heal, soothe, instead of irritating, and immensely augment efficiency and multiply the mental powers. Be always cheerful. Smile. Laugh.

Every thought or emotion or word produces a strong vibration in every cell of the body and leaves a strong impression there. If you know the method of raising an opposite thought or counter-thought, then you can lead a happy harmonious life of peace and power. A thought of love will at once neutralise a thought of hatred. A thought of courage will immediately serve as a powerful antidote against a thought of fear.

When there are diseases, discord, disharmony in the cells of the body owing to influence of vicious thoughts, worry-thoughts, fear-thoughts, hatred-thoughts, jealousy-thoughts, lustful-thoughts you can neutralise the poison or canker in these diseased, morbid cells and establish peace, harmony, health, new vigour and vitality by entertaining sublime, soul-stirring, life-giving, soul-awakening, Sattvic, Divine thoughts by vibrations of OM chanting, by repetition of the different names of the Lord, by Pranayama, Kirtan (singing of the Names of the Lord), study of the Gita and the holy scriptures, by meditation etc.

COURAGE

Courage is bravery, undaunted spirit, fearlessness, intrepidity. It is the quality that enables men to meet dangers without fear.

Courage enlarges your resources but cowardice diminishes them.

Abhayam is courage or fearlessness. In the Sixteenth Chapter of the Gita this virtue comes first. No spiritual progress is possible without courage. Courage is an essential of high character.

There cannot be truth without courage, you cannot do anything in this world without courage. It is the greatest virtue of the mind.

Courage triumphs. Courage succeeds. Courage conquers.

Courage is that quality of mind which enables man to encounter danger, opposition and difficulties with firmness, calmness and intrepidity or without fear or depression of spirits.

A courageous man is cool and calm. At the very time of danger he is extremely serene. He is resolute-minded.

Physical courage and moral courage are necessary to make a man great. Moral courage is a virtue of higher order than physical. It is very ennobling.

Physical courage depends upon bodily strength and intrepidity. Moral courage is that quality which enables one to pursue a course deemed right through which one may incur contempt, disapproval or opprobrium.

True courage is not the brutal force of vulgar heroes, but the firm resolve of virtue and reason. The courage of a soldier in the battle is Rajaso-Tamasic, but the courage of an aspirant or a Sage or a saint is Sattvic. The former is the hardness of the rash and foolish, but the latter is the courage of the wise.

Do not possess Dutch courage, but be really courageous. Dutch courage is a fictitious courage induced by drinking. It evaporates quickly when the influence of alcohol wanes. Courage must become part and parcel of your very nature.

Have the courage of your convictions. Have the courage to act up to or consistently with your views or opinions.

Always pluck up your courage to nerve yourself to something daring.

Courage is the sterner stuff of which heroes are made.

If you have courage and confidence, you can accomplish anything in this world. Courage is the source of all success. Impossible things become possible if you have courage and confidence.

You have strength in proportion to courage. Your ability to perform deeds is in accordance with your courage and confidence.

You may have courage when everything is going right; but it is difficult to have courage in times of panic and danger. The really courageous man is one who knows no fear when danger is on his heels and helps others with a calm attitude of mind.

Bravery, intrepidity, valour, boldness, fortitude, fearlessness, daring, heroism, gallantry, dauntlessness, mettle, pluck—are synonymous with courage.

Cowardice, fear, fright, timidity, pusillanimity, poltroonery are the opposites of courage.

Meditate ceaselessly on the absolutely fearless Atman or the Immortal Soul that dwells in the chambers of your heart. You will become an embodiment of courage.

COURTESY

Courtesy is elegance of manners. It is an act of civility and respect.

Courtesy is elegance or politeness of manners. It is politeness combined with kindness. It is complaisance. It is an act of kindness or favour performed with politeness.

Courtesy is politeness originating in kindliness and exercised habitually. It is courtliness, civility, graciousness. It is a gesture of civility, reverence or respect.

Courtesy denotes an act of kindliness or good breeding.

He who sows courtesy reaps friendship.

Sweet and gracious is that fine sense of courtesy.

Be courteous even in common speech. You will be loved by all.

Courtesy is the sister of charity which keeps love alive and quenches the fire of hatred.

Show courtesy to all. Let it be artless, continuous and uniform. Have courtesy in your heart. Show courtesy in your outward behaviour.

Return a salute joyfully. Salute the person who salutes you with a better salutation. Always salute first to all.

Courtesy sweetens and ennobles life. It makes smooth the road of life, like grace and beauty. It opens the door and allows the stranger into the house. It enlivens the hearts of guests and visitors.

Be pleasant and courteous in your behaviour towards your inferiors and all persons.

Small kindness, small courtesies, small consideration habitually practised in your social intercourse give a great charm to your character.

Courtesy charms at first sight and leads on to great intimacy and friendship.

A man of courtesy is a man of fine and polished manners. All people love him.

Show not scant courtesy at any time to any person. Be liberal in your courtesy.

Urbanity, civility, complaisance, condescension, affability, elegance, courteousness, good breeding are synonymous with courtesy.

DESTINY

Courage is thy birthright but not fear; peace is thy divine heritage but not restlessness. Immortality is thy birthright but not mortality; strength, but not weakness; health but not disease; bliss but not sorrow; knowledge but not ignorance.

Pain, sorrow, ignorance are all illusory; they cannot live. Bliss, joy, knowledge are true; they cannot die.

You are the architect of your own fate. You are the master of your own destiny. You can do and undo things. You sow an action and reap a tendency. You sow a tendency and reap a habit. You sow a habit and reap your character. You sow your character and reap your destiny. Therefore destiny is your own creation. You can undo it if you like. Destiny is a bundle of habits.

Purushartha is right exertion. Purushartha can give you anything. Change your habits. Change the mode of thinking. You can conquer destiny. You are thinking now "I am the body." Start the spiritual (cross-current) and think "I am the Immortal, diseaseless, sexless, Atman." Think "I am Akarta (non-doer) and Abhokta (non-enjoyer)." You can conquer death and attain the Immortal seat of supreme splendour.

By virtuous deeds and right thoughts you can disarm destiny. You have a free will to act. By exertion Ratnakar became Valmiki. By exertion, Markandeya conquered death. By exertion, Savitri brought her husband Satyavan back to life. By exertion alone did Uddalaka attain Nirvikalpa Samadhi.

Therefore, apply yourself tenaciously to Atmic enquiry and meditation. Be vigilant and diligent. Kill the thoughts and desires. Overcome tomorrow's evil by today's right exertion. Destroy unholy desires (Asubha Vasanas) through holy desires (Subha Vasanas). Slay unholy thoughts by holy thoughts and gain victory over your destiny.

Do not yield to fatalism. Do not become impotent. Stand up like a lion. Exert and attain independence or Atma Svarajya. There is a vast ocean of knowledge within you. All faculties are latent in you. Unfold them and become a Jivanmukta (liberated soul).

The positive overcomes the negative. This is the immutable law of nature. Purushartha (self-exertion) is a mightier power. Purushartha is the lion or the elephant, Prarabdha (destiny) is the ant or the jackal. God helps those who help themselves. Vashishtha asked Rama to do Purushartha. Fatalism will induce inertia and laziness. Therefore gird up your loins and exert yourself to the utmost.

May you all attain Self-realisation or Brahma-Jnana in this very birth! May you all live immersed in an ocean of bliss in an illumined state! May you all shine as liberated sages!

DETERMINATION

Determination is resolution, fixedness of purpose, decision of character. It is the act of deciding. It is firmness.

It is a firm resolve as a determination to conquer.

Determination is a manly trait.

Determination is the mental habit of setting upon some line of action with a fixed purpose to adhere to it. It is adherence to aims and purposes, resoluteness as a 'man of determination.'

If you have fiery determination only, you can attain success in all undertakings, in Self-realisation, too.

Decision is literally a cutting off, or cutting short, of debate or questioning.

Determination is a settling of the limits within which one must act.

Resolve is a separating of the essential act from all that might cause doubt or hesitation. It always refers to a single act.

Resolution may have the same meaning, or it may refer to the habit of mind which readily forms and adheres to resolves.

Decision or determination especially marks the beginning of action.

Resolution holds one to the end.

Doubt, faltering, fickleness, hesitation, indecision, instability, irresolution, vacillation, wavering are the opposite terms.

A man of strong, pure, irresistible will can have fiery determination.

Strengthen your will and cultivate determination.

DIGNITY

Dignity is elevation of mind or character. It is grandeur of mien. It is degree of excellence.

Dignity is grave and noble bearing. It is impressiveness of character or manner. It is serenity of demeanour.

Dignity is the state or quality calculated to inspire awe, respect or reverence. It is stateliness.

Against lies, calumnies, etc., dignity is the only weapon.

Dignity of position adds to dignity of character as well as dignity of carriage.

The statesman's dignity is innate.

Dignity is the state or quality of being excellent, worthy or honourable, as the dignity of labour.

If you will only call a headache a cephalalgia, it acquires dignity at once, and the patient becomes rather proud of it!

To stand upon one's dignity is to have or assume an exalted idea of one's own importance, especially if offended.

DISCRETION

Discretion is prudence. It is liberty to act at pleasure.

Discretion is the ability and tendency to choose or act with prudence. It is instinctive perception of what is wise or proper, united with caution. It is sagacity. It is the habit of wise judgement, especially in relation to one's own conduct.

Discretion is liberty of action and decision, as in a particular matter. It is freedom in the exercise of judgement; also action resulting from such liberty or freedom; as "the matter is subject to your discretion."

A man of discretion is wise in avoiding errors or evil or in selecting the best means to accomplish a purpose. He has good discernment. He is judicious.

Discretion is that discernment which enables a person to judge critically of what is correct and proper united with caution.

It is nice discernment and judgment, directed by circumspection and primarily regarding one's own conduct.

Discretion is the victor of the war, valour the pupil.

Discretion is the liberty or power of acting without other control than one's own judgment; as "the management of affairs was left to the discretion of the president."

There are many shining qualities in the mind; but none so useful as discretion.

Discretion in speech is more than eloquence.

Discretion is the salt of life. It preserves life.

Discretion is the perfection of reason. It is your guide in all your duties of life.

Discretion is the better part of valour.

Discretion is found only in men of sound sense and good understanding.

DISCRIMINATION

Discrimination or Viveka is the faculty or power of the Sattvic mind to distinguish between the Real and the unreal, the Permanent and the impermanent, Atma and Anatma.

Discrimination dawns through the grace of the Lord, in a man who has done virtuous actions in his previous births as offerings unto the Lord without expectation of fruits and without egoism.

Viveka or discrimination is strengthened by study of scriptures and Satsanga.

If you have discrimination, surely you will have lasting dispassion.

The edifice of wisdom is built up on the strong foundation of discrimination.

Brahman or the Absolute alone is the Real, Imperishable thing. All things other than Brahman are transient and perishable.

DISPASSION

Dispassion is Vairagya. Dispassion is indifference to sensual enjoyments herein and hereafter. Dispassion is non-attachment to sensual objects.

This is an important requisite for attaining God-realisation.

Man is bound to this world, through Raga or passion or attachment. He is liberated through Vairagya.

Vairagya born of discrimination between the Real and the unreal only will be of a lasting nature. Such a Vairagya alone will help you to attain spiritual progress and illumination. Karana-Vairagya due to loss of property or death of your son will be temporary. It will be of no use to you. It is volatile like ammonia.

Look into the defects of sensual life or sensual pleasure. You will develop dispassion.

Sensual pleasure is momentary, deceptive, illusory and imaginary.

Enjoyment cannot bring about satisfaction of a desire; on the contrary it makes the mind more restless after enjoyment through intense craving.

Sensual pleasure is the cause for birth and death. It is an enemy of devotion, wisdom and peace.

DUTY

Duty is what one is bound by any obligation to do.

Do your duty and leave unto the Lord the rest.

He who knows his duty but does not practise it, is the worst man in this world.

You are not in this world to do what you wish. You must be willing to do that which is your duty.

Regard all duties as sacred. Do your duty unselfishly. Then duty ceases to be irksome. It becomes joyful.

Do your duty in your shop, in your kitchen, in the office, in the school, in the home, very faithfully. Apply your whole heart even in doing little things such as arranging of your papers, cleaning your room, the sorting of your clothes, etc.

Your daily duties are a part of your religious life.

Duty is carrying on promptly and faithfully the affairs now before you.

Duty is the sublimest of ideas, for it implies the idea of God, of the soul, of freedom, of responsibility, of immortality.

The worthy fulfilment of the duties of every stage of life brings honour to man.

Be exact in doing even your little duties. You will derive much joy and happiness.

There is no mean work. Work is worship. All actions are sacred. Performance of duty is practice of religion.

Duty performed is a moral tonic. It strengthens the mind and the heart.

Human happiness and moral duty are inseparably connected.

Do as you would be done by. Do unto others as you wish others do unto you. This is the great moral law.

You are not born to solve the problems of the universe. You are born to find out what you have to do.

This span of life is given to you for lofty duties, not for selfishness, not to be spent worthlessly in idle gossiping, eating, drinking and sleeping, but to improve yourself, to cultivate virtues, serve humanity selflessly and to attain God-realisation.

EARNESTNESS

Earnestness is the state of being earnest. It is enthusiasm tempered by reason.

An earnest man is determined. He is eager to obtain. He is intent, sincere and serious. He shows strong desire. He is ardent in the pursuit of an object. He gives his whole heart to the work on hand.

Do you wish to master any science or accomplishment? Then give yourself to it. Be sincere and earnest. You will attain sanguine success.

Far more than mere talents, enthusiasm and earnestness in work carry the day.

It will be found everywhere that the men who have attained success in business or anything have been the men who have earnestly given themselves to it.

An earnest man finds means. He creates means.

Earnestness strengthens weakness, braves dangers, overcomes pain, sustains hope, lightens difficulties, lessens the sense of weariness in overcoming them, gives endurance.

A man may be the cleverest of men; he may be brilliant. But, without earnestness no one is ever great or does really great things.

You cannot be earnest about anything which does not naturally and strongly engage your thoughts.

Earnestness is the devotion of all the faculties. It gives patience. It is the cause of patience. It gives zeal and enthusiasm.

Earnestness is the best source of mental power. It gives intellect.

There is no substitute for thorough-going, ardent, sincere, earnestness.

An earnest man is serious in purpose. He is zealous and determined especially in matters of moral and religious import, spirit and speech.

There must be a great and earnest soul behind a great cause.

When a man is earnest in his speech, attempt and action, we say: "Rama's speech is earnest speech; Krishna's attempt is earnest endeavour. Siva is an earnest doctor."

ELEGANCE

Elegance is the state or quality of being elegant. It is the beauty of propriety. It is refinement, polish or gracefulness. That which is nice and pleasing to good taste is elegance.

When the mind loses its feeling for elegance, it becomes corrupt.

Elegance is something more than a freedom from awkwardness. It implies a precision, a polish, a sparkling and brilliance.

Though elegance is reckoned among the smaller and secondary morals, yet it is of no mean importance in the regulation of life. It greatly decreases the evils of vice.

Elegance is choice or delicate structure, form or action; beauty resulting from a combination of fine qualities; as elegance of proportion, motion, style or manner.

A clear and sharp-cut enunciation is one of the elegancies of speech.

We say: "Among the Indians, we find profound and elegant scholars."

An elegant thing is marked by grace or symmetry and refinement. It exhibits faultless taste and delicacy of finish. It possesses a fine sense of beauty, purity or fitness. We say: "This is an elegant apartment." We say: "Rama's argument was elegant." It is marked by completeness, simplicity. It is appropriate.

'Elegant' refers to that assemblage of qualities which makes anything choice to persons of culture and refinement. It refers to the lighter, finer elements of beauty in form or motion.

A dress may be elegant, but such expressions as "an elegant field of corn" "an elegant ride" or "an elegant time" are glaring lexical improprieties.

Exquisite denotes the utmost perfection of the elegant in minute details. We speak of an elegant garment, an exquisite lace. Exquisite is also applied to intense keenness of any feeling as exquisite delight, exquisite pain.

Elegance is beauty resulting from perfect propriety or from the absence of anything calculated to produce a disagreeable sensation, said of manners, language, style, form, architecture and the like; as elegance of dress.

That which pleases by its nicety, symmetry, purity or beauty is elegant.

Polished, polite, refined, graceful, pleasing to good taste are elegant manners.

Polished, pure, rich in expressions, correct in arrangement is elegant style or composition.

Symmetrical, regular, well-formed in part, proportions and distribution is an elegant structure.

Rich, costly and ornamented is elegant furniture or equipage.

Nice, sensible to beauty, discriminating beauty from deformity or imperfection, is an elegant taste.

EMULATION

Emulation is an attempt to equal or excel. It is a healthy competition. It is a desire for like excellence with another.

It is a noble passion. It is striving to excel, not by depressing others, but by raising oneself. It keeps within the terms of honour and makes the contest for glory just and generous.

Without emulation nothing great or excellent can be done. Emulation is laudable ambition. It urges you to advance and make improvement. It admires and strives to imitate great actions. But envy is only moved to malice.

Emulation is the shadow of aspiration. It looks out for merits so that it may exalt itself by a victory.

Through emulation one exalts oneself to something that is praiseworthy. He exerts, strives and struggles. He does not have a cut-throat competition with others.

He does not envy the merit of another, he improves his own talents, faculties and capacities. He does not boast of himself; and he does not deride others.

He who emulates does not depress his competitors by any dishonest or unworthy methods. He endeavours to raise himself only by excelling him. By virtuous emulation, the spirit of a man is exalted. He is ever diligent, vigilant and persevering. He always soars higher and higher.

He keeps before his mind the examples of illustrious persons and strives to follow them and reaches their level quickly. He forms great designs and executes them.

But the heart of an envious man is gall and bitter. His heart burns at the success and prosperity of others. He is restless. His heart is filled with hatred and malice. He does mischief to others. He harms and ruins others. He depreciates those who excel him.

In all the pursuits of active and speculative life, emulation is the most powerful spring of the efforts and improvements of mankind.

Emulation regards the abstract, competition the concrete. We speak of competition in business, emulation in scholarship, rivalry in love, politics, etc.; emulation of excellence, success, achievement; competition for a prize; rivalry between persons or nations. Competition may be friendly; rivalry is commonly hostile. Opposition is becoming a frequent substitute for competition in business language. It implies that the competitor is an opponent and hinderer.

Carelessness, indifference, false satisfaction are the opposites of emulation.

ENDURANCE

(TITIKSHA)

Endurance is the state of enduring or bearing. It is a suffering patiently without sinking or yielding to the pressure, without resistance.

Endurance is the capacity or power to endure without opposition. It is ability to suffer pain, distress, hardship or any very, prolonged stress without succumbing or murmuring or complaining, lamenting or repining. It is patient fortitude. It is the ability to bear and continue in spite of destructive forces.

To endure is to bear with strain and resistance with conscious power. To brook is quietly to put up with provocation or insult.

He who endures conquers. Through endurance, will-power and patience are developed. Through endurance evils and difficulties are overcome.

Your strength often increases in proportion to the obstacles imposed upon you. Endure them bravely.

Difficulties and troubles, adversities and calamities have often built the character of men.

The palm-tree grows best beneath a ponderous weight, and even so the character of man.

The greater the difficulty, the more glory in surmounting it. Skilful pilots become famous from storms and tempests.

Through endurance you exhibit your divine grandeur and make alliance with God.

EQUANIMITY

Equanimity is equality or evenness of mind or temper. It is balanced mind in pleasure and pain, success and failure, honour and dishonour, censure and praise.

Equanimity is composure of spirit, especially calmness and steadiness of mind, amidst trying circumstances.

The excellence of equanimity is beyond all praise. That man who is endowed with this virtue is not dejected in adversity, nor elated in prosperity. He is affable to others and contented in himself.

He who is endowed with equanimity has poise at all times under all conditions of life. He bears losses with equanimity.

A Jeevanmukta has always an evenness of mind or equanimity or poise. He has a perfect, unshakable balance of mind, rooted in insight, intuition or Atman.

In this world of pairs of opposites, man is tossed about hither and thither by various waves of emotion. Now he gets gain, successs, honour, praise. The next moment, he gets failure, loss dishonour, censure and disappointment. He who has evenness of mind or poise can pull on in this world joyfully and peacefully.

Root yourself in your own unchanging, all-blissful Atman within, by disciplining the mind and the senses. Then alone will you rest peacefully for ever. No worldly wave can upset you. You will rest silently in the bed rock of your own innermost Self within, which is an ocean of peace.

Samatvam or equanimity is Yoga. To attain this state it needs constant vigilance, perseverance, patience and perfect discipline of body, mind and senses. This is not a day's or week's or a month's effort.

Constantly think of the "Samam Brahman" which is seated equally in all beings. Gradually you will develop equanimity.

Eradicate desires, cravings, attachments, likes and dislikes. Cultivate discrimination, serenity, dispassion, self-restraint, self-control, self-denial. You will be slowly established in equanimity.

FAITH

Faith is belief in the truth of revealed religion. It is confidence and trust in God. It is confidence in one's own Self. It is belief in the statements, utterances and teachings of one's Guru or Preceptor or saints. It is belief in religious scriptures.

Faith is a firm conviction of the truth of what is declared by another by way either of testimony or authority without any other evidence.

Faith is that personal attitude by which divine revelation is subjectively appropriated. It does not originate from logical processes, but from an immediate inner experience.

Men with no assets but tremendous faith in themselves have accomplished wonders.

Have perfect faith in God. Surrender your entire being unto Him. He will take care of you. All fears and tribulations will vanish in toto. You can ever remain at ease.

Faith should not be forced. Trying to compel religious belief leads to unbelief.

Faith in God elevates the soul, purifies the heart and emotions and leads to God-realisation.

Faith is the soul of religion. It creates new hopes and awakens immortality.

Faith is the eye that sees the Lord, and the hand that clings to Him.

Faith is power. Faith is strength. Faith is abundant energy.

He who has faith is strong. He who doubts is weak. Doubt cramps energy. Strong faith precedes great actions.

Much divine knowledge is lost to you through lack of faith.

Faith illumines the spiritual path, builds a bridge across the gulf of death and takes the aspirant to the other shore of fearlessness and immortality.

We give credence to a report, assent to a proposition or to a proposal. Belief is stronger than credence. Conviction is a belief established by argument or evidence.

Assurance is belief beyond the reach of argument.

Faith is a union of belief and trust. Faith is chiefly personal. Belief may be quite impersonal. We speak of belief in a proposition, faith in a promise, because the promise emanates from a person.

Confidence is a firm dependence upon a statement as true, or upon a person as worthy. We have reliance upon the uniformity of nature. We have trust or faith in God.

FIDELITY

Fidelity is faithful and careful performance of duty, or performance of obligations. It is faithfulness to a husband or wife. It is honesty. It is firm adherence.

Fidelity is hearty allegiance to those to whom one is bound in affection or honour. It is loyalty, devotion, as the fidelity of an officer, matrimonial fidelity, fidelity to a father or friend, the fidelity of subjects to their king, the fidelity of a servant to his master.

Fidelity finds its reward and its strength in exalted purpose.

Fidelity is nine-tenths of success in business.

Fidelity is the friend of justice.

Nothing is more noble, nothing more venerable than fidelity. It is a fundamental virtue of mind.

Fidelity is strict adherence to truth or fact; reliability, veracity, honesty; as the fidelity of a report or a witness, the fidelity of a portrait.

Allegiance, constancy, devotion, faith, faithfulness, honesty, integrity, loyalty, truth, truthfulness, are synonymous terms.

Disloyalty, infidelity, treachery, treason are the opposites of fidelity.

Be constant as the Pole Star. Be faithful and devoted.

FIRMNESS

Firmness is steadiness, resoluteness, determination, constancy. We speak of the firmness of foundation, firmness of step, firmness of faith, firmness of purpose or resolution, firmness of mind or soul.

A man of firmness is not easily moved or disturbed. He is unshaken by anything. He is courageous.

Cleverness, talents, faculties, abilities, capacities, eloquence, elegant manners, winsome ways, graceful speech are nothing unless they are protected by the shield of firmness.

Firmness enables a man to overcome obstacles and difficulties very easily. A man of firmness always attains success in all undertakings.

You must have firmness both in suffering and exertion. Then alone will you attain greatness and victory.

Firmness is indeed a noble quality, but it must be guided by knowledge. Otherwise it becomes rashness or obstinacy.

Firmness of purpose is the best instrument for success. It is one of the most necessary sinews of character.

Firmness is then only a virtue when it accompanies the most perfect wisdom.

Firmness is the faculty that gives stability, persistency and obstinacy.

Firmness belongs to the wise act; constancy to the affection and principles—the former prevents us from yielding and the latter from fluctuating.

FORBEARANCE

Forbearance is exercise of patience. Forbearance is command of temper or clemency. It is a great divine virtue.

Forbearance is patient endurance or toleration of offences. It is lenity. It is restraint of passions. Forbearance is refraining or abstaining from, avoiding voluntarily. It is a refraining from feelings of resentment or measures taken in retaliation.

Forbearance is a mysterious mixture of mercy, sympathy, pity, compassion, patience, endurance, forgiveness and strong will.

He who practices forbearance keeps himself in check. He practises self-restraint or self-control and forgiveness. He bears injuries, insults, annoyance and vexatious mocking, patiently, prayerfully and with self-control and thus develops a strong will-power.

Cover the blemishes, faults, weaknesses of others. Excuse their failings. Bury their weaknesses in silence. Proclaim their virtues from the house-top.

Find out occasions to forbear. Pity and forgive weak persons. Cultivate forbearance till your heart yields a fine crop of it.

Lord Jesus and Lord Buddha were embodiments of forbearance. Glory to these divine personages. Follow their example and become divine.

O Man! Forbear! Have patience even under greatest provocation. You will reap a rich harvest of peace and bliss.

FORGIVENESS

(KSHAMA)

Forgiveness is pardoning. Forgiveness is to overlook an offence or debt. It is disposition or inclination to pardon or excuse.

A man who is endowed with forgiveness is merciful and compassionate.

To err is human; to forgive divine.

Pretence of forgiveness is common. Real forgiveness is rare.

If you practise forgiveness, you will become strong and noble. You can control anger easily.

Forgiveness saves the expense of anger, the cost of hatred, the waste of spirits.

Forgiveness ought to be like a cancelled note—torn in two and burnt up, so that it never can be shown against one.

He who practises forgiveness ceases to cherish displeasure or resentment towards a man who has injured him.

Kshama or forgiveness is an antidote to anger.

"Forgive" points to inward feeling and supposes alienated friendship. When we ask for forgiveness, we primarily seek the removal of anger.

"Pardon" looks more to outward things or consequences and is often applied to trifling matters, as when we beg pardon for interrupting. The magistrate grants a pardon, and not forgiveness.

FORTITUDE

I

Fortitude is the mental power of endurance. It is firmness in meeting danger. It is strength, power of resistance or attack.

Fortitude comes from Latin *fortitudo*, from *fortis*—strong, powerful.

Fortitude is strength or firmness of mind to endure pain and adversity patiently, without murmuring, depression or despondency, or to encounter danger undismayed with coolness and courage. It is patient and constant courage.

Fortitude is power to resist or attack.

Fortitude is passive courage or still courage, enduring courage. It is that quality which is able not merely to endure pain, or trial but steadily to confront dangers that can be actively opposed or against which one has no adequate defence. It takes courage to charge a battery, fortitude to stand still under an enemy's fire. Resolution is of the mind. Endurance is partly physical. It requires resolution to resist temptation, endurance to resist hunger and cold.

Active fortitude is demanded when evils are to be encountered and overcome. It comprehends resolution or constancy and intrepidity or courage. Passive fortitude is demanded when evils are to be met and endured. It includes patience, humility, meekness etc.

In itself it is an essential virtue. It is a guard to every other virtue.

This is a world of pain, misery, sorrow, perils, misfortunes, want, injury and disease. Every man has his share of pain and trouble. Cowards crouch beneath their load and men of fortitude bear without repining.

He who fights with the lower nature and overcomes, that man is adorned with the best virtue—fortitude.

Patience, courage, endurance, heroism, resolution and presence of mind are the ingredients of fortitude.

Fortitude will sustain you through all perils, adversities, misfortunes. Just as the dashing of the waves cannot disturb a rock, so also all the tribulations of mundane life will not disturb you.

Fortify thy mind with fortitude, courage and patience. You can surmount all the troubles of this mundane life boldly and can remain ever calm and peaceful. In the hour of danger you will not be embarrassed and confounded. In the days of misfortune you will not sink with despair, or despondency.

Fortitude will sustain you and the steadiness of your mind will bear you out. You will emerge with victory and joy.

Prahlada, Sita, Damayanti, Nalayini and Savitri were all embodiments of fortitude.

II

Fortitude is Dhriti. Fortitude is mental power of endurance. It is firmness in meeting danger. It is strength, power of resistance or passive negative aspects of attack.

The birth of a man is due to his mixed Karmas, mixture of good and evil. Every man will have to meet dangers, calamities adversities, catastrophies, want, pain, injury at some period of his life. He who is endowed with fortitude will bear them calmly with great presence of mind and tide over them with a smiling face.

Fortitude is a sweet mysterious spiritual mixture of courage, calmness, patience, presence of mind and endurance. It is a virtue born of Sattva. It gives great strength of mind to Sadhakas, who tread the path of Truth and even to those who live in the world and tread the path of Pravritti.

That Sadhaka who is not endowed with fortitude leaves his Sadhana during times of peril, privation and sickness. He faints, creaks and loses heart. But fortitude of a man sustains him through all perils, calamities, privations and sickness. It was fortitude that sustained Lord Rama and Sita, Nala and Damayanti, Yudhishthira and his brothers during their life in the forest when they were in great distress. Sri Harishchandra, Jesus Christ, Rana Pratap, Abdul Baba are examples of heroes who possessed immense fortitude.

Fortitude is a friend in need. It is a nursing mother. It is a mental tonic and panacea. It is a shield and an armour to protect one from hunger, thirst, heat, cold. It is an unfailing injection to instil inner strength during times of threatening collapse and heart failure. It is a potent weapon to combat against trying conditions of life and unfavourable circumstances.

The man of fortitude stands firm like the Himalayas during adversities. He keeps the balance of mind under all conditions of life. He is not shaken by heavy sorrows. Just as a rock on the sea-shore stands firm and is not affected by the dashing of waves, so also he stands firm even amidst storms and vicissitudes of this dire Samsara.

Just as the man in the battlefield protects his nose, eyes and other parts through special contrivances from the disastrous effect of explosive bombs, so also the Sadhaka and the wise man protects himself from the explosive gases of worldly adversities through fortitude and comes out victorious.

But the timid, weak man with the dastardly spirit who lacks in fortitude, trembles in the hour of danger shrinks, faints and falls down in utter shame. He sinks in despair. He is bewildered and confused. He does not know what to do. He is like the reed that is shaken even by the least puff of breeze. He loses presence of min Fear, faintheartedness, impotency overpower him. He hopelessly meets with failure and sorrow. He succumbs and yields during times of adversity and misfortunes.

Develop fortitude gradually and stand firm like that yonder Meru or Himavan. Cultivate this virtue again and again patiently.

Fortitude shows power of character. Just as to a man of high office his authority is his strength, to a noble man his pedigree is his strength, to a great leader his status is his strength and to a wealthy man his money is his strength, even so to a man of character fortitude is his strength. It is what sustains him. It denotes self-confidence and self-reliance. Where there is fortitude there discouragement and pessimism dare not approach. Fortitude is therefore the only real lasting strength, for high office, birth, leadership, money all pass away. Character is lasting wealth, fortitude is a lasting power.

May you all attain success in worldly life and God-realisation through fortitude.

FRIENDSHIP

Friendship is attachment for mutual esteem. It is cordiality. It is intimate acquaintance.

Friendship is the mutual liking, esteem or regard cherished by kindred minds, as the basis of the mutual interchange of kind offices. In friendship there is congeniality of sentiment; there is close intimacy or acquaintance leading to sympathy or helpfulness.

Friendship is attachment to a person, proceeding from intimate acquaintance and a reciprocity of kind office or from a favourable opinion of his amiable and respectable qualities.

Man is a social animal. He wants company and talk. He desires to have friends. He cannot live well without friends.

Two persons cannot keep friendship for a long time if they cannot forgive each others' little defects or weaknesses or shortcomings.

Friendship with the upright and sincere men is advantageous.

Friendship with men of vanity, insincerity, double-dealing and crookedness is injurious.

Be slow to make friendship with anybody. Once you have made friendship with some one, be firm and constant.

Sincere friends are rare in this world. You will find selfish friends in abundance. Your only sincere, immortal friend is the Indweller of your heart, the Antaryamin, the Inner Ruler.

You will find the friendship of many people as mere outward show. It is like the harlot's tears.

False friendship decays soon, but true friendship gives new life and animation.

A friend in need is a friend indeed. Be more prompt to go to a friend in adversity than in prosperity.

True friendship is infinite and immortal.

Friendship is a fragile thing and requires as much care in handling as any other fragile thing. Be careful. Let it grow.

Your friend should be one in whose understanding, virtue and opinion you can safely confide.

Be not the tenth friend of him who had nine before and lost them.

A good virtuous man will be your best friend. Make friendship with him at once. Retain his friendship till the end of your life. You will be immensely benefited by his counsels and friendship. He will help you, guide you and serve you.

A true, sincere friend will advise you justly, assist you readily at all times, will defend you courageously when you are in difficulties, and will continue to be your friend unchangeably.

Do not make friendship hastily. If you make friendship with anybody, hold fast to him. Do not be always changing your acquaintances and friends.

True friendship is one of the sweetest joys of life.

Friendship between mean, diplomatic, greedy and crooked people will not last long.

The best of friendship is found not only in prosperity but in adversity. A true friend loves at all times.

There are true, lasting affection, harmony and goodwill between sincere friends.

Friendship augments joy and happiness and decreases misery by the doubling of our joy and the dividing of our grief.

Friendship is a deep, quiet, enduring affection, founded upon mutual respect and esteem. Friendship is always mutual. There is never unreciprocated or unrequited friendship.

Friendliness is a quality of friendly feeling without the deep and settled attachment implied in the state of friendship.

Affection is purely natural. Friendship is a growth. Friendship implies some degree of equality.

Comity is mutual, kindly courtesy, with care of each other's right.

Amity is a friendly feeling and relation, not necessarily implying special friendliness as the comity of nations or amity between neighbouring countries.

Friendship is more intellectual and less emotional than love. It is easier to give reasons for friendship than for love. Friendship is more calm and quiet, love more fervent. Love often rises to intensest form. We cannot speak of the passion of friendship.

A friend is one who is attached to another by affection or who entertains for another sentiments of esteem and respect which lead him to desire his company and to seek to promote his happiness and prosperity.

There can be no friendship without confidence and no confidence without integrity.

FRUGALITY

Frugality is thrift or economy with efficiency.

Frugality is prudent economy in the case of money or goods or provisions of any kind. It is good husbandry or housewifery.

Frugality makes a poor man rich. By sowing frugality, you reap liberty, a golden harvest.

Be frugal, but not niggardly or parsimonious or miserly.

Frugality is a virtue but niggardliness or miserliness is a vice.

The way to wealth depends on industry and frugality. Waste neither time nor money. Make the best use of both.

Without frugality, none can become rich and with it, few would be poor.

Abandon the superfluities or luxuries of life. Be simple. Have the motto: "Simple or plain living and high thinking." You will be free from want. You will enjoy infinite happiness.

Frugality is the daughter of prudence, the sister of temperance and the parent of liberty.

He who is extravagant will soon become poor. He will become dependent. He will be corrupted.

Economy is a wise and careful administration of the means at one's disposal.

Miserliness is the denying oneself and others the ordinary comforts or even necessaries of life for the sake of mere hoarding money.

Economy manages, frugality saves, providence plans, thrift at once earns and saves with a view to wholesome expenditure at fitting time.

Extravagance, lavishness and prodigality are the opposites of frugality.

GENEROSITY

Generosity is nobleness or liberality of nature. The essence of generosity is self-sacrifice. A generous man is bountiful.

Generosity is a disposition to give liberally or to bestow favours heartily. It is the act or practice of giving freely and kindly. It is beneficence or munificence. A generous man has a large or magnanimous heart. His charity is overflowing.

A generous man is endowed with a noble disposition. He is most pliant and courteous in his behaviour to his inferiors.

Generosity is the accompaniment of high birth. A generous man always gives and gives. His heart is filled with sympathy. Sympathy and benevolence are the attendants of generosity.

Generosity during life is different from generosity at the time of death. The former proceeds from real liberality and benevolence, the latter from pride or fear.

Liberality, munificence, magnanimity, beneficence, bounteousness are synonymous with generosity.

Generous refers to the self-sacrificing heartiness of the giver, liberal to the amount of gift. One is generous by a kindness of heart that will rejoice in the welfare rather than in the punishment of the offender. A child may show himself generous in the gift of an apple; a millionaire makes a liberal donation. A munificent gift is vast in amount whatever the motive of its bestower may be. 'Disinterested' suggests the thought of one's own self-denial. One is magnanimous by a greatness of soul that rises above injury or insult.

Ignoble, illiberal, mean, miserly, parsimonious, petty, stingy nature is the opposite of generous nature.

GENTLENESS

Gentleness is the state or quality of being mild and refined in manners and mild in disposition.

Gentleness is tenderness of feeling. It is love and consideration. It is sympathy.

Gentleness is softness or sweetness of disposition. It is mildness. It is docility. It is absence of roughness.

A man of gentleness is amiable, soothing and courteous. He is polite in manners. He is free from rudeness and harshness. He is sweet and soft.

Gentleness corrects whatever is offensive in your manners.

If one is gentle, it does not mean, he is weak and inefficient. Only the strong can be really gentle. Nothing is so strong as gentleness. Rudeness or harshness is sign of weakness, ignorance, impoliteness and inexperience.

Gentleness is a power.

Gentle describes the natural disposition; tame, that which is subdued by training; mild implies a temper which is, by nature, not easily provoked; meek, a spirit which has been schooled to mildness by discipline or suffering.

GOODNESS

Supreme goodness is God.

Goodness is virtue, excellence, benevolence.

Goodness is the state or quality of being good in any sense of that word especially kindness, benevolence, morality, virtue. It is an act or expression showing goodness. It is an act of benevolence, compassion or mercy.

If you do good to humanity, you approach nearly to the gods. "Be good; and do good." The whole ethics and right conduct are contained in this. If you practise this, you will soon attain God-realisation.

A good man always lives with God. He lives in God. He has a divinity within him.

A good man who does good actions attains fame and longevity.

A good deed is never lost. It purifies the heart and leads to the descent of divine light and dawn of divine grace.

He who sows courtesy reaps friendship. He who plants kindness, reaps love.

Goodness is love in action. It is noble to be good.

Goodness is the greatest virtue. Every good deed is a grain of seed for immortality or eternal life. Promote the welfare of the whole world. Work for the solidarity of the world.

Do all the good you can in all the ways you can, to all people you can, in every place you can, at all the times you can, with all the zeal, strength, love and heart and interest you can, as long as ever you can.

Return good for evil. It is the sign of a real man. Love begets love, hatred begets hatred.

Doing good and bringing happiness to others bring goodness and happiness to you.

Good is the conquest over evil. It is not the absence of evil.

Goodness makes life a blessing. Goodness will bring sure success and prosperity in life.

To do good is human. To be good is divine.

Little self-denial, honest service, little words of cheer, encouragement, sympathy and kindness, little acts of kindness, little virtuous deeds, little silent victories over temptations—these will pave a long way to the attainment of eternal bliss, perennial joy, everlasting peace and immortality.

Nations and peoples do not obey the laws of goodness. Therefore, the present world is beset with evils of various sorts.

The law of cause and effect is inexorable and unrelenting. You reap a harvest of suffering, poverty, pain and sorrow, beacuse you have sown the seeds of evil in the past. You reap a harvest of plenty and bliss, owing to your sowing the seeds of good. Try to understand this law. You will then begin to sow only seeds of good.

Entertain good, sublime, divine thoughts. Shut your mind from evil thoughts just as you shut your doors against the approach of enemies, thieves and dacoits. Always perform good actions. Evil cannot enter your mind now.

Cultivate good habits. Goodness is a habit. Goodness of nature is an inclination. Without goodness man is a brute or a vermin. He is a mischievous, wretched, despicable thing on this earth. He is a burden on this earth.

Even a little good thinking and a little doing good are highly beneficent. It will lead to eternal bliss. Then, why not try a little good thinking and good doing?

HINTS ON DEVELOPING
GOODNESS, PURITY AND TRUTHFULNESS

1. The noble soul who always does good to the world and entertains sublime divine thoughts is a blessing to the world at large.

2. A person of good deeds and good, pleasant, sweet speech has no enemy. If you really want spiritual growth and salvation, do good to those men who attempt to poison or hurt you.

3. Purity leads to wisdom and immortality. Purity is of two kinds, internal or mental and external or physical. Mental purity is more important. Physical purity is also needed. By the establishment of internal, mental purity, cheerfulness of mind, one-pointed mind, conquest of Indriyas and fitness for realisation of the Self are obtained.

4. Purity is the best jewel of a Yogi. It is the best and greatest treasure of a sage. It is the best wealth of a devotee.

5. Practice of compassion, charitable acts, kind services purifies and softens the heart, turns the heart-lotus upwards and prepares the aspirant for the reception of the Divine light.

6. Japa, Kirtan, meditation, charity, Pranayama can burn all sins and purify the heart quickly.

7. Truth is the highest wisdom. Truth stands even if there is no public support. Truth is eternal. Truth reigns supreme. Those who are truthful and pure, do not die. Those who are untruthful and lustful are as if dead already.

8. You must have a pure mind if you want to realise the Self. Unless the mind is set free, and casts away all desires, cravings, worries, delusion, pride, lust, attachment, likes and dislikes, it cannot enter into the domain of Supreme Peace and unalloyed felicity or the Immortal Abode.

9. Mind is compared to a garden. Just as you can cultivate good flowers and fruits in a garden by ploughing and manuring

the land and removing the weeds and thorns and the watering plants and trees so also you can cultivate the flower of devotion in the garden of your heart by removing the impurities of the mind such as lust, anger, greed, delusion, pride, etc., and watering it with divine thoughts. Weeds and thorns grow in the rainy season, disappear in summer; but their seeds remain underneath the ground. As soon as there is shower, the seeds again germinate and sprout out. Even so the Vrittis or modification of the mind manifest on the surface of the conscious mind, then disappear and assume a subtle seed-state, the form of Samskaras, and again become Vrittis either through internal or external stimulus. When the garden is clean, when there are no weeds and thorns you can get good fruits. So also when the heart and the mind are pure, you can have the fruit of good deep meditation. Therefore, cleanse the mind of its impurities first.

10. If you do not clean a plate daily, it will lose its lustre. It is the same with the mind too. The mind becomes impure if it is not kept clean by the regular practice of meditation.

11. Speaking truth frees one from worries and bestows peace and strength.

12. Speaking truth is the most important quailfication of a Yogi. If truth and one thousand Ashwamedha Yajnas are weighed in a balance, truth alone will out-weigh.

13. God is Truth. He can be realised by speaking the Truth and observing Truth in thought, word and deed.

14. Truthfulness, self-control, absence of envious emulation, forgiveness, modesty, endurance, absence of jealousy, charity, thoughtfulness, disinterested philanthropy, self-possession and unceasing compassion and harmlessness are the thirteen forms of truth.

15. Some persons hold that a lie, that is calculated to bring immense good is regarded as truth. Suppose an unrighteous king has ordered a sage to be hanged without any cause. If the life of this sage can be saved by uttering a falsehood, the falsehood is only Truth.

16. By speaking the truth always in all circumstances, the Yogi acquires Vak Siddhi. Whatever he thinks or speaks, turns to be true. He can do anything even by mere thought.

17. "This Atman is attainable by the strict observance of Truth." "There is nothing greater than the Truth" is the emphatic declaration of the Srutis. Take the life of Yudhishthira and

Satyavrati Harischandra. They did not part with the truth even at the critical junctures.

GRACEFULNESS

Gracefulness is easy elegance in form and manner. It is marked by propriety or fitness. It is the outward expression of the inward harmony of the soul.

Gracefulness is elegance of manners or deportment. It is beauty with dignity in manner, motion or courteousness.

A graceful figure is a perpetual letter of recommendation.

A graceful man is free from affectation and pretence. He has a dignified personality. He thinks, speaks and acts with propriety.

A man of gracefulness is characterised by grace, elegance, beauty, harmony or ease. He is pleasing in appearance, motion or language. He is graceful in form, action, looks or speech.

Graceful suggests motion or the possibility of motion. Beautiful applies to absolute fixity. A landscape or a sky is beautiful but neither is graceful. Graceful commonly applies to beauty as addressed to the eye though we often speak of a graceful poem or a graceful compliment. Graceful denotes a pleasing harmony of outline, proportion, etc., with a certain degree of delicacy. A Hercules is massive, an Appolo or a woman is graceful.

We speak of graceful attitude, graceful drapery.

We speak "Sita walks and speaks gracefully" i.e., with a natural ease and propriety, elegantly.

GRATITUDE

Gratitude is warm and friendly feeling towards a benefactor; thankfulness.

Gratitude is a sense of appreciation of favours received, accompanied with goodwill towards the benefactor. It is an emotion or sentiment of thankfulness, kindness or goodwill to a benefactor and a disposition to make a suitable return of benefits or services or, when no retuns can be made, a desire to see the benefactor prosperous and happy.

Gratitude is a duty which ought to be paid. It is much more than a verbal expresion of thanks. It is an indication of a noble nature. It is a virtue most deified. It is not only the memory of the benefit received from a good and kind man, but the homage of the heart rendered to him for his good deeds.

Gratitude is the noblest of virtues, the most capital of all duties.

Just as a river pours its waters into the ocean from which it drew its supply, so also a man of gratitude returns a benefit received from others. He looks upon his benefactor with reverence and love. If he is not able to return the benefit, he keeps it in his memory with kindness. He does not forget it during his whole life time.

Be grateful to God, your Creator, for all the bounties He has given you. Pray to Him fervently from the bottom of your heart. Sing His glory. Remember Him at all times. Surrender your entire being to him, obtain His Grace and be happy for ever.

An ungrateful man is a miserable wretch in this world. His lot is pitiable, lamentable and deplorable indeed! This world abounds with ungrateful wretches.

Be grateful. All will admire and revere you. You will reap a rich harvest of peace and immortal bliss.

Harohara. Tat Twam Asi. Om Shanti.

HEROISM

Heroism is courage or boldness.

A hero is distinguished for valour, fortitude, or bold enterprise. He is deified or regarded as a demi-god. Death of a hero puts him in a more exalted rank. He is worshipped in local festivals.

Hero is a man of distinguished bravery. He is very daring.

Heroism is the brilliant triumph of the soul over fear, fear of suffering, fear of death, etc.

Heroism is the sum of herioc qualities as lofty aim, fearlessness, resolution, fortitude.

Courage is generic, denoting fearlessness of danger. Fortitude is passive courage, the habit of bearing up nobly under trials, dangers and sufferings.

Bravery and valour are courage in battle or other conflicts with living opponents.

Intrepidity is firm courage, which shrinks not amid most appalling dangers.

Gallantry is adventurous courage, dashing into the thickest of the fight.

Heroism may call into exercise all these modifications of courage.

The world in all ages has worshipped its heroes, but the standard of heroism has always been improving. We reckon heroism today, not so much on account of the thing done, as for the motive behind the act.

HONESTY

Honesty is integrity, candour, freedom from fraud, frankness, fair dealing.

Honesty is the only virtue upon which individual or national life can safely rest. The society can only endure when it is built with the tempered mortar of honesty, justice and righteousness.

There is one immutable law—honesty. Honesty in the house, in the office, in politics, in business, on the highway, in the courts of justice, in all assemblies—is what we need.

Honesty is not the best policy, but it is the best virtue. It is the highest wisdom.

Honesty is conformity to justice and moral rectitude.

Honesty is a disposition to conform to justice and honourable dealing. It is uprightness of conduct in general. It is justice, fairness, probity, rectitude, uprightness.

The basis of high thinking is perfect honesty.

An honest man is characterised by openness, genuineness or sincerity. He is faithfull, sincere, straightforward, true, trustworthy, upright. He is always disposed to act with careful regard for the rights of others, especially in matters of business or property. He scrupulously observes the dictates of a personal honour that is higher than any demands of mercantile law or public opinion and will do nothing unworthy of his own inherent nobility of soul. He does not steal, cheat or defraud. He will not take an unfair advantage that would be allowed him.

He who is honest in the highest and fullest sense, is scrupulously careful to adhere to all known truth and right even in thoughts.

Deceitfulness, dishonesty, faithlessness, treacherousness, falsehood, hypocrisy, are the opposites of honesty.

No success in Yoga, no spiritual progress is possible without honesty.

HOPE

A desire of some good, with expectation of obatining it, or a belief that it is obtainable, is hope. Hope is anticipation.

Hope is a stimulant. Hope is a tonic. Man lives here through hope alone. He hopes to become better. He hopes to get something which will give him solace, satisfaction, comfort, peace, bliss and immortality.

Great things are never done, even small success is never achieved, when there is no hope.

Hope is the balm and life-blood of the soul. Hope gives you strength. Hope pushes and urges you to struggle, strive, achieve and attain.

Man always hopes to attain something and make himself better and better. The natural flight of the mind is from hope to hope.

Nil desperandum. Never despair. Life begins fresh each morning. Look not into the past. Be always hopeful. You will succeed.

Hope is your companion. Hope is the mother of success. Hope is your prop to lean upon and hope gives you happiness. Hope pushes you to sublime heights of splendour and glory. Hope conducts you through life by an agreeable path. Hope inspires and encourages. It conducts you in an easier and more pleasurable way to your journey's end.

Every man or woman in this world rests on hope. A medical student hopes to become a famous doctor with roaring practice. A young girl hopes to marry a beautiful, intelligent, rich husband. A businessman hopes to become a millionaire. A Munsiff hopes to become a District Judge.

Heart is the last organ that ceases its functioning. Hope is the last thing that dies in man.

You live not on what you have, but on what you hope.

Hope is that which is welcome. Expectation is either welcome or unwelcome. Trust and confidence denote dependence on a person or thing to bring about that which is desired.

The promises of hope are very sweet.

He who hopes helps himself.

Give up vain hopes. Fix not your hopes beyond the bounds of probability.

Be strong to hope, Oh heart!

Oh Auspicious Hope! In thy sweet garden grow the flowers of success and happiness.

HOSPITALITY

Hospitality is the spirit, practice or art of receiving and entertaining strangers and guests without reward and with kindness and consideration.

A hospitable man is generous and bountiful.

Hospitality is Atithi Yajna. It is one of the five Yajnas or daily sacrifices which are to be practised by the householders.

Hospitable people are rare in this world. All shut their doors and feed their stomachs with avidity, cupidity and stupidity.

Hospitality is a direct passport to heaven or higher blissful regions.

If rich people are hospitable, the woes of this world will be lightened.

Let the hospitality of the house with respect to the poor, be kept up.

HUMILITY

Even if you are a man of great erudition, you must be very humble. A learned man with humility is very much revered by all.

If you want to drink water at the tap, you will have to bend yourself. Even so, if you want to drink the spiritual nectar of immortality, you will have to bend. You must be meek and humble.

Humility is the highest of all virtues. 'Blessed are the meek; for they shall inherit the earth' (St. Mathew, Chap. V—51). You can destroy your egoism by developing this one virtue alone. You can influence the whole world. You will become a magnet to attract many persons. All the lives will be drawn towards you. Humility must be genuine. Feigned humility is hypocrisy. It cannot stand.

God helps you only when you feel utterly humble. Therefore develop this virtue to a considerable degree. Become an embodiment of humility. Become humility personified.

There is no virtue greater than humility. Through this one virtue alone you can get salvation. Humility destroys egoism, brings Sama-bhava, Atma-vasya, peace of mind, good sleep and rest, Atma Bhava or Narayana Bhava in all beings and eventually Self-realisation or Vishnu Padam.

INDUSTRIOUSNESS

This is the quality of being diligent. It is assiduity. This is steady application to labour, study or writing.

A man of industrious nature is laborious. He is very hard-working.

This is the opposite of idleness, sloth and indolence.

An industrious man earns the fairest fruits and the richest rewards.

Industry will improve your talents, make up your lack of abilities and supply their deficiencies.

Great persons achieved their greatness by industry rather than by mere brilliance.

The way to wealth and prosperity depends upon industry and frugality.

Industry makes all things easy. It always achieves triumph. An industrious man will never starve. Poverty and failure are unknown to him.

Industry keeps the body healthy and strong, the mind clear, the heart whole and the purse full.

Industrious nature produces cheerfulness, joy; destroys evil tendencies and habits, sweetens enjoyment and seasons your attainments with a delightful relish.

We speak in common parlance: "Sri Tawker is an industrious workman; Sri Bannerjee is an industrious man of letters; Sri Ramaswami had an industrious career."

Goldsmith writes in his "The Traveller":

"Industrious habits in each bosom reign
And industry begets a love of gain."

Be industrious and attain success and prosperity.

INITIATIVE

Initiative is the power or rite of commencing. It is an introductory step or action. It is making a beginning. It is the performance of the first act. It is a first move, beginning or start.

We say: "Rama took the initiative in that noble work."

Initiative is the power to originate or start. It is the aptitude to develop or undertake new enterprises. It is the first active procedure in any enterprise.

It is the power of commencing. It is the power of taking the lead or of originating.

Many people lack the initiative as they are timid, shy, lazy and indolent, as they are lacking in pluck, tact, pushing nature, strength of will, vigilance, diligence, perseverance and courage. Therefore, they are not successful in life.

Be bold. Be cheerful. Be tactful. Be skilful. Be vigilant. Be persevering. Be patient. The initiative will come and you will attain sanguine success in all your undertakings.

INSPIRATION

Inspiration is a superior, elevating, divine influence.

It is the supernatural divine influence exerted upon the sacred teachers and writers by the Spirit of God by which divine authority is given to their writings.

It is the supernatural influence by which prophets, apostles, saints and sacred writers are qualified to set forth divine truths without any mixture or error.

It is the communication of the divine will to the understanding by suggestions or impressions on the mind, which leave no room to doubt the reality of their supernatural origin.

All sacred scriptures are given by inspiration of God.

Inspiration is the infusion or communication of ideas or poetic spirit by a superior being or presiding power.

Inspiration is spiritual inexhaustible wealth. It gives joy, peace and bliss eternal.

An inspired writing convinces and converts sinners, atheists, sceptics. It edifies and comforts believers. It prepares them for emancipation or the final beatitude. It is a safe, infallible, trustworthy, guide, concerning the way of emancipation.

It is majestic, pure, forcible, clear. It is the word of God.

INTEGRITY

Integrity is uprightness of character, honesty, purity. Integrity is the first step to true greatness. A man of integrity is honoured and respected by all. All place confidence in him.

To maintain integrity costs self-denial. It is liable to opposition, but its end is glorious. The whole world will pay homage to it.

Integrity comprehends the whole moral character, but has a special reference to uprightness in mutual dealings, transfers of property and agencies for others.

The moral grandeur of independent integrity is the sublimest thing in this world.

INTUITION

Intuition is direct supermental knowledge of Atman through direct Self-realisation. There is no reasoning here. Intellect ceases to function here. There is no sensation here. Intuition is beyond relativity.

This is an inner spiritual experience which cannot be adequately described in words. Language is imperfect; also it cannot express this whole, ineffable, transcendental experience. Words are merely conventional.

You can realise God or Atman only through intuition.

In intuition everything is clear. All doubts vanish in toto.

Intuition is immediate knowledge in contrast with mediate-knowledge. Through intuition the aspirant perceives the truth of things without reasoning or analysis.

Intuition is knowledge from within. First there is the flash of intuition. Thereupon the aspirant is established in his own Atman or self.

Intuition is immediate knowledge of the Absolute through the eye of wisdom as opposed to knowledge of the objects through the senses and intellect.

Intuition transcends reason, but is not opposed to reason.

Intuition is truth obtained by internal apprehension without the aid of perception or the reasoning powers.

Intuition is the direct perception and apprehension of the divine reality underlying the manifested and the unmanifested universe.

The sage in his flights of intuition ascends to that supramental region where he experiences the Divine Reality or the Absolute. The superconscious experience is very vivid, vital and vibrant. It is intensely real to the sage. He lives in it, moves in it and breathes in it. The intuitive experience-whole is grand, sublime and profound.

The knowledge of God would have been lost to mankind but for the intuition and revelation of the seers and sages.

Intuition is the only way by which the Absolute can be realised and experienced in all its totality and integrality. These mortal limited senses and the finite intellect cannot comprehend the all-pervading Reality.

The mind and senses require time and space to function, but the Reality which is beyond this temporal, spacial and causal order of things can only be grasped and apprehended by intuition.

Reason can give you only conceptual knowledge and conceptual knowledge does not give you knowledge of the Reality in its whole, in its totality, but it divides, fragmentises and breaks things into pieces.

The Indwelling Soul of this material universe is pure consciousness. Indian sages and seers have intuited this Reality in all its integrality and have given to mankind the rich and precious pearl of wisdom of the Self.

KINDNESS

Kindness is the state or quality of being kind. It is goodwill, humaneness, tenderness.

Kindness is that temper or disposition which delights in contributing to the happiness of others. Any act of benevolence which promotes the happiness or welfare of others is kindness.

Kindness is a grace very near the likeness of God.

A kind man is disposed to do good to others. He is benevolent. He is good-natured, sympathetic, friendly, tender, accommodating and amicable.

A kind man wins the hearts of others.

Kindness is the cheapest of all things. Exercise of kindness does not involve much trouble and sacrifice. Smile, serve, radiate joy. Speak kind and sweet words. Cheer up a man in distress.

Kind words soothe, quiet and comfort the hearer.

Kindness is the golden chain by which people are bound together.

Heaven is open to all kind-hearted persons.

A kind man is really the king of a vast domain. He is indeed the Emperor of emperors.

A kind look, a kind word, a kind act, a friendly smile, all cost nothing but bring to others happiness which money cannot buy. They are priceless in their value.

He who entertains kind thoughts is ever calm and cheerful. Kind thoughts increase the flow of vital energy into your body and mind.

Do kind acts now. Do not procrastinate.

Kindness is like a healing balm. It soothes suffering.

Kindness is the language the deaf can hear and the dumb understand.

Little drops of water make the mighty ocean. Even so, little acts of kindness make an ocean of goodwill.

By 'many kindness' is meant not 'much kindness' nor 'great kindness', but kindness manifested in many forms or shown on many occasions, many acts of kindness.

Kindness is a direct passport to the kingdom of Eternal Bliss.

Cultivate kindness. Be kind to all. You will soon attain God-realisation.

LOVE

Love is the living essence of the divine nature which beams full of all goodness. Love is the golden link or tie which binds heart to heart, mind to mind, soul to soul. Love is the crowning grace of humanity.

It is the holiest right of the soul. Love is the masterkey to open the door of Moksha or eternal bliss.

Love is the best thing in this world. It cements broken hearts.

Life is a sweet flower of which love is the honey. The great pleasure of life is love. Love is the whole, the very life-breath of your heart.

Love is indeed heaven upon earth. It casts out all sorts of fears.

This world has come out of love. It exists in love. It finally dissolves in love.

Love inspires, illumines, designates and leads the way. Love inspires love.

Love never reasons but profusely gives. It is not affected by offence or insult. It looks not with the eyes, but with the heart. It looks through a telescope.

Love makes great sacrifices. Love is anxious to help and serve others and make others happy. Love forgives.

Love is a saviour of life unto life. Love is a divine elixir. It bestows immortality, supreme peace and everlasting joy.

God is an embodiment of love. He is an ocean of love. If you wish to attain God-realisation, you must also become an embodiment of love.

The only greatness lies in unselfish, pure love. There is not even a tinge of selfishness in pure love.

The love of a mother is never exhausted. It never changes. It never tires. Mother's love endures for ever. Love is not getting or bargaining, but giving. Love is goodness, honour and peace and pure living.

Pure love is bliss. Pure love is sweet. Pure love is without selfish attachment. Pure love is immortal, divine essence. Pure love is a divine flame. It is ever brilliant. It is never exhausted.

It is the very essence of pure love to be willing to suffer for the good of others, to place its happiness in the happiness of others.

Pure love strengthens and ennobles the character, gives a higher, pure motive and a nobler aim to every action of life and makes a man strong, noble and courageous.

True, pure love or divine Prema is eternal, unchanging, infinite. It takes unselfish interest in other people's welfare, interest in other lives than its own.

Physical love is animalism. It is passion exalted and refined. It is gross and sensual.

Love of body or skin is passion. Love of God is Prema or devotion. It is pure love. It is love for love's sake.

To love any one for attaining some selfish gain is selfish love. It binds you to this earth.

To love all beings with Narayanabhava as manifestations of the Lord is pure love. It is divine love. It leads to liberation.

Pure love redeems, purifies the heart and transmutes you into divinity.

A husband loves his wife not for the sake of his wife, but loves her for the sake of his own self. He is selfish. He expects sensual pleasure from her. If leprosy or small-pox destroys her beauty, his love for her ceases.

All loves are simply stepping stones to the love of God.

Cultivate pure love slowly in the garden of your heart through Japa, prayer, Kirtan, faith, devotion, service of saints, humanity and all beings, meditation and company of saints, etc.

Love all. Embrace all. Include all in the warm embrace of your love. Cultivate cosmic love or unreserved love.

Love your neighbour as your own self. Love God with all your heart, mind and soul.

Hatred ceases not by hatred but ceases by love. Return love for hatred.

Love your enemies, love your inferiors. Love all animals. Love your Guru. Love all saints and sages.

Love little, but love long. Love must be of an enduring nature.

Speak lovingly. Act lovingly. Serve lovingly. You will soon enter the Kingdom of Heaven or Supreme Peace.

Love not perishable, mundane objects. You will come to grief and destruction if you love them.

Love God. Love your own immortal Self or Atman. You will be blissful for ever. You will become immortal.

Eat in love. Drink in love. Bathe in love. Talk in love. Sleep in love. Write in love. Think in love. Serve in love. Walk in love. Become an embodiment of love.

UNIVERSAL LOVE

The only Sara Vastu in this world is Prema or Love. It is eternal, infinite and undecaying. Physical love is passion (Moha) or infatuation. Universal love is only Divine love. Cosmic love and universal love are synonymous terms. God is love. Love is God. Selfishness, greed, egoism, vanity, pride, hatred, contract the heart and stand in the way of developing universal love.

Develop universal love gradually through selfless service, Satsanga with great souls, prayer, recitation of Guru Mantras, etc. When the heart is contracted through selfishness in the beginning, man loves only his wife, children, a few friends and relatives. As he evolves, he loves the people of his own district, then the people of his own province. Later on he develops love for men of his country. Eventually, he begins to love other people of different countries. In the long run he begins to love all. He develops universal love. All the barriers are broken now. Heart is expanded infinitely. It is very easy to talk of universal love. But when you want to put it into actual practice, it becomes extremely difficult. Petty-mindedness of all sorts comes in the way. Old wrong impressions which you have created by your wrong mode of life in the past, act as stumbling blocks. Through iron determination, strong will- power, patience, perseverance and Vichara (right enquiry), you can conquer all obstacles quite easily. The grace of the Lord will descend on you if you are sincere.

Universal love terminates in Advaitic unity or oneness or Upanishadic consciousness of seers and sages. Pure love is a great leveller. It brings equality and equanimity. Hafiz, Kabir, Mira, Gouranga, Tukaram, Ramdas—all have tasted this universal love. What others have achieved you can also attain.

Feel that whole world is your body; your own home. Melt or destroy all barriers that separate man from man. The idea of superiority is ignorance or delusion. Develop Viswa-prema, all-embracing love. Unite with all. Separation is death. Unity is eternal life. The whole world is Visva-Brindavan. Feel that this body is moving temple of God. Wherever you are, whether at home, in office, railway station or market, feel that you are in the temple. Consecrate every act as an offering unto the Lord. Transmute every work into Yoga by offering its fruits to God. Have Akarta, Sakshi Bhava if you are a student of Vedanta. Have Nimitta Bhava if you are a student of Bhakti Marga. Feel that all beings are images of God. *Isaavasyamidam Sarvam*—this world is indwelt by the Lord. Feel that one power of God works through all hands, sees through all eyes, hears through all ears. You will become a changed being. You will enjoy the highest peace and bliss.

May Lord Hari take you all to His bosom and bathe you with waters of sweet love!

May your heart be filled with cosmic love!

COSMIC LOVE AS AHIMSA

Much has been written and said about cosmic love. An exhortation to develop selflessness and cosmic love has become part of religious preaching. It is as it should be. For, selflessness and cosmic love are the very alpha and beta of spiritual life. They form the foundation of life divine, and their influence is felt throughout the superstructure. It would be quite true to say that these twin-virtues form the most essential prerequisites, the disciplines, the test of progress, the Supreme Attainment and its later manifestation. Selflessness and cosmic love are the Sadhana, the Sadhya and Siddhi. They are the guiding light of the Sadhaka, and the aura of the Siddha. In neither can it be absent! Hence the supreme importance of our understanding aright the true meaning of selflessness and cosmic love, or, shall we say selflessness or cosmic love, for, on a closer scrutiny we shall find that the two are in fact one. One who is truly selfless, who has given up love of the self, finds himself in Cosmic Love. One in whose heart the rarest flower of cosmic love grows has hardly a thought for his own self, much less a love for it: he is utterly selfless.

Cosmic love as Sadhana is the golden mean between Raga (inordinate love or attachment) and Dvesha (hatred). It is very important for an aspirant to remember that *cosmic* love is the very antithesis of love of any one particular thing or being. Love of one is Moha (delusion) and Raga (attachment). It is the root of bondage to Samsara. Cosmic love, on the other hand, is liberating and has to be distinguished from Raga. Therefore, do the scriptures and saints ask the Sadhaka to develop Vairagya (the antidote to the poison of Raga) to the highest degree.

Again, Vairagya is good so far as it goes. But it should not lead the Sadhaka to the self-exclusiveness which is none other than a subtle form of selfishness. Here, too, there is need for caution. The aspirant who zealously cultivates Vairagya might turn away from the world, might shun company and comforts; but he might become extremely selfish. He might all the time be thinking of himself, his Sadhana, and his Vairagya. Naturally, he would come to regard everything and everyone that does not fall in line with his views, his behaviour, his standards of conduct, and his Sadhana as inimical to himself. Now, this, again is extreme. Vairagya is not contemptuous aversion, but the absence of Raga or inordinate love or attachment. Contemptuous aversion, on the other hand, is subtle Dvesha (dislike or hatred), subtle Himsa—the negation of Ahimsa.

Vairagya should be the natural corollary to Ahimsa. Attachment to everything other than the Self or Atman should be given up. Love of self, of the body, of the modes of thought that take the form of pet dogmas and ideologies—everything other than the Self should be given up. For, one who worships these "little" things, the unrealities, the objects of phenomena, is bound to get entangled in the Dvandvas of "love" (Raga) and "hate" (Dvesha). To illustrate; one may have no attachment whatsoever to one's family, to one's property to one's own body even—but he may be attached to some pet ideology. It may outwardly seem that he has great Vairagya, that he is perfectly selfless. You will find on closer analysis that it is not really so. Adoration of a pet ideology means, in however subtle a degree, an aversion to (if not hatred of) some other opposing ideology; and, though one may strive not to translate this aversion into personal animosity towards those who hold different views yet it lurks at the back of one's mind. There is attachment (Raga) to that ideology; and so there is no Vairagya. There is adoration of something born of the self, however subtle it may be—so, there is no selflessness either. Cosmic love is (by the same test) found to be absent.

Now, we have to find That which is not attachment, nor self-exclusiveness. That certainly is cosmic love, which knows no hatred in however subtle a degree or sublimated a form. It is impossible to define this Cosmic Love—*Anirvachaneeyam Prema-Svarupam*. The wise Patanjali Maharshi, therefore, enjoined upon the Sadhakas to get established in Ahimsa. Note the wisdom that prompted him to give a negative nomenclature, Ahimsa. Harbour not evil thoughts; utter no evil word; harm none. Here, then is a Sadhaka that carefully, wisely and efficiently avoids all the extremes, all chances of perversion. When the Sadhaka thus gets established in Ahimsa, the Light of Self-knowledge dawns in him. He realises that the Self that resides in him, resides as the Self of all beings. That state in which this knowledge fully manifests itself is Cosmic Love.

Such a sage (for a Sage is one in whom Cosmic Love resides) does not shun society; he hates none. He loves all, not as a matter of gracious condescension, but as a natural course of conduct of one who does not love his own self above anything else, who hates none, nothing, and in whom there is not the slightest trace of hatred or ill-will. He loves the Self which pervades all creatures. As this Self is all-pervading, he is attached to none, nothing. He identifies himself with all, because he is free from self-adoration. Selfless service springs from him as the breath springs from all living beings. Whomever he comes into contact with in the normal course of his daily life, he adores as the manifestation of his own Self. He wishes them well. He is filled with goodwill, as he has cast ill-will out of his heart. The very practice of Ahimsa has enabled him to root out selfishness. A selfish man can never truly practise Ahimsa. Love of self always means no-love of something else; eagerness to acquire something for oneself must necessarily mean effort to deprive some one else of it. The sage who is established in Ahimsa or Cosmic Love, on the other hand, takes as much delight in others' enjoyment as in his own. When he finds that some one is suffering, he rushes to relieve. Not because he loves that particular person; but because he has realised that his own Self pervades the other person, because the goodwill or cosmic love that fills his heart naturally flows towards the suffering man and endeavours to remove his affliction. This service he renders naturally—service for the sake of service; love for love's sake—these expressions can be understood only if you watch the behaviour of one whose heart is filled with Cosmic Love. It is a love that does not clamour for reciprocity; it is service which does not look back for appreciation or reward. In this love, in this service, the Sage of Cosmic Love makes no distinction whatsoever. All are equal to him. Otherwise, it would not be Cosmic Love, it would not be Ahimsa, it would not be selflessness. He is tranquil and peaceful, for Cosmic Love has extinguished the fire of selfishness, lust, anger and greed, that consume the peace of an ordinary man. He is ever happy for he has no desires, and Cosmic Love keeps him ever happy-at-the-happiness-of-all, and he lives in the Consciousness of the Immortality of the Self, in the indestructibility of the soul of man.

Glory, glory to the Sage of Cosmic Love! May Cosmic Love dwell in the hearts of all.

MAGNANIMITY

Magnanimity is greatness of soul. It is elevation of dignity, of mind. It is that quality of mind which raises a person above all that is mean or unjust. It is generosity. It is nobility.

Magnanimity is generosity in sentiment or conduct towards others. It is exaltation above envious, cowardly, vindictive or selfish motives. It is loftiness of character or action. It is large-heartedness.

Magnanimity is that elevation or dignity of soul which encounters danger and trouble with tranquillity and firmness, which raises the possessor above revenge and makes him delight in acts of benevolence, which makes him disdain injustice, and meanness and prompts him to sacrifice personal ease, interest and safety for the accomplishment of useful and noble objects.

A man of magnanimity is elevated in sentiment. He is brave and unselfish. He scorns temptations, what is mean and base and despises earthly pomp and splendour.

Of all virtues, magnanimity is the rarest.

Mighty of heart, mighty of mind—magnanimous is indeed to be great in life.

Generosity, high-mindedness, chivalrousness, large-heartedness, nobleness of soul are synonymous with magnanimity.

MANLINESS

Manliness is bravery.

Manliness is not merely courage. It is the quality of soul which frankly accepts all conditions in human life and makes it a point of honour not to be dismayed or wearied by them.

Dignity is manliness. Nobility is manliness.

Manliness is freedom from childishness, boyishness or womanishness.

A manly man possesses characteristics of a true man as bravery, resoluteness, etc.

Every virtue or the higher phase of manly character begins in this—in truth and modesty before the face of all maidens; in truth and pity, or truth and reverence to all womanhood.

'Manly' refers to all the qualities and traits worthy of a man.

We speak of manly decision, manly gentleness or tender-ness—such as firmness, bravery, undaunted spirit, dignified nature, nobility and stateliness.

MANNERS

'Manners' is good behaviour or respectful deportment. It is good character. It is good breeding.

'Manners' is the demeanour or bearing peculiar to one. It is personal carriage. It is mien. It signifies polite, civil or well-bred behaviour.

A man of good manners is free from rudeness. He is well-behaved. He is complaisant, civil, courteous and polite.

Good manners constitute good behaviour. They consist of courtesy and kindness. They are the art of making those people easy with whom you converse. They give colour to life.

Manners are the result of much good sense, some good nature and a little self-denial for the sake of others.

A man of good manners is always sociable and complaisant.

Good manners are the best thing in the world to get a good name and make friendship.

A man of good manners eats quietly, moves quietly, lives quietly and loses even his money quietly.

Good manners are stronger than laws.

Good manners make the road of life smooth. They render a superior amiable, an equal agreeable and an inferior acceptable. They smooth distinctions, sweeten conversation, and make everyone in the company pleasant with himself. They produce good nature, mutual benevolence, soothe the turbulent, encourage the timorous and humanise the fierce.

Manners are minor morals. They are the shadows of virtue. They are a passport to regard. They are the blossom of good sense and good feeling.

Pride, ill-nature, want of sense, arrogance, impatience are the great sources of ill-manners.

Good manners are a part of good morals. They are a rare gift. They easily and rapidly ripen into morals.

Be silent as to yourself. Say little or nothing about yourself.

MEEKNESS

Meekness is the state or quality of being mild and gentle of temper. It is submissiveness. It is humility. It is gentleness of disposition. It is submission to divine will. It is that low, sweet root from which all divine virtues shoot.

Blessed are the meek, because they will soon attain eternal peace.

Meekness abounds in goodwill. It excludes revenge, irritability, morbid sensitiveness.

A meek man bears patiently the resentments of others.

Meekness is the noblest self-denial. It is abstinence from self-love and self-conceit.

Meekness is a solid foundation of all the virtues.

Meekness is the essence of true religion. It is a fundamental virtue of a saint. It is not a weak and timid quality. It is a power. Meekness is nobility. It is always grace. The flower of meekness grows on a stem of grace.

God delights to dwell in the hearts of the meek.

The first, the second and the third thing in religion is meekness. Meekness is the avenue to spiritual glory. It makes a man divine.

Meekness is the root, mother, nurse, of all virtues.

Meekness is the one road to lead you to God.

Meekness, courtesy, benevolence, politeness, gracefulness are virtues of the same stock.

The first test of a saint or a truly great man is his meekness.

Meekness reveals the divine light.

God walks with the meek. He reveals Himself to the meek.

MERCY

Karuna Sagara Narayana
Karuna Sindhu Sadasiva.

God is an ocean of mercy or Karuna. He is all-merciful. If you want to have communion with Him, if you want to unite with Him, if you wish to dwell in Him, you must also become an embodiment of mercy.

Mercy is a fundamental attribute of a saint. If you do not find mercy in him, do not take him for a saint.

Mercy is an enemy of cruelty, atrocity, harshness, rudeness, ferocity. It is a friend of gentleness, softness, sweetness.

Mercy among the virtues is like the moon among the stars.

Mercy is a great power. It is intense strength. It gives strength.

Mercy opens the door to freedom, immortality and eternal bliss. It makes the narrow heart as wide as the sky. It gives wings to soar high to the realm of Supreme Peace.

Mercy transforms you into divinity. It is mightiest in the mightiest.

Sweet mercy is nectar. It is nobility's true mark or Linga. It is a celestial shower of Grace and love. It is a magnet.

Mercy is the greatest attribute of God. Mercy softens and purifies a sin-hardened heart.

Mercy shines with even more brilliance than justice. It bestows Chitta-Prasada or peace of mind. Therefore, be merciful.

Mercy is tenderness and forbearance shown in sparing an offender in one's power. It is a forgiving disposition.

Mercy is compassion or benevolence. Mercy is sublime goodness. It knows and understands the sufferings of others and is ready to help them.

The heart of a merciful man is more soft than butter. Butter melts near fire, but the heart of a merciful man melts when he sees the sufferings of others even at a distance.

The ingredients of mercy are tenderness of heart, fellow-feeling, good feeling, sympathy, compassion, supreme goodness, kindness, affection, love, charity, generosity, selflessness and sacrifice.

Mercy, compassion, sympathy and pity are virtues of the same genus. Mercy is the foremost amongst them. It is divine. It includes not only compassion, but also forgiveness, love and service. The man of mercy serves and loves the person who has wronged him.

Compassion comes next. Compassion is a fellow-feeling or sorrow for the sufferings of another. Compassion combines the tenderness of pity and the dignity of sympathy with the active helping nature of mercy; but it is exercised only in the case of those who are suffering and are unfortunate. Mercy has forgiveness, tolerance, forbearance and cosmic love also, in addition to the qualities that make up compassion.

Sympathy and pity are merely feeling for the others. Whereas compassion embraces in its love human beings and animals, sympathy is felt only for one's own equals or those who are above oneself. But, sympathy is not dynamic like compassion or mercy.

Pity is feeling for the suffering of inferiors. It implies a certain amount of vanity and arrogance in the person who pities another. On account of this vanity, pity almost always ends in words!

The thoughts, words and deeds of a merciful man are full of sympathy and compassion. He always shares what he has with others. He sacrifices even his own needs and comforts for the sake of others.

If you have a hard heart, try to do little acts of kindness and mercy. Give a cup of milk to the poor sick man. Give a small blanket to the poor man during winter. Feed a poor man or Sadhu once a month. Visit a Hospital and serve the sick patients. Thus cultivate mercy.

Feel for others' sufferings. Be merciful in your judgement of others. Remember your own defects, frailties and weaknesses. Be slow in your criticism of others and generous towards those who do wrong actions.

Show mercy to others. Others will also be merciful to you. You will receive mercy when it shall be most needed. This is the immutable law of God.

Remember again and again Lord Buddha and his actions and other saints. Study 'Lives of Saints' and 'Saints and Sages.' You will gradually develop mercy.

The sun, the tree, the river, are impartial. Even so you will have to show mercy towards your friend and your enemy.

Remain in the company of sages and saints. Meditate on the Lord. Repeat His Name. Sing Kirtan and His glory. You will develop mercy.

Meditate in the early morning on the quality of mercy. When you move in the world, feel 'I will be merciful today. I will perform acts of mercy.' Slowly mercy will become part and parcel of your nature.

Show mercy to animals and persons who are in distress. Wipe their tears. You will indeed be blessed.

Follow the example of Sri Swami Chidananda who has a wonderful heart filled with mercy. He dressed a dog which had an ulcer with maggots. He dressed a leper for three months, with his own hands.

Charitable institutions, charitable hospitals, decrepit homes, construction of wells, tanks, poor feeding homes, Annakshetra, Dharmashalas, animal welfare leagues, social service institutions—are all manifestations of mercy.

May mercy arise in your heart. May your heart be filled with mercy.

MODERATION

Moderation is freedom from excess. It is the act of restraining or tempering or lessening or repressing.

A man of moderation keeps himself within measure or bounds. He regulates his food and other things. He is temperate. He is reasonable.

Moderation is the inseparable companion of wisdom.

Moderation gives a charm to life. It bestows longevity and good health.

The choicest pleasures of life lie within the circle of moderation.

Moderation or temperance is the keeping of the proper mean between extremes and the tempering of excitement or passion. It is not so much a virtue in itself as a means to obtain it.

Moderation is an important quality which is to be cultivated by a student of ethics or an aspirant. Moderation is freedom from excess in anything. Moderation is calmness of mind. Moderation is equanimity. Moderation is skill in Yoga. Without moderation no success is possible in Yoga, and material pursuits also. All the luminaries of the world of the past have observed moderation.

You should be moderate in eating, drinking, sleeping, reading, laughing, copulation, talking, exercise, etc. Lord Krishna says, "Verily Yoga is not for him who eats too much, nor who abstains to excess, nor who is much addicted to sleep, nor even to wakefulness. Yoga kills all pains in him who is regulated in eating and amusement, regulated in performing actions, regulated in sleeping and waking" (Gita, VI. 16, 17). If you eat too much you will get too much sleep. Various diseases of stomach, intestines and liver will develop. All the internal organs will be overtaxed. Too much copulation will drain your energy and cause weakness, low vitality and various diseases. Too much talking will disturb peace of mind.

Lord Buddha plunged into extreme austerity in the beginning of his spiritual practices. He gave up food entirely. He did rigorous tapas. He suffered very much. His body became emaciated. He did not make much spiritual progress. Then he adhered to the golden medium. He began to take food in moderation. He regulated his spiritual practices. Only then he attained illumination. He always taught disciples to stick to the middle path only. He learnt lessons from experience.

It becomes difficult for some to control the tongue. If the dishes are palatable, they go beyond the limits of moderation. They overload the stomach. College students who have plenty of money with them go to the sweetmeat shops and eat sweetmeats for Rs. 5 at a time. They cannot get up till the stomach is completely filled up. Complete filling of stomach is unhygienic and unscientific. Half the stomach only should be filled with food, quarter with water; one quarter of the stomach must be free for expansion of gas. This is Mithahara or moderation in diet. You can check overloading of stomach through complete fasting.

Always get up when there is still inclination to eat. Giving up salt for two or three days in a week will help you to reduce the quantity of your food. Reduction of food will not kill you. It will keep you quite healthy. It will help you to attain longevity.

Some students begin to study hard forcing away sleep with strong tea, burning midnight oil just before appearing for the final examination. They lead a happy-go-lucky life for ten months. This is very bad. That is the reason why they fall sick on account of undue strain during the period of examination. Study must be well regulated. You must prepare your lessons thoroughly every day.

Some aspirants give up their food and try to live on Neem leaves for 40 days. This is foolish tapas. They fall sick, become weak, and are not able to do any Sadhana. Lord Krishna condemns this: "The men who perform severe austerities enjoined by the scripture, wedded to vanity and egoism, impelled by the force of their desires and passions, unintelligent, tormenting the aggregate elements forming the body and Me who is seated in the inner body, know these to be demonaical in their resolves." Do not spoil your health in the name of Tapascharya. Do not go to extremes in anything.

Sadhana also must be well-regulated. The period of meditation must be gradually increased. The period of Sirshasana must be gradually increased. The reduction of sleep must be gradual. When Sadhana is done by fits and starts there will be no spiritual progress.

Some people make friendship quickly with others, love them intensely for sometime and break it quickly on account of some trivial causes. They are extreme in their manifestations of emotions. They love either intensely or hate intensely. The emotions also must be well-controlled. Do not move too much with anybody. Be moderate in this direction also. You can keep lasting friendship with everybody.

Be moderate in your expenditure. Regulate your expenses. Some are imprudent. They thoughtlessly spend in one month too much and borrow in the next month.

Be moderate in thinking. Kill all irrelevant, nonsensical, loose thoughts. Do not think too much. Entertain sublime, divine thoughts.

Be moderate in work. Do not overwork. Overwork is cause for many diseases. If you overwork, you cannot meditate.

He who is perfectly moderate in everything is a real Yogi. He enjoys happiness here and in the next world also. He moves about happily and is always cheerful. He keeps perfect health and a higher standard of vigour, vim and vitality. He attains longevity and fame. He attains spiritual and material success.

Therefore stick to golden or happy medium. Follow always the middle path. Give up extremes in everything and be happy for ever.

May moderation be your motto and ideal!

MODESTY

Modesty is a shining light. It prepares the mind to receive wisdom and the heart to receive the Truth.

Modesty is the colour of virtue. It is not only an ornament but also a guard to virtue.

Modesty gives new lustre to one's character. It is a discerning grace. It is the citadel of beauty and virtue. It is a beautiful setting to the diamond of talent and genius. It is the greatest ornament of an illustrious life. It is the appendage of sobriety.

Modesty is ever amiable. It resides in a heart which is enriched with noble virtues.

Modesty is a feminine virtue. It is humility. It is purity of thought and manners. It is becoming behaviour. It is chastity. It is purity. It is moderation.

Modesty is the sense of propriety. It is the absence of all tendency to overestimate oneself. It is absence of anything suggestive of sexual impurity. It is decency. It is purity of manners, chiefly in reference to women.

Modesty is freedom from excess, exaggeration or extravagance. It is decent reserve or propriety of manner or speech. It is purity of thought, character, feeling or conduct. It is decorousness.

We speak of maidenly modesty. We speak of modest scholar. "He is too modest to speak."

There is no conceit in a modest man or woman. As a plain garment gives very good beauty to a woman, so a decent behaviour or modesty is the greatest ornament of wisdom.

A modest man or woman is unostentatious or unassuming, unpretentious. He is disinclined to bring himself into notice or limelight. He is free from show or gaudiness.

A modest man does not brag. He turns away his ear from his own praise. He is free from vanity and pride. He is very very simple.

A modest woman is bashful. She is not forward.

An egoistic man will always speak of himself, but a modest man ever shuns making himself the subject of his conversation.

The speech of a modest man is inspiring, and elevating. It touches your heart. It penetrates your heart. It breathes love and wisdom. It gives lustre to truth.

Make no display of your talent or attainments. Do not blow your trumpet. Be modest. All will admire and acknowledge your talents, abilities and achievements. A pot full of water makes no sound. Empty vessels make much sound. Modesty is eloquence itself.

A modest man wins the heart of all. He is respected and adored by all. Therefore be modest. Cultivate modesty to a maximum degree.

NOBILITY

Nobility is the quality of being noble. It is greatness of mind or character. It is dignity, excellence, generosity.

Nobility is the state or quality of being noble in character as distinguished from selfishness, cowardice and meanness. It is dignity and grace of character. It is magnanimity, greatness, nobleness.

Nobility is that elevation of soul which comprehends bravery, generosity, magnanimity, intrepidity, and contempt of everything that dishonours character.

It is not wealth nor ancestry, but honourable conduct and and a noble disposition that makes you great.

Nobility without virtue, is a fine setting without a gem. Virtue is the first title of nobility.

If you are endowed with a generous mind, this is the best kind of nobility.

Nobility is a graceful ornament to a man or woman. True nobility is derived from virtue, not from birth.

The true standard of quality is in the mind. He who thinks nobly is really noble.

Nobility is the finer portion of the mind and heart linked to divinity.

The essence of true nobility is neglect of self.

Sweet mercy is the true badge of nobility.

OBEDIENCE

Obedience is willingness to obey commands.

Obedience is submission to or compliance with a command, prohibition, known laws, or rule of duty. It is the performance of what is required or enjoined or the abstaining from what is prohibited. Obedience is submission to authority as obedience to a person or to a law.

To obey is better than sacrifice.

He who obeys only can command or rule.

The man who commands efficiently must have obeyed others in the past and the man who obeys dutifully is worthy of being some day a commander

From obedience spring all other virtues.

True obedience neither procrastinates nor questions.

Obedience is the mother of success, and is wedded to safety.

Let your child's first lesson be obedience.

Wicked men obey from fear; good men from love.

Command is anxiety; obedience is ease.

Goodness is a river that follows from the lotus feet of the Lord by the path of obedience.

If the heart is not satisfied, obedience is not truly performed by the body.

OPTIMISM

Optimism is the doctrine that everything is ordered for the best. It is a disposition to take a bright, hopeful view of things.

Optimism is the doctrine or view that everything in nature and the history of mankind is ordered for the best, the order of things in the universe being adapted to produce the highest good.

It is the doctrine that the universe is tending toward a better state. It is the disposition to believe that, however things may appear to the contrary, whatever is or occurs is right and good. It is sanguine temperament opposed to pessimism.

Pessimism is the opposite of optimism.

An optimist sees an opportunity in every difficulty; a pessimist sees a difficulty in every opportunity.

There is a bright side to every situation. Adopt a hopeful, confident state of mind. The trouble is half overcome before you start on it.

An optimist gets the best out of life. He hopes the best and makes the best of people and circumstances and thinks the best of people.

Optimism is hope. It is happy life. It saves people.

How can the existence of evil be reconciled with the goodness of God? Optimism solves the question by affirming that evil is the necessary antecedent of good.

Optimism makes you happy and cheerful. The accident is not as terrible as you feared. The hill is not so steep as you thought before you begin climbing. The difficulty is not as great as you expected. Things come out better than you hope.

PATIENCE

Patience is the quality of being patient or able calmly to endure. It is the quality of sustaining pain without repining.

A man of patience is not easily provoked. He is calm and serene even under adverse conditions.

Patience is strength. It is the support of weakness. It is the greatest and sublimest power. Patience can work wonders. It can move mountains. Patient working can achieve anything in this world. It will surmount every obstacle in the search after truth. A patient man can have what he will.

Everything comes if you only will wait. To know how to wait is the great secret of success. Patience lies at the root of all pleasures. Patience develops will-power and the power of endurance.

Patience is not passive. It is indifference. It is concentrated strength. It is the pillar of human peace on this earth.

Patience is a chief ingredient of wisdom. It is the finest and worthiest part of fortitude and forbearance. It is the key of contentment. It is the courage of the conqueror.

Be patient in little things. Learn to bear the daily trials and annoyances quietly and calmly. You will develop great strength and bear severe calamities, privations, sufferings and adversities.

Patience strengthens the spirit, sweetens the temper, stifles anger, develops the will force, extinguishes jealousy, subdues pride, controls the organ of speech, restrains the hand.

Patience is the sister or daughter of fortitude. Patience is genius.

Patience is bitter, but its fruit is extremely sweet.

Patience is the soul of peace. It makes a man divine. The best of men, all the saints, sages, Yogis and Sannyasins had immense patience. It was their ornament or crest-jewel

Patience is a specific remedy for control of anger. It is a penicilin injection to kill anger.

Patience is passive fortitude. It is the habit of mind shown in passive endurance of the evils to which man is liable.

Patience is unflinching, undaunted perseverance. Genius is patience. It is the exercise of unaltering endurance and perseverance in any work or activity or in pursuit of a desired end.

We say: "Ram has patience in study."

Patience may also have an active force denoting uncomplaining steadiness in doing, as in tilling the soil, removing the shell of "chilgosa", etc. There is untiring energy.

Endurance hardens itself against suffering and may be merely stubborn. It may be made to have a passive force, as when we speak of "passive endurance."

Fortitude is endurance animated by courage. Patience is not so hard as endurance, so self-effacing as submission. Submission is ordinary and resignation always applies to matters of great moment, while patience may apply to slight worries and annoyances.

Forbearance is abstaining from retaliation or revenge. Patience is keeping kindliness of heart under vexatious conduct. Long suffering is continual patience.

Patience refers to the quietness or self-possession of one's own spirit; resignation to his submission to the will of another.

There is patience in or amidst sufferings. There is patience with or toward opposers or offenders. There is patience under affliction. We do not speak of patience of heat or cold or hunger.

In patience there is quiet endurance or forbearance under distress, pain, injury, insult, suspense, calamity, provocation.

A man of patience has a calm, unruffled temper. He has endurance without murmuring or fretfulness or retaliation.

Patience is also the act or quality of waiting for justice or expected good without discontent.

A patient man is not hasty. He is not overeager or impetuous.

PATIENCE AND PERSEVERANCE

Patience and perseverance are noble qualities that are born of Sattva. No success either in the material world or in the spiritual path is possible without these qualities. These qualities develop the will-power. Difficulties do crop up at every stage and these are to be overcome by patient efforts and perseverance. The success of Mahatma Gandhi was due to these qualities. He never got discouraged by failures. All great persons of the world have achieved greatness and success and eminence through patience and perseverance. You will have to develop these virtues slowly.

A patient man always keeps his head cool. He keeps a balanced mind. He is not afraid of failures and difficulties. He finds out methods to strengthen himself. For the practice of concentration of mind one should have assinine patience. Many people get discouraged when they encounter some difficulities and give up the work as hopeless. This is very bad. Aspirants should not give up their Sadhana when they come across some difficulties.

The ants collect small particles of sugar and rice and store them up in their abode. How patient and persevering they are! In the Bible you will find the words; "Go to the ant, thou sluggard, and observe its ways and be wise." The bees collect a drop of honey from each flower patiently and store the honey in the honey-comb. How patient and persevering they are! How patient are the engineers who construct big dams and bridges over seas and big rivers. How patient was the scientist who found out that diamond was only carbon. See how patient is Sir J.C. Bose in his laboratory when he is making experiments with plants! The saint who is living in the caves of the Himalayas is more patient than these men in his practices of mind-control.

A patient man cannot be irritated even a bit. Patience helps a man in the conquest of temper. Patience gives immense strength. Do all your routine of the day patiently. Slowly develop virtues. Be eager to develop them. Have a mental image of "OM PATIENCE", in your mind. The habit will slowly develop. Meditate on this virtue in the morning. Try to do all actions of the day patiently. Never grumble or murmur. Think of the advantages of patience and I assure you that you will become an embodiment of patience ultimately.

PATRIOTISM

Patriotism is love of and devotion to one's country.

Patriotism is the passion which influences one to serve one's country, either in defending it from invasion or protecting it from invasion or protecting its rights and maintaining its laws and institutions in vigour and purity.

It is the spirit that, originating in love of country, prompts to obedience to its laws, to the support and defence of its existence, rights and institutions, and to the promotion of its welfare.

He who truly loves and serves his motherland is a patriot.

Love of one's country is one of the loftiest virtues.

Your country's welfare is your first concern. He who promotes that best, best proves his duty.

The noblest motive is the public good.

That patriotism which animates and prompts to deeds of self-sacrifice, of valour, of devotion and of death itself—that is public virtue, that is the sublimest of public virtues.

First patriotism. Then comes Vedantism.

PEACE

The peace that passeth all understanding has been, since the remotest times, the axis round which Indian culture has revolved in all its aspects.

Peace is a state of quiet. It is freedom from disturbance, anxiety, agitation, riot or violence. It is harmony, silence, calm, repose, rest. Specifically it is the absence or cessation of war.

Peace is the very nature of the soul, or Atman. All the Vrittis or modifications of the mind are dissolved in the soul. There is no Sankalpa or thought.

Selflessness, desirelessness, non-attachment freedom from I-ness and mine-ness, cravings, devotion to God or Atman, self-restraint, control of senses and mind bring happiness and peace of mind.

National peace comes from goodwill, sympathy, tolerance and right understanding between nations.

Develop cosmic love, kindness, forgiveness; understand the views of others.

Peace is not in the heart of the carnal man. Peace is not in the heart of ministers, advocates, businessmen, dictators, kings and emperors. Peace is in the heart of Yogis, sages, saints and spiritual men.

Peace comes from prayer, Japa, Kirtan, meditation, good and sublime thoughts and understanding.

Peace should be built on right understanding between nations, mutual goodwill, a striving after a common welfare and a higher good.

Speak, move, act in peace. Realise that stupendous peace of God which passeth all understanding.

Nothing can bring you peace but yourself. Nothing can bring you peace but the victory over your lower self, triumph over your senses and mind, desires and cravings.

If you have no peace within yourself, it is vain to seek it in external objects and outward sources.

Greed, lust, jealousy, envy, anger, pride, egoism, are the six enemies of peace. Slay these enemies by the sword of dispassion, discrimination and non-attachment. You will enjoy perpetual peace.

Peace is not in money, estate, bungalows, wealth and possession. Peace does not dwell in outward things, but within the soul. Withdraw yourself from external objects, meditate and rest in your soul. You will realise everlasting peace now.

Peace is a precious jewel. It is a priceless treasure.

Peace is the happy, natural state of man. It is his birthright. War is his corruption; his disgrace; his shame.

The peace of God fills your heart. Realise this Supreme Peace through meditation and devotion.

PERSEVERANCE

Perseverance is continued application to anything which one has begun. It is a going-on till success is attained.

Perseverance is steadfast pursuit or prosecution of a resolution, business or course marked out. It is persistence in purpose and efforts. It is assiduous endeavour.

God is with those who persevere.

If you have perseverance, you can do all that you wish.

The tendency to persevere, to persist in spite of hindrances, discouragements and impossibilities—it is this that distinguishes the strong soul from the weak.

A man of perseverance never meets with failures. He always attains success in all his undertakings.

When you start any work, you should not leave it till you attain complete success. Pursue it resolutely.

A man of diligence, vigilance and strong resolution grows into a genius.

The nerve that never relaxes, the eye that never blenches, the thought that never wanders—these are the masters of victory.

Victory belongs to the most persevering. Perseverance gives power to weakness, and opens to poverty the whole wealth of the world.

With steady perseverance, great difficulties come to an end.

'Continue' denotes 'to do as one has done hitherto'; 'to persevere' is to continue in a given course, from a desire to obtain an object; 'to persist' is to continue from a determination of will not to give up.

PHILANTHROPY

Philanthropy is goodwill towards all men. It is love of mankind especially as shown in good deeds and services to others.

Philanthropy is disposition or effort to promote the happiness or social elevation of man as man or of mankind on a large scale.

Philanthropy is desire or effort to mitigate social evils and increase and multiply social comforts, as based on broad and sound views of man's nature and condition. It is comprehensive benevolence, but often specified in its objects. It is active humanitarianism. It is love of the entire humanity. It is goodwill to all men shown by kindly actions.

He who tries to benefit mankind is a philanthropist.

A true philanthropist lives not for himself but for the world. He has a generous feeling for the welfare of the whole world.

A philanthropist is characterised by kindness to one's fellow-beings. He works for the good of mankind. He is benevolent. He is a humanitarian.

PITY

Pity is a feeling for the sufferings of others. Where pity dwells, the peace of God is there.

It is the feeling of grief or pain, awakened by trials, misfortunes or distresses of others, joined with a desire to help or relieve. It is sympathy with the suffering of others, inclining to help.

Sympathy (feeling or suffering with) implies some degree of equality, kindred or union. Pity is for what is weak or unfortunate and so far, at least, inferior to ourselves; hence pity is often resented where sympathy would be welcomed.

We have sympathy with one in joy or grief, in pleasure or pain, pity only for those in suffering or need. We may have sympathy with the struggles and triumphs of a conqueror; we are moved with pity for the captive or the slave.

Pity may be only in the mind, but mercy does something for those who are its objects.

Compassion, like pity, is exercised only with respect to the suffering or unfortunate; but combines with the tenderness of pity, the dignity of sympathy and the active quality of mercy.

Commiseration is as tender as compassion, but more remote and hopeless. We have commiseration for sufferers whom we cannot reach or cannot relieve.

Condolence is the expression of sympathy.

Barbarity, brutality, cruelty, ferocity, hard-heartedness, harshness, inhumanity, mercilessness, pitilessness, ruthlessness, are the opposites of pity.

PLUCK

Pluck is courage. Pluck is spirit. Pluck is confidence and spirit in the face of difficulties. Pluck is undismayed energy and resolution.

Pluck is endurance. Pluck is resolution in the face of difficulties.

A man of pluck can achieve great results.

When your luck is out, put a 'p' before it. You can start a fresh life now and attain anything you want!

President Chadbourne put pluck in place of his lost lung and worked thirty-five years after his funeral had been arranged.

PLUCK OR KNACK

This quality is most essential for a businessman as for any other man. Knack is dexterity or adroitness. When a man flourishes in business, people say: "Mr. Banerjee has got good business knack. He has got the pluck." Aptitude is another term which is synonymous with pluck or knack. Politeness, courtesy, good behaviour, are all hidden in this quality 'pluck.' When any man enters a shop for some purchase, the salesman has to approach him with great gentleness and address him politely:

"Well, Sir, could I do anything for you? Kindly take your seat here, Sir. Will you have some tea or a cold drink?" A rough and rude man cannot prosper in business. Gushing nature is also hidden in business.

A man of business knack is very careful in his accounts. He has a good memory. He knows the current market prices of all goods. He knows economy with efficiency. He knows the places from where he can get things at very cheap rates. He knows how to advertise. He has presence of mind. He is not afraid of failure or loss. He will make it up very quickly by starting some other side-line. The mind of a businessman who has pluck is always very inventive. A man of pluck is very intelligent.

Doctors and lawyers also want this pluck if they wish to become very successful practitioners. Some people are born with knack. You can also develop it in no time if only you will. A man with pluck or gushing nature can work wonders in the world. Even religious preachers are in need of knack. Then alone can they influence people and spread their teachings far and wide. Sri Sankara was very aggressive. He formed an army of Naga Sadhus for fighting against the Buddhists. Guru Govind Singhji had great pluck and a remarkable pushing nature. Though he was a spiritual man, he had the martial spirit. Religious teachers have to adopt various methods of work according to the times, conditions and needs.

POLITENESS

Politeness is refinement of manners. It is good breeding. It is polished, smooth, refined nature.

Politeness is ease and gracefulness of manners. It is polish or elegance of manners. It is gentility, good breeding.

Politeness moderates and softens your sentiments. It is an easy virtue, costs little and has great power.

Politeness is the flower of humanity. It consists of treating others just as you love to be treated yourself.

A polite man is loved and respected by all. It brings good name.

Politeness is a mixture of courtesy, discretion, civility, complaisance and circumspection.

Politeness tells not only on the manners, but on the mind and the heart. It renders the feelings, the opinions and the words moderate and gentle. ,

Politeness is kindness kindly expressed. Put it in practice daily. Be polite. All will be charmed with your manners.

A polite man is agreeable and pleasant.

Politeness is the result of good sense and good nature. It makes one a perfect gentleman.

Politeness is a mirror in which every one shows his own image. Politeness is good nature regulated by good sense.

Politeness requires humility, good sense and benevolence.

Politeness is kind feeling toward others. It is the result of good sense, some good nature and some self-denial for the sake of others.

There is politeness of the heart. Politeness of outward behaviour springs from the politeness of heart.

A polite man exhibits in manner or speech a kindly regard for the comfort or happiness of others. He is polished and courteous in behaviour. He is polished in language.

Politeness is polish or elegance of manner, courtesy or complaisance in speech.

Affability, amenity, civility, courtesy, complaisance, courteousness, comity, courtliness, decorum, elegance, gentility, polish, refinement, urbanity, suavity are synonymous with politeness.

Arrogance, coarseness, discourtesy, impertinence, impoliteness, impudence, uncivility, insolence, rudeness, rusticity, sauciness, boorishness, bruskness, clownishness, uncouthness are the opposites of politeness.

A polite man observes such propriety of speech and manner as to avoid being rude. He observes more than the necessary proprieties, conforming to all that is graceful, becoming and thoughtful in the intercourse of refined society.

A man may be civil with no consideration for others, simply because self-respect forbids him to be rude, but one who is polite has at least some care for the opinions of others. If he is polite in the highest and truest sense he cares for the comfort and happiness of others in the smallest matters.

'Civil' is a colder and more distant word than polite.

'Courteousness' is fuller and richer, dealing often with greater matters and is used only in a good sense.

'Genteel' refers to an external elegance which may be showy and superficial. It is inferior to politeness and courtesy.

'Urbane' refers to a politeness that is genial and successful in giving others a sense of ease and cheer.

'Polished' referes to external elegance of speech and manner without reference to spirit or purpose.

'Cultured' refers to a real and high development of mind and soul, of which the external manifestation is the smallest part.

'Complaisance' denotes a disposition to please or favour beyond what politeness would necessarily require.

'Politeness' denotes ease and gracefulness of manners and a desire to please others by anticipating their wants and wishes and avoiding whatever might give them pain.

Courtesy displays itself in the address and manners. It is shown more especially in receiving and entertaining others and is a union of dignified complaisance and kindness.

PROMPTNESS

Promptness is readiness and quickness of decision and action. It is alacrity.

Promptness is favourable to fortune, reputation, influence and usefulness.

Promptness is the soul of business.

A man of promptness at once plans, resolves, executes and succeeds.

Promptness is your duty. It is a part of good manners.

Time is most precious. Know the true value of time. Snatch, seize and enjoy every moment of it. Utilise every second profitably and usefully. No idleness, no delay, no procrastination. Never put off till tomorrow what you can do today.

Be prompt in giving reply to your letters. This will produce a very deep and good impression on those who receive your reply.

PRUDENCE

Prudence is a universal virtue. It enters into the composition of all the rest. Where there is no prudence, fortitude loses its name and virtue.

Prudence is a necessary ingredient in all the virtues. It is the pivot on which many virtues turn. Prudence will protect you.

Prudence is the habit of acting with deliberation and discretion. It is principally in reference to actions to be done and due means, order, season and method of doing.

Prudence differs from wisdom only in degree. Wisdom is more consummate habit of prudence. Prudence is a lower degree or weaker habit of wisdom.

Folly, audacity, foolhardiness, foolishness, heedlessness, imprudence, indiscretion, rashness, recklessness, thoughtlessness, unwaryness, are the opposites of prudence.

Prudence is wisdom applied to practice. A prudent man is cautious and wise in conduct. He is careful. He is discreet. He is dictated by forethought. He is frugal.

Prudence is the best safeguard. Sensible men often learn from their enemies. That man is prudent who neither hopes nor fears anything from the uncertain events of the future. Happy is that man who learns prudence from the doings and experiences of others, as he does not purchase it by personal suffering.

A prudent man takes care to avoid practical mistakes or entanglements. He is cautious. He is endowed with circumspection. He has good judgement and foresight, in practical affairs, He is economical. He has consideration. He has foresight, forethought, judgement, judiciousness and wisdom. He watches, guards and saves. As he has forethought, he thinks in accordance with the wise views of the future.

A prudent man is habitually careful to avoid practical errors and to follow the most profitable course. He is worldly wise also. He is very attentive to his own interests. He exercises sound judgement. He is wisely thoughtful. He is careful and judicious. He foresees evil and hides himself. He has practical wisdom. He is sagacious.

A prudent man is cautious or circumspect in determining on or adopting an action or line of conduct. He is careful of the consequences of any measures, actions or business undertaken.

It would be the point of prudence to defer forming one's ultimate irrevocable decision so long as new data might be offered.

Hear the words of prudence. She will guide you in the right path. She will give you wise counsels. Give heed unto her counsels. Store them in your heart. Follow them cautiously. All the virtues lean upon her.

Learn wisdom from the experiences of others. Correct your faults from their failings. Have foresight. You will never be in want or trouble. Use not today what tomorrow may want.

Cultivate prudence to a maximum degree.

PUNCTUALITY

Punctuality is the keeping of the exact time of an appointment.

A punctual man is scrupulously exact in keeping time, engagements and appointments.

Punctuality is faithfulness to a time promised.

A man of punctuality is observant and exact in points of time, as in working hours, appointments and the like. He arrives promptly on occasions as relating to a fixed time.

Punctuality is the stern virtue of men of business and great men.

A man of punctuality is always succeessful in life.

Better be two hours too soon than one moment too late.

When a Secretary of Washington, excusing himself for being late, said that his watch was too slow, the reply of Washington was "You must get a new watch, or I must get a new Secretary."

The most indispensable qualification of a doctor, a cook, an officer, a Professor, is punctuality.

I have always been half an hour before my time. This is the secret of my success.

Strict punctuality is the cheapest virtue. Want of punctuality is a want of virtue.

The vast majority of persons are indolent by nature and habit. It is very difficult to find a man of real, undeviating punctuality.

Method is the very hinge of business and all important works. There is no method without punctuality.

"Better late than never" is not half so good a maxim as "Better never late."

Be punctual. You will have success in all undertakings.

PURITY

Purity is freedom from sin or defilement. Purity is chastity in thought, word and deed. Purity is freedom from lustful, sexual thoughts. It is moral cleanness.

Purity (Saucha) is of two kinds—internal purity and external purity. Freedom from Raga-Dwesha, purity of intentions, purity of motives, and purity of Bhava, constitute internal purity. Purity of body through bath, etc., purity of clothes, purity of surroundings like the house and its neighbourhood, constitute external purity.

Purity is the main part of virtue. Purity lives and derives its life solely from the spirit or soul.

Your soul is Nitya Suddha (eternally pure). Through your contact with the mind and the senses, you have become impure. Regain your original purity through, Japa, Kirtan, prayer, meditation, enquiry of 'who am I', the practice of Pranayama, Study, Satsanga and Sattvic food.

Without purity, no spiritual progress is possible. Atman is purity. You should attain this ever-pure Atman through the practice of purity, through the virtue purity, through Brahmacharya in thought, word and deed.

I pray: "O adorable Lord! Make my mind pure. Free me from all impure thoughts. Make my mind as transparent as a crystal, pure as the Himalayan snow, brilliant as the shining mirror."

What greater undertaking lies before you than purifying your life of all enmity, impurity, hartred, lust and filling it with love, purity, peace and goodness?

PUSHING NATURE

Pushing nature is also called 'gushing nature.' That is the opposite of shyness. The man is aggressive. He tries to penetrate into all places like ether. Some doctors and advocates are starving. Why? Because they have not got this pushing nature. They are very intelligent and clever, but unfortunately they are so incorrigibly shy. They cannot influence other people. The man of gushing nature can talk sweetly and is very adventurous. He is very very bold.

A man of pushing nature is very active. He knows how to please other people and win others' hearts. He knows how to serve people and to get into their confidence. He creates work for himself. He cannot remain idle. He always plans, schemes, and speculates. He wants to rise up in the ladder of fortune and in the estimation of the world. He is of a very joyous nature. Very jovial and can mix with all. He knows how to adjust himself with other people of different temperaments. Pushing nature is necessary for success in life and God-realisation. You will have to cultivate it to the maximum degree. Desire fervently to develop this habit and try your best to make it your intimate friend. Then your other intimate friend, the sub-conscious mind and the Will, will do the work for you. Have a clear mental image of the thing you want. That is all that is needed.

Europeans have this nature in a large measure. Englishmen came in the biginning to India as mere traders and started the East India Company. Then slowly and slowly they became the rulers of this soil only through their pushing nature. People of Malabar have got this pushing nature. You can find Malabaris in every nook and corner of this fair earth. Vasco Da Gama had this pushing nature. He discovered a sea-route to India. So did Colombus who discovered America. The people of Japan are remarkable for their pushing nature. That is the reason why they have risen to prominence in so short a time. Japan is a small piece of land. They compete in the field of industry and commerce with almost any other country in the world.

Pushing nature keeps a man always active and is useful for the religious aspirant too. Business people should possess this quality to an enormous degree. This is an important qualification for all.

REGULARITY AND PUNCTUALITY

No man can reasonably expect success in life and God-realisation if he does not possess these two qualifications. Perfect discipline can only be maintained by regularity and punctuality. There cannot be any success without discipline. Discipline is an enemy of mind. The mind is very terribly afraid when it hears the terms discipline, regularity, Tapas, Vairagya, renunciation, Sadhana etc. These practices bring death of the mind or Manonasa.

Man evolves quickly by regular practices. He who meditates regularly gets Samadhi quickly. He gets the meditative mood easily without any exertion. He who does physical exercises regularly gets rapid development of body. That man who is irregular and does his actions by fits and starts cannot reap the fruits of his efforts.

Learn your lessons from nature. Mark how the seasons rotate regularly! Mark how the sun rises and sets, how the monsoon comes, how the flowers blossom, how the fruits and vegetables crop up, how the revolution of the moon and the earth take place, how the days and nights, weeks and months and years roll on! Nature is your Guru and guide. The five elements are your preceptor and teacher. Open your eyes and receive instructions and follow.

Regularity and punctuality and discipline go hand in hand. They are inseparable. College and school students in India imitate the West in fashion, style, cropping the hair etc. These are all vile imitations. Have you imbibed from them the important virtues such as punctuality and regularity? See how an Englishman adjusts his time to the very second! How very punctual he is! The number of specialists and research scholars is larger in the West than in India. There may be a few geniuses in India like Tagore, Bose, Aurobindo and a few sages and Yogis. But there are innumerable specialists and scholars in the West. They are more studious, regular and punctual than the Indians. They are reputed for this one qualification viz., punctuality. A European manager does not like his clerks if they are unpunctual. He will issue immediate notice to that man who is not punctual. That man who is regular and punctual will get sure success in all departments of life. There is no doubt of this.

Indians are famous for their "Indian punctuality." If there is an announcement in the newspaper that there will be a meeting in the Town Hall at 4 p.m. Indians will slowly begin to gather at 5.30 p.m. only. This is what is known as Indian punctuality. If there is an announcement in the notice that there will be a Kirtan at night at 8 o'clock people will come at 9-30 only. If there is a difference of a few minutes it does not really matter. I have had enough experiences in my Sankirtan and lecturing tours.

Indians should be ashamed now of their defect and should try to rectify it soon. Wake up Indians, wake up!

The one·important qualification that gave success in my life is this one important virtue, punctuality. Even Europeans used to admire my punctuality. I used to be very punctual wherever there was appointment. It produced a greater impression. I never missed trains. I was always punctual at the station. An unpunctual man misses always his trains. He fails in his business. He loses all his customers. The professor dislikes students who are unpunctual. If a man fails to attend the courts punctually of course he has to lose his case.

Have regular habits in all walks of life. Be regular in going to bed and in rising up early in the morning. "Early to bed and early to rise makes a man healthy, wealthy and wise." Be very regular in your meals always. Be regular in your studies, in your physical exercises, in your meditation etc., and you will have a very successful life and a happy one too. Regularity should be your watch-word.

RENUNCIATION

Immortality or Self-realisation is attained through Tyaga or renunciation alone.

Renunciation strengthens the mind and the will and bestows peace.

Renounce the objects. This is Vishaya-tyaga. Renounce attachment to the objects. This is Sanga-tyaga. This is mental discipline.

Without Tyaga, not an iota of spiritual progress is possible.

The secret of renunciation is the renunciation of egoism, mine-ness, Vasanas and Trishnas, subtle desires and cravings, the Bheda-Buddhi that differentiates, and the Kartritva-Abhimana, doership or agency.

Complete renunciation does not come in a day. It takes a long time.

Satsanga with saints and sages, study of books which treat on Vairagya and Tyaga such as "Necessity for Sannyasa", etc., are aids in the practice of renunciation.

He who has renunciation is the real King of kings, Emperor of emperors.

Renunciation is the greatest force on this earth.

REPENTANCE

Repentance is contrition for sin, producing newness of life. It is remorse for past, sinful conduct.

Repentance is a turning with sorrow from a past course. It is sorrow for something done, with desire to make things right by undoing the wrong and doing the right.

Repentance is the destroyer of sins. It purifies the heart. Every tear has a cleansing virtue.

Repentance creates a movement toward a new and better life. It has a tremendous purifying power.

True repentance is to cease from sinning.

Repentance is sorrow or grief, on account of some wrong actions or past misdeeds.

Repentance is a heavy sorrow for past evil actions and a sincere resolution and endeavour to the utmost of our power to conform all our actions to the law of God.

Repentance without a change of heart and conduct, without amendment, is of no use.

Death-bed repentance will not produce any tangible effect.

There must be repentance with a contrite or penitent heart. There must be a sincere and thorough changing of the mind and disposition in regard to sins. Otherwise, it is of no avail.

Repentance is sorrow for sin with self-condemnation and complete turning away from the sin.

Penitence is transient and may involve no change of character or conduct.

Remorse is a biting or gnawing back of guilt upon the heart, with no suggestion of divine forgiveness.

Regret is sorrow for any painful or annoying matter. One is moved with penitence for wrong-doing.

There may be sorrow without repentance, as for consequences only, but not repentance without sorrow.

Contrition is a subduing sorrow for sin, as against divine holiness and love.

Self-congratulation, self-complacency, self-approval, impatience are the opposites of repentance.

RESOLUTION

Resolution is fixed determination. It is steadiness. It is constancy or fixed purpose.

A man of resolution is determined. He has a fixed purpose. He is constant in pursuing a purpose. He is unshakably firm and steady. He is bold and unflinching. He is a man of resolute will. He has steadiness of purpose and firmness in adhering to it, especially in the face of dangers or difficulties. He has active fortitude.

He who is firm and resolute in will attains success in all undertakings. Failure is unknown to him.

Put on the dauntless spirit of resolution. March on, hero! Your efforts will be crowned with sanguine success. All obstacles will be removed at once.

Resolution is omnipotent. A man of resolution scales all barriers which stand in his way. All difficulties vanish for him. Courage, steady perseverance, fortitude and strength are the companions of resolution.

A man of resolution has the nerve which never relaxes, the eye which never blenches, the thought which never wanders, the purpose that never wavers. He always attains victory.

Resolution is your soul help in need. Be fixed and resolute. March on steadily. Gird up your loins. Persevere. You can conquer the whole world.

A man of resolution pulverises the Himalayas, swallows the fire and drinks the waters of the ocean in a minute. He can accomplish anything in the three worlds in the twinkling of an eye.

Even if the whole world opposes him, he marches forward with undaunted spirit.

All great men who have achieved greatness and who have accomplished superhuman deeds in this world possessed resolution.

Wherein there is resolution, there is the dynamic, irresistible, strong will. Resolution and strong will, go hand in hand.

Be resolute. Stick to resolves. Strengthen your resolves. You will develop your will.

RESOURCEFULNESS

Resourcefulness is means of any kind.

A man of resourcefulness is fertile in resources or expedients or contrivances. He is skilled in methods of efficiency. He possesses abundant means.

That which is resorted to, relied upon or made available for aid or support is resource.

An expedient to which one may resort for aid or safety is resource.

We speak of "a business resource;" "a woman's resource is patience;" "a country of inexhaustible resources;" "Rama has a resourceful brain. He can deliver lectures on anything at any time without any preparation;" "Sri Vyasa tried the resources of philosophy."

Resources are—pecuniary means, funds, money or any property that can be converted into supplies; means of raising money or supplies; available means or capabilities of any kind; as "In the Russo-Japanese war the resources of Russia were several times more than those of Japan."

He who has a resourceful brain can become the General of an Army, the Admiral of a Navy, the inventor of scientific instruments.

RIGHT CONDUCT

Ethics or ethical science treats about Sadachara or right con duct or morality or duty. Ethics is the science of morals, that branch of philosophy which is concerned with human character and conduct.

Conduct is behaviour. Deportment, carriage, demeanour, conduct and behaviour are synonymous terms. The way in which rational beings should behave towards each other as well as towards other creatures is dealt with in the science of morals or ethics.

To speak the truth, to practise Ahimsa, not to hurt the feelings of others in thought, word and deed; not to speak harsh words to any one; not to show any anger towards anybody; not to abuse others or speak ill of others and to see God in all beings is Sadachara. If you abuse anyone, if you hurt the feelings of others, really you are abusing yourself and hurting the feelings of God only. Himsa is a deadly enemy of Bhakti and Jnana. It separates and divides. It stands in the way of realising unity or oneness of Self.

That act or exertion which does not do good to others, or that act for which one has to feel shame, should never be done. That act on the other hand, should be done, for which one may be lauded in society. This is a brief description of what right conduct is.

Lord Manu says in his Smriti, "Achara (good conduct) is the highest Dharma, declared by the Smriti and the Sruti. Therefore let the twice-born that knoweth the Self ever diligently engage therein. Thus beholding the path of Dharma issue from Achara, the sages embrace Achara as the root of all Tapas."

Righteousness, truth, good works, power and prosperity all originate from conduct. You will find in the Mahabharata "The mark of Dharma is Achara (good conduct). Achara is the mark of good. Higher than all teachings is Achara. From Achara Dharma is born; Dharma enhances life. By Achara man attains life; by Achara he attains prosperity, and by Achara he attains fair name, here and hereafter. He who is the friend of all beings, he who is intent on the welfare of all with act, thought and speech—he only knoweth Dharma!"

Dharma is extremely subtle (Ati Sukshma), intricate and complex. Even sages are perplexed. Dharma gives wealth, satisfaction and liberation in the end. Dharma tops the list of the four Purusharthas viz., Dharma, Artha, Kama and Moksha. Dharma is generally termed as 'Duty,' 'Righteousness' etc. Any action that is best calculated to bring Sreya (Moksha) is Dharma. That which brings well-being to human beings is Dharma.

All that is free from any motive of injury to any being is surely morality. For indeed the moral precepts have been made to free the creatures from all injuries. Dharma is so called because it protects all. Indeed morality saves all creatures.

The conduct is the root of prosperity. Conduct increases fame. It is conduct which prolongs life. It is conduct which destroys all calamities and evils. Conduct has been said to be superior to all the branches of knowledge. Knowledge is power; but character is better power.

It is by conduct that one acquires a long life, and it is by conduct that one acquires riches and prosperity. It is a means to attain the goal of life. Without good conduct no one can achieve the goal. Good conduct brings in fame, longevity, wealth and happiness. It eventually leads to Moksha. It is conduct that begets virtue, and it is virtue that prolongs life. Conduct gives fame, long life and heaven. Conduct is the most efficacious rite of propitiating the celestials. The self-create Brahma Himself has said, "That one should show mercy to all orders of men."

Virtue is singled out by conduct. The good and virtuous are so on account of the conduct they follow. The marks again of good conduct are afforded by the deeds of those that are good or righteous. Indeed, it is by conduct that one acquires fame that depends upon great deeds both in this world and next. Forsooth, one may, by his conduct alone, conquer the three worlds. There is nothing which virtuous persons cannot obtain. A person of good deeds and good, pleasant and sweet speeches has no peer. People have great regard for that man who acts righteously and who does good acts even if they only hear of him without actually seeing him.

The man whose conduct is improper or wicked never acquires long life. All creatures fear such a man and are oppressed by him. If, therefore, one wishes his own advancement and prosperity, one should in this world, follow the path of righteousness and conduct himself righteously. Good conduct succeeds in removing the inauspiciousness and misery of even one who is sinful.

The man of right conduct has ideals, principles and mottoes. He strictly follows them, removes his weaknesses and defects, develops good conduct and becomes a Sattvic man. He is very careful in behaving with his elders, parents, teachers, Acharyas, sisters, brothers, friends, relatives, strangers and other creatures. He attempts to know what is right and what is wrong, by approaching Sadhus and Mahatmas and studying scriptures very carefully and then treads with joy the path of righteousness or Dharma.

The man of right conduct always cares for the welfare of all beings. He lives in harmony with his neighbours and all people. He never hurts the feelings of others, and never speaks lies. He practises Brahmacharya. He checks the evil tendencies of the mind and prepares himself through the practice of right conduct to attain the bliss of union with Paramatma or Self.

An aspirant went to Veda Vyasa and said: "Oh Maharshi, Avatara of Vishnu, I am in a dilemma. I cannot properly comprehend the right significance of the term 'Dharma.' Some say it is right conduct. Others say that, that which leads to

Sreya (Moksha) and happiness is Dharma. Anything, any action that brings you down is Adharma. Lord Krishna says 'Even sages are puzzled to understand perfectly what is Dharma? What is Adharma? *Gahana Karmano Gatihi*—mysterious is the path of action.' I am bewildered Oh Maharshi, kindly give me a very, very easy definition of Dharma to enable me to follow Dharma in all my actions." Maharshi Vyasa said "Oh aspirant! hear me, I shall suggest an easy method. Remember the following sayings with great care when you do any action. Do as you would be done by. Attend to this carefully. You will be saved from all troubles. If you follow these wise maxims, you can never give pain unto others. Practise this in your daily life. Even if you fail one hundred times, it does not matter. Your old Samskaras, Asubha Vasanas are your real enemies. They will come in the way as stumbling blocks. But persevere. You will succeed in the attainment of the Goal." The aspirant strictly adhered to Vyasa's instructions and attained liberation.

This is a very good maxim. The whole gist of Sadachara or right conduct is here. If one practises this very carefully, he will not commit any wrong act. To work in accordance with the Divine will is right; to work in opposition to the Divine will is wrong.

God, Religion and Dharma are inseparable. All human beings are characterised by righteousness and they in course of natural progress and improvement attain to the dignity of God. Man evolves through practice of Dharma according to his caste and order of life and eventually attains Self-realisation, the ultimate goal of life, which brings infinite Bliss, Supreme peace, unbroken joy, highest knowledge, eternal satisfaction and Immortality. Ethical perfection is a pre-requisite to Self-realisation.

Metaphysics rests on Morality, Morality rests on Metaphysics. Morality has Vedanta as its basis. The Upanishad says, "Thy neighbour, in truth, is thy very Self and what separates you from him is mere illusion." Sadachara is the basis for the realisation of Atmic unity or oneness of life or Advaitic feeling of oneness everywhere. Ethical culture prepares you for the Vedantic realisation of "*Sarvam Khalvidam Brahma*—All indeed is Brahman. There is no such thing as diversity."

GLORY OF RIGHT CONDUCT

A man who has attained ethical perfection by the continued practice of Right Conduct or Yama and Niyama has got a magnetic personality. He can influence millions. Character gives a strong personality to man. People respect a man who has good character. Moral people command respect everywhere. He who is honest, sincere, truthful, kind and liberal-hearted always commands respect and influence at the hands of all people, Sattvic virtues make a man divine. He who speaks truth and practises Brahmacharya becomes a great dynamic personality. Even if he speaks a word there is power in it and people are magnetised. Character-building is of paramount importance if a man wants to develop in personality. No development of a strong personality is possible without celibacy.

A man may die but his character remains. His thoughts remain. It is the character that gives real force and power to man. Character is power. Without character the attainment of knowledge is impossible. That man who has no character is practically a dead man in this world, he is ignored and despised by the society. If you want success in life, if you want to influence others, if you want to progress well in the spiritual path, if you wish to have God-realisation, you must possess an unblemished or spotless character. The character of a man survives or outlives him. Sri Sankara, Buddha, Jesus and other Rishis of yore are remembered even now because they had wonderful character. Character is a mighty soul-force. It is like sweet flower that wafts its fragrance far and wide. A man of noble traits and good character possesses a tremendous personality. Personality is character only. A person may be a skilful artist, clever songster, an able poet or a great scientist, but if he has no character he has no real position in the society.

You must be polite, civil and courteous. You must treat others with respect and consideration. "Good manners and soft words have brought many a difficult thing to pass." He who gives respect to others gets respect. Humility brings respect by itself. Humility is a virtue that subdues the hearts of others. A man of humility is a powerful magnet or loadstone.

Note carefully how the Rishis of yore gave instructions to their students when they have finished their course of study. "Speak truth. Do your duty. Do not neglect the study of Vedas. Do not swerve from truth and duty. Do not neglect your welfare and prosperity. Do not neglect the learning and teaching of Vedas. Do not neglect the duties towards God and forefathers. May the mother be thy God (*Matru Devo Bhava*). May the father be thy God (*Pitru Devo Bhava*). May the preceptor be thy

God (*Acharya Devo Bhava*). Do such actions as are blameless and not others. Those Brahmins that are superior to us, they should be comforted by thee with seats, etc. Give with faith. Do not give without faith. Give with joy, with modesty, with fear, with kindness."

Righteousness is eternal. Do not leave the path of righteousness even if your life is in danger. Do not leave righteousness for the sake of some material gain. A virtuous life and a clean conscience give great deal of comfort to man while living and at the time of his death also. A holy man with piety is far superior to the mighty potentate. God is much pleased with a pious man. Lord Krishna says "Even if the most sinful worshippeth Me, with undivided heart, he too must be accounted righteous, for he hath rightly resolved." There is a great hope even for a cut-throat, if he makes a strong determination and takes up the spiritual path.

Dear friends: Do your duties in a satisfactory manner in accordance with Sadachara. Apply yourselves diligently to all kinds of your daily duties. Consult the Sadacharis and Mahatmas whenever you are in doubt. Build up your character. This will give you success in life. Struggle hard daily to remove old evil habits. Establish daily virtuous healthy habits. Character will help you to attain the goal of life. Character is your very being. Struggle hard to practise Sadachara. Stick to Sadachara with leech-like tenacity. Practise it and realise Sat-chit-ananda state right now in this very second. May character confer on you the Atmic Bliss and Self-realisation! May Joy, Bliss, Immortality and Peace and poise abide in you for ever!

RIGHTEOUSNESS—THE BREATH OF LIFE

Righteousness is the Kalpa-Vriksha on which the fruits of peace, happiness and prosperity grow in abundance. The righteous men are happy here. They enjoy the satisfaction of having lived a life in accordance with the Divine Law of Dharma. Righteousness is the fire that reduces the Samsara wood-pile into ashes within the twinkling of an eye. The righteous man is liberated here and now.

Be righteous. You will enjoy both Bhukti (prosperity, happiness) and Mukti (Liberation). Righteousness takes you nearer to God. When you lead a life of strict righteousness, you live in constant communion with God; for God is righteousness.

The unrighteous man knows no peace nor happiness. *Satyameva Jayate Na Anritam*. An unrighteous man is doomed to failure and abject misery. His lot is pitiable indeed. His life is full of anxiety, fear, remorse and regret. He can never find happiness here; for his happiness depends on illusory objects here. Happiness is the other half of righteousness; where there is righteousness there happiness resides, too.

Ascend the ladder of Truth and reach the summit of Truth Absolute. Light the candle of Love and behold the Supreme Lord of Love, Who resides in every heart. Wear the garment of purity and enter the Kingdom of the Ever-pure Atman. Breathe the air of unity and attain union with the Supreme One, the All-pervading Brahman.

That is the purpose of your life on earth. That is the purpose for which you have taken this human birth; not to eat, drink and make merry. Every moment is precious. Every moment rolls silently by and drops into the ocean of eternity; you cannot recall it. Live well. Love all.

Universal love is the very foundation of righteousness. Selfless service is the corner-stone. Dispassion, discrimination, cultivation of virtues, and a strong yearning for liberation are the pillars. The superstructure is eternal happiness, peace, prosperity and immortality. In this temple is the Supreme Lord enshrined. Adore Him there. You will soon attain Him.

It is only when you are convinced that true happiness can be had only in God and not in the objects of this world that you can really be righteous. This is not pessimism. This is glorious optimism. You will sometimes get your cherished objects of enjoyment; you will later on lose them, and often you may not get them at all! Not so is the case with God. He is your very Self. He is nearer to you than your jugular vein. He is closer to you than your life-breath. You can never be without Him. If you realise that happiness can be had only in Him, and if you seek His constant communion, you will be ever immersed in bliss. Is this not optimism of the highest order?

What have you to do to get this happiness? You will have to be indifferent towards the objects of the world. This is not a loss to you. Is it a loss to throw a bug out of your bed? Is it a loss to pull out a thorn that has entered your foot, and to throw it out? To renounce craving for sensual pleasure is itself a great joy. From such a renunciation springs righteousness.

A righteous merchant will not be greedy. He will not hoard. He will not indulge in falsehood, blackmarketing and adulteration. He will see his God in his customers. He will conduct his business in the spirit of worship of this God. Glory, glory to such businessmen. The world is in need of them today.

A righteous employer will look upon his employees as his co-pilgrims on the path to God. He will treat them with love and kindness. He will look after them as he will look after himself. He will see God in all.

A righteous employee will consider that his employer is an Amsa of God Himself. He will serve the employer with faith and devotion.

Every righteous man will strive day and night for the attainment of the goal of his life, viz., God-realisation, and thus contribute to the peace and welfare of the world at large. He will radiate peace. He will work for the welfare of humanity. To such a man even the Devas pay their homage. He is verily a God-on-earth. He is fit to be worshipped by all.

May you all become righteous, pious, noble and wise! May you all shine as Jivanmuktas and Yogis in this very birth! May God bless you all with health, long life, peace, prosperity and Kaivalya Moksha!

SELF-ANALYSIS

Self-analysis is self-examination. It is self-scrutiny through introspection. It is good to check up daily your thoughts, words and actions.

Sum up at night what you have done in the day and in the morning what you have to do.

Keep watch over your thoughts, words and actions. Be vigilant. Be on the alert. Be diligent. Be circumspect.

Finish your daily stock-taking of your thoughts, speeches and actions at night just before you go to sleep.

Daily self-analysis or self-examination is indispensably requisite. Then alone can you remove your defects and can grow rapidly in spirituality. A gardener watches the young plants very carefully. He removes the weeds daily. He puts a strong fence around them. He waters them at the proper time. Then alone do they grow beautifully and yield fruits quickly. Even so, you should find out your defects through daily introspection and self-analysis, and then eradicate them through suitable methods. If one method fails, you must adopt a combined method. If prayer fails, you should take recourse to Satsanga or association with the wise, Pranayama, meditation, dietetic regulation, enquiry etc. You should destroy not only big waves of pride, hypocrisy, lust, anger, etc., that manifest on the surface of the conscious mind, but also their subtle impressions which lurk in the corners of the sub-conscious mind. Then only are you perfectly safe.

These subtle impressions are very dangerous. They lurk like thieves and attack you when you are napping, when you are not vigilant, when your dispassion wanes, when you slacken a bit your daily spiritual practice, and when you are provoked. If these defects do not manifest even under extreme provocation on several occasions, even when you are not practising daily introspection and self-analysis, you can rest assured that the subtle impressions also are obliterated. Now you are safe. The practice of introspection and self-analysis demands patience, perseverance, leech-like tenacity, application, iron will, iron determination, subtle intellect, courage etc. But you will gain a fruit of incalculable value. That precious fruit is Immortality, Supreme Peace and Infinite Bliss. You will have to pay a heavy price for this. Therefore you should not murmur when you do daily practice. You should apply your full mind, heart, intellect and soul to spiritual practice. Then only is rapid success possible.

Keep daily spiritual diary and practise self-analysis (self-examination) at night. Note down how many good actions you have done, what mistakes you have committed during the course of the day. In the morning resolve: "I will not yield to anger today. I will practise celibacy today. I will speak truth today."

SELF-CONTROL

Self-control is control or restraint exercised over one's self.

Self-control is the power or habit of having one's inclinations, and emotions, desires and appetites, senses and mind under control.

Control yourself first. Then you can control others.

Self-control clears the mind, strengthens judgement and elevates your character. It gives you freedom, peace, bliss and joy. It strengthens your will.

He who conquers himself is greater than the commander-in-chief who conquers a country.

Self-control is the master-key that opens the realm of eternal bliss and immortality.

There is no triumph more glorious than that of the victory obtained over your own self.

Control your senses and mind. You will attain Self-realisation.

Obtain self-mastery. Conquer thyself. Till you have done this, you will only be a slave of the senses.

He who is subject to his passions is the worst slave on the surface of this earth. He who rules his passions, desires, cravings and senses is the real king of kings. He is the Supreme Ruler or President of Self-Government. Crowns and sceptres are nothing for him. His is the best Government.

Every temptation that is resisted, every evil thought that is subdued, every desire or craving that is destroyed, every bitter word that is withheld, every wrong action that is checked paves a long way to the attainment of everlasting peace and bliss.

He who can command and govern himself can govern and command others.

Self-control gives you power to withstand trial, to bear suffering and to face danger.

Self-control leads to the highest merit. Self-control is the eternal duty of man. Self-control surpasses in merit charity and study of the Vedas.

Self-control increases your energy. Self-control is highly sacred. Through self-control you will be purified of all your sins, and gifted with energy and character. You will acquire the highest blessedness.

There is no other duty equal to self-control. Self-control is the highest virtue in the world. Through self-control you can enjoy the highest happiness both in this world and in the next. Gifted with self-control you will win great virtue.

The self-controlled man sleeps happily and awakes happily and moves in the world happily. He is always cheerful. Self-control is the best of all vows.

The man who is without self-control always suffers misery. He brings upon himself many calamities, all begotten by his own faults.

Forgiveness, patience, abstention from injury, impartiality, truth, sincerity, control of the senses, cleverness, mildness, modesty, firmness, liberality, freedom from anger, contentment, sweetness of words, benevolence, freedom from malice—all these combined make up self-control.

It also consists of respect for the preceptor and mercy for all. The man of self-control avoids both adulation and slander. Depravity, infamy, falsehood, lust, covetousness, pride, arrogance, fear, envy and disrespect are all shunned by the man of self-control.

He never incurs obloquy. He is free from envy.

That eternal region in Brahman which originates from Vedic penances and which is concealed in a cave can only be acquired by self-control.

The self-controlled man is never fettered by the attachments originating from earthly connections and sentiments.

That is a forest where the man of self-control lives. That is ever a sacred place. Of what use is a forest to a man of self-control? Of what use is the forest to him who has no self-control?

The man of self-control acquires great reward in the next world. He acquires esteem in this world and attains to a high end hereafter. He acquires the state of Brahman. He attains liberation.

SELF-DENIAL

Self-denial is the denial of one's self. It is the non-gratifying of one's own appetites or desires in the interests of one's own higher good, or the welfare of others. It is refusal to gratify self, especially when done with a moral or religious motive.

The more you deny, the more you shall obtain from God, the more you will grow in spirituality.

The first lesson in the Yoga-Vedanta School is self-denial.

Self-denial is necessary for building a strong and noble character. Self-denial is an excellent guard of virtue.

O Adhyatmic hero! O brave conqueror! Practice self-denial. Wage war against your own lower appetites, impulses and desires, and enter into the illimitable domain of eternal bliss and become an Atma-Samrat (Self-King).

The penalty of evading self-denial is just you get the lesser instead of the larger good.

Practise self-denial. Teach self-denial. You can create for the world a better destiny.

The practice of self-denial is the highest education. Wthout it all other education is mere chaff or straw.

Know how to deny yourself. This is the secret of all success.

He who carries on a successful warfare against his own appetites, passions and desires and keeps them under perpetual control is the greatest conqueror or hero.

Abstinence, self-abnegation are synonymous with self-denial.

SELF-EXAMINATION

Self-examination is a scrutiny or enquiry into one's own state, conduct, motives, mental and moral condition and thoughts, etc., especially with regard to one's religious feelings and duties.

Self-examination consists of self-introspection and self-analysis.

Self-examination will lead you to the Knowledge of your own nature. It will improve your heart and correct all your mistakes, defects, weaknesses and faults. It will bestow wisdom on you.

When you are alone, watch your thoughts. Examine your heart. Find out your defects and foibles.

Before retiring to bed, take stock of your thoughts, speeches and acts of the day. Find out "What evil quality have I mastered today?" "What temptations have I resisted?" "Which virtue have I developed today?" "Which Indriya have I controlled?" You will evolve quickly.

SELF-HELP

Self-help is the use of one's own powers and abilities to attain one's ends.

SELF-CONFIDENCE

Self-confidence is the state or quality of having confidence in oneself or in one's own unaided powers, judgement or opinions. Self-confidence is self-reliance. Self-confidence is the attribute of greatness. A man of self-confidence will always attain success and victory.

SELF-RESTRAINT

Self-restraint is the restraint of the lower nature or passions or the senses by the force of one's own will. Self-restraint is restraint over one's appetites or desires. Self-restraint is self-control.

SELF-DISCIPLINE

Self-discipline is discipline of the body, senses and the mind. Through self-discipline, the body, the senses and the mind are brought under one's control. Asanas, Pranayama, Pratyahara, Yama, Niyama, are aids in the practice of self-discipline. The emotions and impulses are kept under perfect control.

SELF-IMPROVEMENT

Exercise thyself. Improve thyself. Know thyself. Fortify your heart with virtuous principles. Discipline your body, senses and mind. Grow daily and evolve quickly.

Enlighten your mind with useful knowledge. Annihilate evil habits, evil thoughts, evil speech and cultivate good habits, good thoughts and good speech.

Talk a little. Hear much. Reflect alone. Hear the wise counsels of sages, saints and Yogis.

Make good resolves. Stick to them tenaciously. Strengthen them.

Waste not time. Time is most precious. Seize spare moments and utilise them to your best advantage. Do Japa. Practise meditation. Study religious books. Cultivate virtues. Increase your earning capacity. Serve the society. Serve your country. Serve elders. Serve teachers. Serve your parents. Serve sick people. Serve the poor. Your heart will be purified quickly.

Look into your own character and conduct. Read your own heart.

Keep the picture of great men and sages before your mind's eye. Remember their teachings and sayings. Follow their ideas. Practise their instructions.

Remove one vicious habit every month and cultivate one virtue every month. You will have quick self-improvement.

Be willing to learn from whatever source possible. Have an open heart.

Whatever you dislike in another person, take care to correct in yourself.

Try to do a thing better today. The only way you can make tomorrow a better day is to think and do today what invites a better tomorrow.

Serve. Pray. Reflect. Cogitate. Meditate. Sing the Lord's glory and name. Think rightly. Speak gently and sweetly. Thus grow, evolve and improve thyself.

SELF-RELIANCE

Self-reliance is reliance on one's own abilities, powers, resources or judgement. Self-reliance is independence, of character.

Rely on your own self. Help thyself and God will help thee.

You will always be poor without your own industry and labour.

God helps those who help themselves.

He who depends upon himself lives happily. He is a man of manly character and wisdom.

Self-reliance constitutes the true source of your success, vigour, strength and growth. It invigorates and sustains you.

Dependence on others enfeebles you and brings failure. You can never prosper.

He who has no faith in himself and his powers is the weakest man.

There is a vast, limitless magazine of power and wisdom within you. Rely on your own self and tap it.

He conquers who believes he can. He attains success who believes he can attain success.

Think for yourself. Get knowledge wherever possible. Listen to the opinions of those who are more experienced than yourself, but do not allow anyone to do your thinking for you.

Self-reliance is a very important virtue. Self-reliance gives immense internal strength. This is an important qualification for material spiritual success. The vast majority of persons have got a leaning mentality. They have lost their powers of self-reliance. Luxurious habits have rendered people very weak. A doctor and a lawyer want servants to put on their shoes and socks. They cannot draw a pot of water from the well. They cannot walk even a furlong.

In olden days our forefathers washed their own clothing and did all sorts of work for the house. They could even split fuel. They could draw water from the well for hours together. They could walk 40 miles daily. They had wonderful physique and vitality. They had longevity of life. They were absolutely free from any kind of disease. Pyorrhoea, appendicitis and blood pressure were Latin and Greek to them in those days.

Nowadays man depends on others for everything. He has lost this virtue of self-reliance. He has forgotten all about Atmic-Sakti. He has no idea of the vast magazine of power and knowledge within in the Atman. His mind goes outwards. He has no inner life.

You must know how to cook your own food. You must give up servants. You must wash your own clothes. You must walk daily to your office. Give up the false idea of prestige and position. Sir T. Muthuswami Iyyer, the late reputed High Court Judge of Madras used to walk to the court. His name is still remembered for his virtue of self-reliance.

Householders want now a magical pill from the hands of Sannyasins for their spiritual uplift. They do not want to do any kind of Sadhana. Everyone of you should yourself place each step in the spiritual ladder. You are your own redeemer. You are your own saviour. Remember this point well. No one can save another. Stand on your own legs and get success in the world and in the spiritual path. Tap the source by closing the eyes and draw power.

SELF-SACRIFICE

Self-sacrifice is the act of yielding up one's life, interests, etc., for others.

Self-preservation is the first law of nature. Self-sacrifice is the highest rule of grace.

Self-sacrifice is self-abnegation. It is the sacrifice, surrender or subordination of one's own self or one's personal happiness, or comfort, for the sake of duty or to advance the interests of others.

Self-sacrifice kills egoism and leads to the descent of divine grace and divine light. A Karma Yogi annihilates this ego through self-sacrifice.

Self-sacrifice is the sacrifice of oneself or of self-interest for the good of another.

SERENITY

(SAMA)

Serenity is the state or quality of being serene. It is calmness or coolness of mind or peace.

Serenity is evenness of temper. Serenity is undisturbed state of mind.

A serene mind is unclouded or unruffled.

In a serene mind alone the Divine Light descends.

Serenity comes when you annihilate all desires and cravings. Desires and cravings produce restlessness.

If you are serene, it is the greatest manifestation of power and strength.

Do not hurry. Do not worry. Regret not. Do not fret and fume. Control irritability. Control your temper. Be contented. You will have serene mind.

Practise daily prayer, Japa, meditation. You will have serenity.

Serenity does not come in a day, or week. You will have to struggle hard for a long time in cultivating this fundamental divine virtue.

Serenity is the topmost virtue in the group of Shad-Sampat or six-fold wealth of the four-fold Sadhana of Jnana Yoga.

Be serene. Meditate and know that you are the All-pervading, Immortal Atman or the Soul.

SILENCE

Silence is the state of being silent. It is absence of sound or speech. It is calmness.

Silence is Brahman or the Absolute.

Silence is like sleep. It conserves energy and refreshes you.

Silence is a strong weapon which so few of us are strong enough to wield.

Silence is death for a talkative man. It is nectar for an aspirant or a Muni.

True silence is the rest of the mind. All thoughts subside. There is perfect peace.

Silence is a great virtue. It avoids disputes and unnecessary discussions and prevents sin.

Silence is eloquence. Silence is greater than speech.

Be silent and hear the inner voice of the Soul.

Silence from words is good; but silence from desires and passions is better as it promotes quietness of spirit. The best of all is silence from all thoughts as it leads to Self-realisation.

There is a great power in silence. Silence gives peace and strength. Many sublime conquests are effected in silence.

Be silent and know thyself.

SIMPLICITY

Simplicity is plainness, artlessness, unaffectedness, straightforwardness, guilelessness, cunninglesssness, absence of ostentation.

Simplicity is freedom from duplicity, affectation or pretension.

In dress, in food, in character, in manners, in style, in all things, the supreme excellence is simplicity.

There is a majesty in simplicity. Simplicity is Nature's first step and the last of art.

Be what you say. Say what you are. Write as you speak. Speak as you think.

Be simple like a child. The door of Moksha will be opened unto you.

The greatest truths are the simplest; and so are the greatest men.

Goodness and simplicity are indissolubly united.

A simple, frank man is the most agreeable man.

Purity and simplicity are the two wings with which man soars high to the Kingdom of God.

SINCERITY

Sincerity is honesty of mind. It is freedom from pretence. It is frankness.

In sincerity there is honesty of purpose and character. There is freedom from hypocrisy, deceit or simulation. There are genuineness, truthfulness and integrity.

Sincerity is to speak as you think, to do as you pretend and profess, to perform and make good what you promise, and really to be what you would seem and appear to be.

The foundation of steadiness and constancy in friendship is sincerity. Nothing is steadfast which is not sincere.

Profound, great and genuine sincerity is the first characteristic of a virtuous man and an aspirant.

Sincerity is a trait of true and noble manhood.

A sincere man is trusted by all. He is honoured by all.

All virtues increase and strengthen by themselves if you are sincere.

Sincerity is the basis of every virtue.

A sincere man says what he thinks, nothing more or less. He cannot say one thing and mean another.

A sincere man speaks the truth. He is guileless and undissembling, plain, upright and incorruptible.

Sincerity is a fundamental characteristic of the person. Honesty is but a part of sincerity. It denotes simply the absence of intentional or fraudulent concealment. 'Sincere' and 'honest' denote personal characteristics. 'True' denotes a characteristic of a thing.

Sincerity is being in reality what one is in appearance.

A sincere man is clear, pure, unfeigned, frank, honest, true and virtuous.

Sincerity is the basis of every virtue. It is the face of the soul. It is the first of virtues.

Sincerity is the indispensable ground of all conscientiousness.

Sincerity is the foundation of that steadfastness and constancy which you seek in friendship. Nothing is steadfast which is not sincere.

It does not matter what you believe, if you are only sincere.

All virtues increase and strengthen themselves by the practice of sincerity. The shortest and surest way to live with honour in this world is to be sincere, is to be in reality what you would appear to be.

Hypocrisy and deceit are unknown to a man of sincerity. He has dignity of his character. He never stoops.

In common parlance it is said "Rama has made a promise in sincerity;" "Krishna has sincere intention;" "Sri Rama's regret was sincere;" "Sri Krishna is my sincere friend."

A sincere man is honest in intention, action or profession. He is true, plain, incorruptible and upright.

A man of sincerity is always consistent with himself. He is courageous. He has a clean conscience and pure heart. He is free from fear and tribulations. His tongue and his heart are in unison. The words of his mouth are the thoughts of his mind. Whatever he promises he puts into action.

An insincere man cannot make even an iota of spiritual progress.

Sincerity and honesty designate personal characteristics. True denotes a characteristic of a thing.

A sincere man and one who is honest always gets success in his work. He is very much liked by his superiors. These are Sattvic virtues. Honesty is the best policy in the West but is is a sacred virtue in the East. That man who is endowed with these two noble qualifications can penetrate into any region of the world. People will receive him with outstretched hands. Sincere and honest people are very, very rare.

A sincere man feels for the troubles of others and tries his level best to alleviate their sufferings. He is very sympathetic. He is very, very soft-hearted. A sincere man is also generous. He is free from any crookedness, cheating, diplomacy and double-dealing. People place their implicit faith in his words. A sincere man is always reliable. He is quite unassuming. There is not a bit of hypocrisy in him. He is quite frank and honest and true. He will not find any difficulty in getting a job anywhere. People are quite eager to take a sincere man in their service. A sincere man has always the well-being of his master in his mind. He works very hard.

Sincerity is one of the important qualifications in the path of spirituality. Throughout the Gita the one ringing note is that the aspirant in the path of Self-realisation should possess the important virtue, sincerity. The Sanskrit term for sincerity is Arjava.

Look at the sincerity of Lakshmana and Bharata and their unflinching devotion to Lord Rama. Wherever there is sincerity there is devotion also. Savitri was very sincere to her husband Satyavan. Maitreyi was very sincere to her husband Yajnavalkya. So she received the Atma-Vidya from him. Mira was very sincere towards her beloved Lord Krishna. She had the good fortune to have Darshan of Giridhar Gopal. A sincere friend, a sincere devotee, a sincere husband, a sincere wife, a sincere son and a sincere servant are gods on earth. There is no virtue greater than sincerity. It should be developed at all costs by one and all.

BE SINCERE, FRIEND

Sincerity is a virtue born of Sattva. It is known as Arjava in Yoga philosophy. It is one of the virtues mentioned in the thirteenth and sixteenth chapters of the Gita, which are necessary for the attainment of Brahma Jnana or wisdom of the Self. It is a Daivi Sampat. It is an aspect of Satyam or truthfulness. It is a Vritti or modification of the Sattvic Antahkarana.

A sincere man is respected in society. Every man places confidence in him. He says, "Mr. X is the most sincere man. I have not seen a man like him in my life. I have great reverence for him. I have intense faith in him."

An insincere man is a dead man while living. He is a burden on this earth. Of what avail is knowledge of the Universities and titles, of what avail is Tapas, practice of Asana and Pranayama, wearing of matted lock and rosaries on the neck, putting on orange-coloured robe, of what avail is renunciation and position in society, of what avail is wealth and possessions if a man is insincere?

A man who is endowed with this noble virtue gets success in all his attempts. He struggles hard with great sincerity. He never shirks responsibilities. He plods on and perseveres. He works diligently. He is vigilant.

If one possesses even this one laudable trait, all the other virtues will cling to him. Sincere people are rare in this world.

Therefore be sincere, friend, at all times. Develop this virtue to a maximum degree and attain Brahman or the Absolute. Brahman is an embodiment of sincerity. Therefore attain Brahman through sincerity.

A man of sincerity does hard work with intense love and devotion. He takes all responsibilities of his master, preceptor or employer on himself. What ten people can do, he does that himself with zeal, enthusiasm, fervour and love. Sincerity is a great dynamic spiritual force. It gives immense strength. Double-dealing, diplomacy, cunningness, crookedness, petty-mindedness are unknown to him. He is frank and straightforward. He will not hide or conceal anything. He will not conceal his thoughts. His thoughts will agree with his speech and his speech with his actions.

An insincere man never sticks to his promises. He breaks his promises and gives some excuse or other. People do not place any faith in his words. He cannot talk forcibly. He has no strong will-power. He tries to pose for a sincere man by trying to please his friends in a variety of ways, by gifts, artificial sweet and nice speech born of cunningness and other cunning methods. But he does not know that there are better intelligent people to detect the crow which shines in borrowed feathers. He is soon found out.

Man knows fully well that insincerity is not good and yet he clings to it. He cannot leave his evil trait. He does not try to eradicate this evil quality. What is the cause for this? This is due to delusion got up by Avidya or Maya. Mysterious is Avidya; Mysterious is the force and working of evil Samskaras! This delusion can be rent asunder only by Satsanga and service of preceptor.

O friend Venu! You have become insincere on account of intoxication from selfishness and greed. You do not know what you are exactly doing. You have a clouded understanding. Your conscience will prick you severely at one time. Your heart will bleed when you come to your senses. Your heart must bleed through repentance with a contrite heart. Then only can you purify yourself. Do Japa. Sing Lord's Name. Fast on Ekadasi. Do not take even a drop of water. You will develop sincerity and through sincerity you will achieve freedom, peace and perfection.

Large-heartedness, simplicity, unpretentiousness, harmlessness, rectitude, forgiveness, purity, steadfastness, self-control, fearlessness, cleanliness of life, absence of wrath, peacefulness, uncovetousness, mildness, modesty, absence of fickleness, vigour, forgiveness, fortitude, absence of envy and pride are intimately connected with sincerity.

Hyprocrisy, arrogance, conceit, wrath, harshness, unwisdom, deceitfulness, falsehood, diplomacy, cunningness, crookedness, petty-mindedness are connected with insincerity.

An officer wanted to do some constructive religious work. He wanted to build an institute. He was sending his savings regularly to his son for the purpose. But the insincere son kept all money in the name of his wife and cheated his own father. A certain Guru sent his disciple to spread his message. The disciple started his own institution and became a President-Founder himself. But he did not thrive on account of his insincerity. He did some mischief here and there and had to conceal himself to escape from the police warrant. Vice brings its own punishment at once in this world. Insincere people cannot thrive or prosper. They will meet with failure, dishonour, misery here and torture in hell hereafter.

If the husband is insincere, the wife begins to entertain suspicion; there is always quarrel and disharmony in the house. If the head clerk is insincere, the office work suffers, the office superintendent gets displeased and he gets a sack. If the Minister is insincere he is discharged at once by the Maharaja. An insincere man in any social or spiritual organisation creates much disharmony and disturbance and the whole work suffers a great deal.

Even disciples who get initiation from their preceptors become insincere and faithless and ungrateful. An insincere disciple betrayed Lord Jesus. Some of the disciples of Lord Buddha became his traitors and enemies. They left their Guru and did much harm and mischief. Even now there are plenty of insincere disciples who cheat even their Guru. What a shame! What a sad state! Their lot is highly deplorable! Such disciples will meet with miserable death. They will be tortured in the

Maharaorava hell. They will be thrown in lower wombs in the next birth and suffer from incurable diseases.

Padmapada was the most sincere disciple of Sri Sankara. He was able to walk over the river on account of the grace of his Guru. At each step there was lotus. Hence his name Padmapada. Sri Sankara was the most sincere disciple of Sri Govindapada. He never wrote anything without paying his adorations to his Guru first. A sincere disciple only will flourish in the spiritual path. He will earn undying fame. He only will reach the goal of life and attain immortality.

May the Lord abound with sincere people and sincere disciples who can turn out stupendous useful work! May your heart be filled with faith, devotion and sincerity!

SYMPATHY

Sympathy is feeling for another. It is compassion. It is pity. It is oneness with others in their striving and suffering.

Sympathy is a feeling of compassion for another's suffering. It is fellow-feeling. It is the quality of being affected by the condition of another, with feelings corresponding in kind, if not in degree.

A few more smiles of silent sympathy, a look of sympathy, a few more tender and gentle words, a few more kind acts, will pave a long way to contribute to the happiness of the suffering humanity.

True sympathy is putting yourself in another's place.

To ease another's headache is to forget your own. To mitigate another's grief is to alleviate or dispel your own.

Sympathy is the key that fits the lock of any heart.

Shame on those hearts of granite that cannot melt at the sufferings of others.

Open your hearts to sympathy. Sympathy prepares the mind for receiving the impressions of virtue.

There can be no politeness or courtesy without sympathy. Sympathy is the universal solvent.

SWEETNESS

Really sweet people are rarely found in this universe. Though sweetness is a feminine virtue, yet it is not found in the females too. Most of the females are harsh and gall-hearted though their speech appears to be sweet for the time being. A businessman, a lawyer, a doctor and a sister of ill-fame are all apparently sweet till they get money from their clients. This is not natural, lasting, beneficent, elevating sweetness. It is false glittering. It is commercial or mercenary.

A really sweet man is divine. He does not expect anything from others. His very nature is sweet. He brings joy to others by his innate sweetness.

Sweetness is born of Sattva. It is the sweet potent divine golden residuum after Rajas and Tamas have been squeezed out through protracted Yoga-Sadhana. It is the concentrated quintessence of Sattva. It is the sweet aroma that is wafted from the blossoming of the rare sweet flower of perfected soul—Siddha Purusha, adept or Arhat through long and intense Tapas, discipline, Yoga-practice and communion through mind—melting in Silence.

Sweetness must be an essential attribute of a spiritual propagandist and public worker. Without possessing this virtue, no propagandist can turn out efficient and solid work. He who wants to establish a Mutt or Ashram or spiritual institution must possess this ennobling virtue. All public workers and Ashramites must equip themselves with this divine quality.

The Rajasic ego should melt in the crucible of Yoga. Then this golden sweetness will shine in its glory. Rajas must be churned out. Then the butter of sweetness will float on the surface of the Sattvic mind.

Be sweet in speech. Be sweet in behaviour. Be sweet in manners. Be sweet in singing Kirtan. Be sweet in lecturing. Be sweet in look. Be sweet in serving others. Be soft, gentle courteous and polite too. This will increase your sweetness.

Develop this sweetness through service, self-restraint, Mouna, prayer, Pranayama, meditation, introspection, self-analysis, control of anger.

Sweetness is Radha Tattwa: Sweetness is the stuff out of which the heart of Radha is fashioned. Truthfulness, Prema, sincerity, cosmic love, Ahimsa are all modifications of sweetness. Sweetness is a rare divine blend of all these Sattvic attributes. It is millennium potency.

An argumentative, intolerant, impatient, proud, irritable, fault-finding man cannot cultivate sweetness.

May you all be endowed with this noble quality of sweetness which will enable you to root yourself in Brahman, the embodiment of Rasa, divine bliss.

Glory to Brahman, the Sweetness of sweetness.

TACT

Tact is adroitness or cleverness in managing the feelings of persons dealt with. It is new perception in seeing and doing exactly what is best in the circumstances. It supplies the place of many talents.

Tact is a quick or intuitive appreciation of what is fit, proper or right. It is fine or ready mental discernment shown in saying or doing the proper thing or especially in avoiding what would offend or disturb. It is skill or facility in dealing with men or emergencies.

Tact implies self-restraint, good temper, quick and kindly sympathy with the feelings of others. A tactful man will always have success in life. Tact removes all obstacles and surmounts all difficulties.

Tactfulness demands a quick and sound judgement, good commonsense, kind feeling and an instinctive perception of character.

Talent is power, tact is skill; talent is wealth, tact is ready money.

A tactful man says the right thing at the right time to the right people.

Tact is the open eye, the quick ear, the keen smell, the lively touch and the judging taste.

Tact loses no time; loses no opportunities. It takes all hints. It is ever alert, nimble and vigilant. It makes no false steps.

The principal elements of tact as a quasi-moral affair would seem to be (1) sensitiveness of feeling, (2) insight into the motives of others, (3) experiences as to the consequences of conduct, and (4) subtlety of reasoning, especially with reference to details.

TEMPERANCE

Temperance is moderation especially in the indulgence of the natural appetites and passions. In a narrower sense it is moderation in the use of alcoholic liquors and even entire abstinence from such.

Temperance is the spirit and practice of rational self-control. It is habitual moderation.

Temperance is self-restraint in the conduct of one's life or business. It is suppression of any tendency to passionate actions. It is calmness, patience.

Temperance is self-restraint in the indulgence of any natural affection of appetency. It is moderation in the pursuit of a gratification or in the exercise of a feeling as temperance in eating, temperance in drinking, temperance in the use of books, temperance in joy or grief.

If you are temperate your head will be clear, your health will be better, your heart will be lighter and your purse will be heavier.

Temperance is the foundation and source of health, strength and peace.

Temperance gives Mother Nature her full play and enables her to exert herself in all her force and vigour.

The ingredient in the liquor is the devil. It will excite you to do all sorts of mischievous and disgraceful actions. It will sap your vitality. Therefore, give up liquor at once.

Temperance puts money in the purse, contentment and peace in the house, vigour in the body, intelligence in the brain and spirit in the whole constitution. Therefore, be temperate.

It bestows vigour of body, health and strength, purity of mind, unclouded reason, refined sentiment and tranquillity of mind. It is the best guardian of youth and support of old age. It is the physician of the soul as well as the body. It is the Goddess of health and universal medicine of life.

Cultivate understanding. You can avoid the allurements of voluptuousness and fly from her temptations.

Your insincere friends will tempt you. They will take you to the bars and induce you to drink. The liquor will sparkle in the cup and entice you. It will preach "Here is joy and happiness." Now is the hour of danger. Let understanding and reason stand firmly in your guard.

Give up the company of drunkards at once. They will deceive and betray you. They will bring you to utter ruin.

The enjoyments in the bar will lead on to diseases and death. Beware. Beware. Beware. Are the drunkards not meagre? Are they not sickly? Are they not joyless and spiritless?

If you wish to keep the mind clear and the body healthy, abstain from all kinds of liquors.

Temperance is the foundation of all social and political reforms.

If temperance prevails, then education can prevail. If temperance fails, then education must fail.

Temperance is reason's girdle, the strength of the soul and the foundation of virtue. It is the strongest fence and defence against diseases.

Temperance keeps the senses clear and makes you quite fit to do great and hard work. It makes you cheerful and joyful. It cleanses the blood, clears the head, eases the stomach, strengthens the nerves and perfects digestion.

Liquors produce temporary excitement. Then follow depressions of spirits, cheerlessness, nervousness, irritability, gastric pain, loss of appetite, headache, prostration, debility, weakness, etc.

An intemperate man walks with tottering steps. There is no strength in his limbs. His heart is filled with shame, care, grief, sorrow and repentance. Diseases and wants oppress him.

A temperate man sings, dances and whistles. He has rosy cheeks. There is lustre in his eyes, joy in his face, and radiant smile on his lips. He is full of vigour, vim and vitality. He is always cheerful, brave, active and lively. He sleeps soundly. His mind is serene and restful. He has peace and poise. He has coolness and clearness of head.

Cultivate temperance and lead a happy life.

Temperance Movement is a political agitation for the restriction or abolition of the use of alcoholic liquors.

Temperance Society is usually an association of total abstainers from alcoholic liquors.

Temperance drink is any non-alcoholic beverage, especially one that is flavoured as Sarsaparilla, etc.

Temperance hotel is a hotel in which no intoxicating liquors are served.

TOLERATION

Toleration is enduring of offensive person or opinions.

Tolerance is freedom from bigotry. It is a spirit of charitable leniency.

Tolerance is a disposition to tolerate or not to judge or deal harshly or rigorously in cases of differences of opinion, conduct or the like.

You have not the monopoly of wisdom. Do not criticise destructively. Your neighbour's way and opinion may not be yours. It may nevertheless be as good.

Never condemn rashly but judge righteously. Be charitable and kind to one another. Be tolerant.

Religious tolerance is necessary. It will establish religious harmony in the country.

There are diversities of opinion even among the best men. This should not breed hatred. No two minds are alike in nature.

Intolerance is a crime.

Have a wide vision. Have a broad outlook. Give space in your heart for everybody, for every religionist. Be broad as the sky.

Tolerance in religion is absolutely the best fruit of all the struggle and labours.

TOLERANCE LEADS TO BLISS

As there are men of various temperaments, capacities and tastes, various schools of thought, cults and societies are necessary. The followers of cults or sects should have a large heart to include other sects also. The fundamental principles or essentials of all religions are the same. One should have perfect tolerance towards other faiths. Cults and Mandals help the beginners to grow but all cults culminate in Vedanta eventually.

During the life-time of the founders only some cults, Mandals, sects, societies and other institutions function well. After they pass away, the followers do not keep up the integrity and goodwill of the institution. Gurudom creeps in. Selfishness penetrates and overwhelms the heads of the institution. They become money-making concerns. The original sweet spiritual aroma fades and vanishes gradually. The followers unsettle the minds of others by decrying their faith and eulogising their own cult or society and thus produce much harm to the people at large.

People begin to trade in the name of religion. That is the reason why some of the cults, sects, Mandals and societies, instead of becoming dynamic spiritual centres, become fighting centres eventually.

The followers do not do any rigorous Tapas and meditation. They do not go in for seclusion for rigorous Tapas and Sadhana. They are not endowed with dispassion, renunciation and discrimination. They have tall talk. They simply talk of 4th region, 5th place, 7th sphere etc. The institution which was once enjoying spiritual fame and glory during the life-time of the founder, dwindles into a mere social institution gradually on account of lack of a spiritual dynamic personage to run the institution. Mere intellectual grasp of truths or eloquence or oration will not really make one a Yogi or a sage.

Those who say that Lord Krishna and Lord Rama are lower personages, know nothing of religion and philosophy.

A renowned doctor, an M.D., of the Punjab, went to see the chief of a particular faith at a certain place. He heard him saying "Lord Krishna is a lower personage." At once he left the place and had no faith in him. He told me later on that he had full faith in the Sloka of the Gita: "There is nothing whatsoever higher than Me, O Dhananjaya; all this is threaded on Me as rows of pearls on a string." Ch. VII-7.

To say that Lord Krishna is on an inferior stage, that one can have Santi through this faith only, is highly deplorable. Some say, "Join our cult, faith or society, you will have Darshan of the Lord within fifteen days. If you join our faith or cult you will go beyond Para Brahman also. You can have peace and Mukti through our faith and cult only." This is perfect intolerance and narrowness.

Just listen to what Lord Krishna Himself says in the Gita: "In whatever way men approach Me, even so do I reward them. My path do men tread in all ways, O son of Pritha." Ch. IV-11.

May Lord bless you with broad tolerance and large heart. May you be free from carping and cavilling. May you all recognise the Oneness or Unity of Atman. May you embrace others with divine love. May you all realise the unity of all religions. May you not indulge in religious controversies and debates.

May you all silently rest in your own All-blissful and silent Self and enjoy the Eternal Bliss within through deep meditation!

Om Santi!   Santi!   Santi!

TRUTH ALONE TRIUMPHS

(Satyameva Jayate)

Truth is simple; it is made to appear complex by the distracted intellect. The sublimest things are always the most simple.

Truth can never be defeated by untruth. Truth shall always win victory over untruth. When the path of Truth is trodden, everything else also is done. When the root is watered, all the branches are automatically watered.

The path of Truth is a precipitous one. It is slippery and as sharp as the razor's edge. Hard it is to tread, difficult a path it is. Giants among spiritual men walk over it to the City of perfection.

The Absolute is All. Truth is Absolute. You are That. This is the essence of spiritual teaching.

Truth is utterly public. It cannot be hidden even if one would try to do so. Truth persists and is expressed even in the extreme of untruth. The extreme of Truth is the Absolute. Untruth is a shadow of Truth. The world is untruth and the Absolute is the Truth. The world is represented by sex and ego; the Absolute is represented by the Noumenal Gnostic Being.

Truth is not expressed even by Existence-Consciousness-Joy! It is only the nearest relative of Truth. Truth is even greater, grander, mightier, truer!

All is well with him whose heart is turned towards the Truth. No disease, physical or mental, can assault him.

The mover towards the Truth is mighty, lives long, knows everything and is ever delighted; for he is nearing the Almighty.

Truth is: untruth is not; hence it is not absolutely correct even to say that Truth is One, for Truth is Existence Itself and is neither one, nor not-one. Truth is undivided.

The Absolute baffles the mind of even the greatest scholar. It eludes the grasp of even the mightest intellect. It is experienced as Pure consciousness where intellect dies, scholarship perishes and the entire being itself is completely lost in it. All is lost, and all is found!

The Absolute is perfectly scientific, logical, symmetrical, balanced, systematic, reasonable, rational! It is not irregular and haphazard. It is not a supra-natural mystery but the natural fact of life. The infinite and indivisible nature of existence is not a wonder; it is the actual condition of being even as brilliance is of fire, liquidity of water, weight of lead. It is the highest Perfection of Eternal, Immortal, Real Life.

Everything that changes itself is untruth. Hence Truth is infinite. Truth alone endures, while everything else perishes. Everyone, right from Brahma down to a blade of grass, moves towards Truth, some consciously, some unconsciously. They differ only in degree of consciousness or to the extent of mental purification or subtlety of condition. Every leaf that flies in the air, every breath that flows from us, in other words, every act of universal life, is a step taken nearer the Truth; for, Truth is the eternal Home of all beings. Into it they all enter and find permanent satisfaction and peace. It is Truth, that triumphs over falsehood, not falsehood over Truth, whatever the apparent and immediate experience may be.

TRUTH

Truth constitutes the essence of the Vedas. Control over passions constitutes the essence of truth. Self-denial or refraining from the worldly enjoyments forms the essence of self-control. These attributes are always present in a virtuous man.

Truth is one eternal Brahman. Truth is the one undecaying penance. Truth is the one undecaying Swarupa. Truth is the one undecaying Veda. The fruits attached to truth have been described as the highest. From truth originate righteousness and self-control. Everything depends upon truth.

There is no penance like truth. Truth creates all creatures. Truth sustains the entire universe. It is with the help of truth that one goes to heaven. That which exists in the past, present and future is truth.

Truth is the origin of creatures. Truth is their progeny. It is by truth that the world moves. It is by truth that the sun gives heat. It is by truth the fire burns. It is on truth that Heaven rests. Truth is sacrifice, penance, Vedas, the verses of Sama, Mantra and Saraswati.

Truth is knowledge. Truth is the ordinance. Truth is observance of vows and fasts. Truth is the prime syllable, Om.

There is truth where righteousness is. Everything multiplies through truth.

Truth is righteousness. Righteousness is light and light is bliss. Ahimsa, Brahmacharya, purity, justice, harmony, forgiveness, peace are forms of truth.

Truth is duty. Truth is Yoga. Truth is a great sacrifice. Everything depends upon truth.

Impartiality, self-control, modesty, endurance, goodness, renunciation, meditation, dignity, fortitude, compassion and abstention from injury are the various forms of truth.

Truth is immutable, eternal and unchangeable. It is won through Yoga. It is won through practices which do not oppose any of the other virtues. You will gain universal goodwill by continual devotion to Truth.

The quality by which an esteemed and good man puts up with both what is agreeable and disagreeable is forgiveness. You can cultivate this by the practice of Truthfulness.

You should always practise forgiveneses. You should ever be devoted to Truth. The wise man who can renounce joy, fear and anger can develop fortitude.

Abstention from injury to all creatures in thought, word and deed, and kindness are the permanent duties of the good.

All the above virtues, though seemingly different, have but one and the same form, namely, Truth. All these hold up Truth and strengthen it.

It is impossible to exhaust the merits of Truth. That is the reason why the Brahmanas and the gods speak highly of Truth.

There is no duty which is higher than Truth and no sin more dreadful than untruth.

From Truth originates gifts, sacrifice with presents, the three-fold Agnihotras, the Vedas and everything else which lead to righteousness.

Once upon a time, Truth and all religious observances including a thousand virtues were weighed on a scale. When both were weighed that scale on which Truth was, proved weightier.

Harishchandra practised Truth. He adhered to Truth at the risk of his life, and attained immortality and eternal bliss and undying fame. He still lives in our hearts.

Truth always exists in a pure and unmixed state. Truth is always a duty with the good. Truth is eternal duty. Truth is the greatest refuge of all. Hence respectfully bow to Truth.

Brahman is Truth. You can attain Truth only be practising Truth. Therefore be firm in Truth. Realise Truth by practising Truth.

TRUTHFULNESS

Srutis emphatically declare *"Satyam Vada*—speak truth. *Satyameva Jayate Nanrutam*—Truth alone triumphs but not falsehood." God is Truth and Truth must be realised by speaking the Truth. A truthful man is absolutely free from worries and anxieties. He has a calm mind. He is respected by society. If you observe speaking truth for twelve years, you will get Vak Siddhi. Then whatever you speak will come to pass. There will be power in your speech. You can then influence thousands.

Your thought should agree with your words and the words should agree with your actions. In the world people think of one thing, say another thing and do another thing. This is horrible. This is nothing but crookedness. You must carefully watch your thoughts, speeches and actions. The little gain that you get by telling lies is no gain at all. You pollute your conscience and infect your subconscious mind. The habit of telling lies is carried to your next birth also and you undergo suffering from birth to birth. Have you ever thought over this matter? Be very serious and stop the evil habit of telling lies from this very second.

The name of Harishchandra is even now a household word because he was a truthful man. He stuck to his principles of speaking truth at all costs. He never cared for his wife or dominion. He underwent all sorts of suffering. He was truthful to the very last. Visvamitra tried his level best to make him a liar. He failed in all his various schemes. Truth alone triumphed in the end.

Write in bold types the words "SPEAK TRUTH" on card boards and hang them in different places in your house. This will remind you, when you are about to speak any lie. You will check yourself at once. A time will come when you will be established in the habit of speaking truth. Punish yourself by fasting if you tell a lie and record the lies in the diary. Gradually the number of lies will decrease and you will become a truthful man.

SPEAK THE TRUTH

Truth is a common word that is commended by one and all every moment of our life from generation to generation, from time to time and from day to day. It is an ideal to be worshipped and followed. It is so important that man should stick to it at all costs. God is Truth and Truth is God. You render all your worship to truth as you do to the Almighty. It is an essential of life. It is a blessing in itself. It has the splendour of the Sun. It has the blessing of the Lord. It is complete in itself. Truth has a strong foundation in itself. It is bold, it has no fears. It has no limit of space or time. It is a fearless free bird in the sky. It does not care for status. It is wealth in itself.

Truth can be compared to a road of pasture, while falsehood can be compared to a bush of thorns. In a man who indulges in false thoughts, there is a lurking fear at every moment, an uneasiness, a fear of the self, a want of confidence and a feeling that something wrong may happen. Truth is the path of righteousness which certainly leads to success only in the long run. It is a straight road with no doubtful cross-roads. We have heard in the History of Sri Harishchandra what a lot of suffering the king passed through to establish the goodness of truth. In the day-to-day world, it seems as though it is impracticable to strictly follow a path of truth, but if it is practised as your ideal and goal in life, you have your way. All the stumbling blocks on your road to truth will melt away as you proceed along the direct road.

There are certain fallacies that arise in following the straight path of truth. It is absolutely no harm for a mother who fondly nurses the child in just diverting the attention of the child by saying that the small piece of sweetmeat has been carried away by the crow a short while back, and when she shows to be extremely sorry for it and brings round the ideas of the child by saying 'Papa, do not mind it, I shall bring a bigger cake for you in the evening.' The father out of affection for the child gives hope to the boy of seven that if he completes the five sums from his tough arithmetic book before the end of the day, he will be having a prize of two penny; but it so accidentally happens that the father winds himself in his blanket and pretends to be asleep, by the time the boy completes the sum and runs fast to the mother and says 'Mama, I have completed my contract, but, alas, father has gone to bed and I do not like to disturb him as he is very much tired.' It is absolutely no untruth if you do not interfere with others, wound their feelings, harm others or spoil others. If you refuse a small loan, certainly with something for you to fall back upon, if you refuse to lend your pen or any object that you would like not to lend, these cannot be counted as untruths.

If your falsehood disturbs the peace in you, the peace of others and if your untruth spoils the career in others, there is no greater sin in this world than this. You will be having your time for repaying the same in your own coin to your own self with so much of remorse. You are certainly erring and it is so much of swerving from the path of righteousness, which road definitely deviates from the road of Self-realisation. Truth is an ideal to be worshipped, to be followed, to be adhered to at any cost. It is the be-all and end-all of human existence.

When you are only a petty officer with no status of your own, why do you assume so much about your own self, and feed others with vain promises? Can you not afford to be plain in your dealings and guide your friend in the right way? To keep your friend for a longer time in suspense, than to dispose of him with a few kind words of advice directing him definitely for a short distance in the right path—does this help either you or your friend in any way?

Always be bold, be plain, never have the shyness of a nerveless man. Follow the straight road. Serve others to a small definite extent that you are capable of. Do not imagine too much of yourself. Always be plain. Love the neighbour and give him only proper advice or no advice at all. Do not misguide him. Do not give false hopes. Do not say "I shall try, I shall let you know in a day or two, I shall see what I can do in the matter." Such indefinite words do not cost you anything, they cost your neighbour all the world, because he has wasted much of his time in depending upon you and particularly lost by ill-guided advice, the most important period of his life, when probably he cannot afford to mend his faults. Art is long and time is short is the old saying. Time should never be killed. A man of untruth definitely kills his time, as also the time of others. Once you feel yourself you have misguided him, you think for yourself and you will realise that you have definitely swerved from the right path, and this pricks you for a very long time.

Therefore stick to the path of truth at all costs. Truth has a lustre of its own. It shines for itself and sheds light on others. When you stick to it as your only religion, you will be liked by all around you. You cannot afford to harm any one by simply adhering to the path of truth. Nay, you will be respected you will be feared, you will have a peaceful and a blissful heaven around you. There is no kingdom wider in space, there is no bliss more blissful, there is no enjoyment more happy, there is no pleasure more worth this life than the straight road of truth. In the long run there is a world of love between yourself and your colleagues in whatever walk of life they may be, there is a world of smile all around you, for you have no burden to carry, no sense of past thoughts and you are absolutely free.

The whole world aspires for every kind of freedom, the heart in every man aspires to be free of unnecessary thoughts, people around you would like to have a free talk to you, and such being the ideal before you all—why can you not stick to it? Strictly speaking there is no inexplicable 'Circumstance' as you call it to speak the untruth. Untruth is only a means and it leads to no destination. It is all for the nerveless, it is for the weak, it is for the timid to speak the untruth. It is for the shy and the wavering to think and to speak untruth.

For a man treading the right path, everything can be approached with absolute boldness, with free will, and with smiling pleasure; because he releases all his thoughts and he does not attach any importance to the self as distinct from the other. To him service alone counts, he is calm and serene with what little he does and he has always a bold and a sure step before him. There is no ego in him. He loses himself in his love for others. Service, service and service alone is his ideal. The result of service does not come into the picture at all; for he does not imagine any kind of result nor does he entertain any room for idle imaginations. 'Karmanyeva Adhikarasthe-ma Phaleshu Kadachana' is the end and aim of his life. He is not hampered by negative results. The whole world is an indifferent drama before him. He is never moved at all. He simply witnesses the drama and passes away most serenely. Such a silent career is the most successful career in any era of life. May the Almighty bless us in treading the path of truth and Ahimsa.

WILL-POWER

Will is the power of choosing or determining. It is volition.

Will is the power of controlling one's own movements and internal states, feelings and thoughts by conscious and especially by deliberate choice. It is the faculty of self-determination distinguished from all those activities of the mind and body which are initiated or directed wholly by external stimuli and which are, therefore, constrained or impulsive, and from all that play of the intellectual and emotional life which falls under the control of instinct, association and habit, purely. It must always be recognised, however, that the element of choice or volition is a matter of indefinite degrees, and that the control of attention is the primary and most disctinctive evidence of the presence in the mental life of so-called will.

With Aristotle free-will was rational desire, implicating a sort of force comparable to that of a rushing wind.

Will is that faculty or power of mind by which we determine either to do or not to do something which we conceive to be in our power. It is the faculty which is exercised in deciding among two or more objects, which we shall embrace or pursue. It is the power of control which the mind possesses over its own operations.

The combination of the two elements of emotion and self-determining force toward the gratification of emotion controlled the ancient two-fold division of the faculties into understanding and will.

The modern three-fold division into intellect, feeling and will arose from a more searching and thorough analysis of the socialised faculties.

The still more recent and more nearly complete analysis of students of psychology would seem to favour the use of the word 'will' as a term to cover, not any one faculty, but the entire active side or aspect of mental life so far as it is consciously voluntary and culminates in deliberate choice.

Desire, wish, will are states of mind which every one knows and which no definition can make plainer.

If with the desire there goes a sense that attainment is not possible, we simply wish; but if we believe that the end is in our power, we will that the desired feeling, having or doing shall be real.

This self-determining side of man's mental life and development, as the basis of civic and moral responsibility, has always been recognised by reflective thinking and in the popular mind, although in different ways and with differences in the extent of its application. In the conception of will, the two elements of desire or willing intention, and of power or efficiency to realise desire, have both quite uniformly been united.

Great souls have willing; weak souls have only wishing.

According to Vedanta, will is Atma-Bala or spiritual force, born of Atman or soul.

He who has a firm, strong, pure, irresistible will can accomplish anything in this world. He can move the whole world. He can move the three worlds.

When you are free from desires, cravings, the will grows stronger and stronger. Ultimately, you obtain freedom of the will.

Do total surrender unto the Lord. Then your individual will will become one with the Divine Will. Then you shall find every burden light and every duty a joy.

Do God's Will as if it were thy will, and He will accomplish thy wish as if it were His own.

To will what God wills is the only way which gives you perfect peace and rest.

HOW TO DEVELOP THE WILL-POWER

Attention, power of endurance, overcoming aversion, dislikes and irritations, fortitude in suffering, Tapas (austerities such as standing on one foot, sitting in the hot sun) or Panchagni Tapas before five fires, standing in cold water in piercing winter, raising the hands above and keeping in the same position for an hour, fasting, patience, command of temper, forbearance, clemency, mental power of endurance, firmness in meeting danger, power of resistance or attack, Satyagraha, keeping up daily diary—all pave a long way in developing the will. One should patiently hear the words of others even though they are not interesting and charming. He should not fret and fume. Patient hearing develops will and wins the hearts of others. One should do actions or tasks that are uninteresting. This also develops the will-power. The actions that are not interesting will become interesting after some time.

Never complain against bad environments. Create your own mental world wherever you remain and wherever you go. There are some difficulties and disadvantages wherever you go. If the mind deludes you, at every moment and every step, try to overcome the obstacles and difficulties by suitable means. Do not try to run away from bad, unfavourable environments. God has placed you there to make you grow quickly.

If you get all sorts of comforts in a place you will not grow strong. Your mind will be puzzled in a new place when you cannot get these comforts. Therefore, make the best use of all places. Never complain against surroundings and environments. Live in your own mental world. Nothing can upset your mind. You will find Raga-Dvesha even in the eternal snowy regions of the Himalayas, near Gangotri. You cannot get an ideal place and ideal surroundings in any part of the world. Kashmir is very cool, the scenery is very enchanting but Pissus (small insects like fleas) trouble you at night; you cannot sleep. Banaras is a centre of Sanskrit learning but it is famous for hot winds in summer. Uttarakasi in the Himalayas is beautiful but you cannot get vegetables or fruits there; the cold is so very biting in winter. This world is a relative plane of good and evil. Remember this point at all times. Try to live happily in any place, under any condition. You will become a strong and dynamic, pocket and unlock the Elysian regions, the spiritual realms and the immortal abode. You can get sanguine success in any undertaking. You can conquer any difficulty.

The practice of concentration is of great help to strengthen the will. You must have an intelligent understanding of the habits of the mind, how it wanders and how it operates. You must know easy and effective methods to control the wandering of the mind. The practice of thought-culture, the practice of concentration, the practice of memory-culture, are all allied subjects. All these are of immense help in the practice of will-culture. You cannot draw a line of demarcation to denote where the practice of concentration or memoryculture ends and the practice of will-culture begins. There is no hard and fast rule. For further particulars on the practice of concentration, please see my book "Concentration and Meditation."

Mr. Gladstone and Mr. Balfour could go to deep sleep the moment they went to bed through mere willing. They had such a strong will. Even Mahatma Gandhi had this practice. They could get up in the morning at any time they wanted, to the very minute. The sub-conscious mind was their obedient servant. It would wake them up at the very second. Every one of you should develop this habit through will and become a Gandhi, a Gladstone or a Balfour. Generally, the vast majority of persons simply roll in their beds for hours together and do not get sound sleep even for half an hour. It is the quality of sleep and not the quantity that gives refreshment. Sound sleep for even an hour is quite sufficient to refresh the body and revitalise the mind. The moment you go to bed, simply relax the mind and give the suggestion "I will have good sleep now." Don't think of anything. Napoleon had this habit. Even when the bugle was blowing and the drums were beating on the battle field, he would be snoring. His sub-conscious mind would wake him up at the very second he wanted to get up. With a cool mind Napoleon would appear like a lion on the battlefield. One should train himself to sleep in running cars, trains and when moving in the aeroplanes even in a sitting posture. This practice is of immense help for busy medical practioners, advocates and businessmen, who have to do immense work daily and a good deal of travelling. Life has become so very complex nowadays that busy people do not find time to get enough sleep. Whenever they find some leisure, even for five minutes, they should close their eyes in any place and go to sleep for a short time. This would give great rest. They can continue their further activities. This kind of practice is a blessing to busy people. Their nerves are under great tension and pressure. By relaxing them every now and then, they could refresh themselves and keep quite fit for further activities. One should be able to sleep on the platforms of Howrah or Bombay railway stations when trains are moving at all times. This is a wonderful practice that gives immense strength. Dr. Annie Besant used to write editorial columns, when moving in the cars. There are some busy doctors who read newspaper even when they are in the water closet. They keep their minds fully occupied. The practice of keeping the mind fully occupied is the best of all practices for keeping up physical and mental Brahmacharya. Those who want to become magnetic and dynamic personalities or prodigies should utilise every second to the best possible advantage and should try to grow mentally, morally and spiritually every second. Idle gossiping should be given up entirely. Every one of us should realise the value of time. Will is bound to become dynamic if one utilises his time very profitably. Application and tenacity, interest and attention, patience and perseverance, faith and self-reliance, can make a man a wonderful world-figure.

ZEAL

Zeal is boiling or passionate ardour for anything. It is enthusiasm. It is intense eagerness, especially disinterested eagerness in promoting some end. It is enthusiastic devotion. It is fervour.

Success is due less to ability than to zeal. Give yourself to your work body, mind and soul. Success is surely yours.

Your offerings please God according to your zeal and not according to their nature.

Zeal is like fire.

JUSTICE

Justice is integrity, impartiality.

A man of justice is lawful, upright, exact, true and righteous, equitable.

Justice reigns. Injustice is fleeting and illusory.

He who believes in justice remains calm through all trials and difficulties.

Justice consists in doing no injury to men. Justice is decency. A man of justice gives no offence to any man.

The peace of society depends on justice. Lawyers, solicitors, judges, public prosecutors, police inspectors and superintends and all Government officials should be just. Let the hand of justice lead them aright.

When justice prevails in the Government, there is foundation for social security, general happiness of humanity and the improvement and progress of the nation.

In Government relations, justice is the giving to every person exactly what he deserves. Equity is giving everyone as much advantages, previleges or consideration as are given to any other. In personal and social relations justice is the rendering to everyone what is due or merited whether in act, word or thought. In matters of literary work or reasoning justice is close, faithful, unprejudiced and unbiased adherence to essential truth or fact. We speak of the justice of a statement or of doing justice to a subject.

Justice is the bread of the nation. Justice alone triumphs.

Justice is the greatest and simple principle which is the secret of success in all Government. It is the first virtue of officers.

Do not misappropriate. Be not covetous. Return your loans to others. Pay your debts to others. Cast not an evil eye on the property of others. Let no temptation allure you nor any provocation excite you.

If you acted unjustly, pray, repent, do Japa of Lord's Name. Correct yourself immediately and be careful in future.

Give up black-marketing at once. Do not cheat others. You will suffer. You will be thrown in lower births. You will be punished in the hell severely. You will get incurable diseases. You will meet with premature death. Your conscience will torment you.

Do not charge too much when you sell things. Be moderate. Get a small profit.

Oppress not the poor. Exploit not the credulous, the ignorant and the weak.

Betray not. Be faithful to your master. Be faithful to your trust. Cheat not the man who relies on you.

Be always impartial, honest and just in your dealings with others.

Bear no false witness against anybody.

To be perfectly just is an attribute of the divine nature. A just man is a glorious man. He is a veritable God on this earth.

Impartiality is the life of justice. Justice is the constant desire and effort to render to every man his due.

An honest man always thinks justly.

Understand well the consequences of injustice. You will become just.

Be just and fear not.

Justice without wisdom is not possible. Justice is in conformity with the laws.

If you want to enjoy peace, be just.

Justice is the idea of God. It is the ideal of man. It is man's rule of conduct. Therefore, be just. Practise justice.

A just man conforms to the requirements of right or of poisitive law. He renders exactly what is due as in punishments and reward.

Justice applies to either ethics or law, denoting something that which is morally right and fair, and sometimes that which is right and fair according to positive laws.

Equity, fairness, fairplay, impartiality, integrity, justness, lawfulness, rectitude, righteousness, truth, uprightness are synonymous with justice.

Integrity, rectitude, righteousness and virtue denote conformity of personal conduct to the moral law and thus necessarily include justice which is giving others that which is their due.

Corruption, dishonesty, faithlessness, one-sidedness, partiality, treacherousness, unrighteousness, unfairness are the opposite of justice.

O man! Be just always. Examine your heart. Hear the whisperings of conscience. You will reap a rich harvest of peace and bliss.

MEDITATION ON 12 VIRTUES

Meditate on these 12 virtues for 10 minutes daily:

Humility in January.
Frankness (*Arjava*) in February.
Courage in March.
Patience in April.
Mercy (*Karuna*) in May.
Magnanimity in June.
Sincerity in July.
Pure love in August.
Generosity in September.
Forgiveness in October.
Balanced state in November.
Contentment in December.

Meditate also on Purity, Perseverance, Diligence, Sahasa and Utsaha. Imagine that you are in the actual possession of these virtues. Say unto yourself: "I am patient. I will not get irritated from today. I will manifest this virtue in my daily life. I am improving." Think of the advantages in possessing this virtue, "Patience" and disadvantages of irritability.

The spiritual path is rugged, thorny and precipitous. It is too long. The feet may become tired and bruised. The heart may pant. But the reward is very great. You will become immortal. Persevere. Plod on diligently. Be on the alert. Be agile and nimble like the squirrel. There are no resting places on the path. Hear the small inner voice. It will guide you if you are pure and sincere.

LIST OF VIRTUES TO BE DEVELOPED

(Take a copy of this and hang it in a prominent place in your house.)

(A) Major Virtues

Alms-giving
Balance of mind
Brahma Chintana
Courage
Diligence
Equanimity
Feeling His presence at
    all times and in all actions
Generosity
Mouna
Obedience to all
Perseverance
Purity of heart
Self-control and sacrifice
Serving nature
Sincerity
Tolerance
Truth-seeking
Vairagya
Work without attachment

Always speaking truth
Brahmacharya
Calm and cheerful nature
Desirelessness
Discipline
Fearlessness
Forbearance
Frankness
Humility
Nobility
Patience
Power of endurance
Renunciation
Serenity
Simplicity
Strong will-power
Tranquillity of mind
Unfailing devotion
Unshakable faith in God

(B) Minor Virtues

Abstinence
Accepting one's own
    faults and weaknesses
Austerity
Aversion to slander
Bearing insult and injury
Chivalrous nature
Compassion to living beings
Contemplation
Control of Indriyas

Absence of Greed
Affection
Always uttering your
    Ishta Mantra
Avoiding bad company
Charity towards all
Cleanliness
Constancy
Contentment
Dauntlessness

Detachment
Equal-mindedness
Firmness
Fortitude
Freedom from malice and
 overweening conceit
Heroism
Joyful nature
Kindness to all
Loving nature
Mercy
Modesty
Non-injury in thought,
 word and deed
Not caring for public criticism
Observing elegant manners
 and principles
Quick and nimble in
 every action
Satisfaction
Satsangh with Mahatmas
Selfless service
Steadfastness in knowledge,
 and devotion and sacrifice
Sublime thoughts
To be kind and generous
 towards all
Vigour

Enterprise
Fasting on principal days
Forgiving and forgetting
 one's ill-treatment
Gentleness
Giving nature
Innocence
Keeping up one's own word
 at any cost
Magnanimity
Moderation in everything
Non-covetousness
Non-stealing
Non-violence
Nursing the sick with Bhava
Politeness
Praising others
Reducing sleep
Resourcefulness
Righteousness
Self-effacement
Speaking well of others
Steadiness
Study of scriptures
Sympathy towards all
To talk little and sweet
Uprightness

WORD-PICTURE OF VIRTUES

1. **Temperance**—Eat not to dullness; drink not to elevation.

2. **Silence**—Speak not but what may benefit others or yourself; avoid trifling conversation.

3. **Order**—Let all your things have their places, let each part of your business have its time.

4. **Resolution**—Resolve to perform what you ought; perform without fail what you resolve.

5. **Frugality**—Make no expense but to do good to others or yourself; i.e., waste nothing.

6. **Industry**—Lose no time; be always employed in something useful; cut off all unnecessary actions.

7. **Sincerity**—Use no hurtful deceit; think innocently and justly, and, if you speak, speak accordingly.

8. **Justice**—Wrong done by doing injuries, or omitting the benefits that are your duty.

9. **Moderation**—Avoid extremes; forbear resenting injuries so much as you think they deserve.

10. **Cleanliness**—Tolerate no uncleanliness in body, clothes or habitation.

11. **Tranquillity**—Be not disturbed at trifles, or at accidents common or unavoidable.

12. **Chastity**—Rarely use venery but for health or offspring, never to dullness, weakness, or the injury of your own another's peace or reputation.

13. **Humility**—Imitate Jesus and Socrates.

(Have similar word-pictures for other Virtues you wish to cultivate.)

SONG OF EIGHTEEN 'ITIES

Serenity, regularity, absence of vanity,
Sincerity, simplicity, veracity,

> Equanimity, fixity, non-irritability,
> Adaptability, humility, tenacity,

Integrity, nobility, magnanimity,
Charity, generosity, purity,

> Practise daily these eighteen 'ities,
> You will soon attain immortality.

Brahman is the only real entity,
Mr. So and so is a false non-entity,

> You will abide in eternity and infinity,
> You will behold unity in diversity,

You cannot attain this in the university,
But you can attain this
In theYoga-Vedanta Forest University.

THE EIGHTEEN 'ITIES

For everyone's success in life, and especially for a Sadhaka's success in the spiritual life, it is essential that he should develop certain cardinal virtues. Virtue is strength, power and the key to peace. A virtuous man is ever happy, peaceful and prosperous. People ask me for a specific mention of the virtues that one should develop. The "Song of Eighteen 'Ities" enumerates the virtues that everyone should cultivate. Take up any one virtue and develop it to a very high degree of perfection; eradicate in toto its opposite evil quality even in its most subtle form. Meditate on these virtues, their benefits; the methods of cultivating these virtues. The Eighteen 'Ities are:

(1) **Serenity**: Be tranquil within. Let that inner peace and inner joy radiate through a serene countenance. A serene countenance is peaceful, smiling, serious, and does not betray any violent emotions. It is like the surface of a still lake.

(2) **Regularity**: Be regular in your daily habits, work and Sadhana. Get up at a particular time daily; go to bed at a particular time. Be clock-like in your daily activities. You will be free from worry, anxiety, haphazard and shabby work. You will do the right thing at the right moment.

(3) **Absence of vanity**: Do not boast of your birth, position, qualifications and spiritual attainments. Remember the evanescent nature of all things phenomenal. Praise others. See good in all. Treat even the lowliest creatures as your equal.

(4) **Sincerity**: Let your words agree with your thoughts; let actions agree with your words. Let there be harmony between your thoughts, words and actions.

(5) **Simplicity**: Be artless. Be simple in your speech. Do not twist words and topics. Be plain, avoid diplomacy, cunningness and crookedness. Be simple in your dress. Be simple in your diet. Develop a child-like nature.

(6) **Veracity**: Be truthful. Stick to your promises. Do not exaggerate. Do not twist facts. Think twice before you speak. Speak truthfully, speak sweetly; be precise in what you say.

(7) **Equanimity**: Be calm. Bear patiently insult, injury, suffering, failures, and disrespect. Be not elated by praise, pleasure, success and honour. Look upon both with equal vision. Behave alike towards friends and foes. Never let a thing disturb your inner peace.

(8) **Fixity**: Remeber you can achieve nothing if you are fickle-minded. Do Vichara. Choose your goal or ideal. Always remember that. Never let it go out of your mind even for a moment.

(9) **Non-irritability**: Irritability is the precursor of violent outburst of anger. Watch for the disturbance in the mental equilibrium. Watch for the ripples of anger that might arise in the lake of the mind. Quell them then and there. Do not allow them to assume greater proportions. Then you will attain non-irritable state of peace and love.

(10) **Adaptability**: Understand the nature of the people with whom you came into contact. Adjust your mode of approach to them, your conduct towards them in such a way as would be pleasing to them. Joyfully bear with the eccentricities of other people. Always react in a harmonious manner. Serve all and love all. Have the Bhavana that the Lord is in all as the Self of all.

(11) **Humility**: Respect everybody. Bow with folded palms before everybody. Do not talk in a loud voice in the presence of elders and venerable persons. Look at the toes while you walk. See the Lord in all and feel that you are His servant and so the servant of all. Consider none as inferior to you.

(12) **Tenacity**: This is the natural friend of fixity. Once you have fixed your aim and chosen your path, stick to it. Do not waver. Be steadfast. Never compromise on your fundamental principles. Have the mental attitude "I may give up my life; but I will not swerve the Path, I will not break my vows."

(13) **Integrity**: Develop an integral personality. Tie all the loose ends of your character. Become a man of high moral principles. Lead a Dharmic life. Let righteousness waft its fragrance from you. Everyone will trust you, obey you, respect you and revere you.

(14) **Nobility**: Shun mean-mindedness as dung and poison. Never look into other people's defects. Appreciate everyone's good qualities. Be dignified in bearing. Never stoop to low thoughts, words of actions.

(15) **Magnanimity**: Take a broad view of things. Ignore other people's faults. Be great and high-minded in whatever you do. Avoid silly talk and childish prattle. Let not the mind dwell on little things and insignificant incidents.

(16) **Charity**: Give, give and give. Radiate thoughts of goodwill and love. Forgive other people's faults. Bless the man who injures you. Share what you have with others. Feed and clothe all. Disseminate spiritual knowledge, to one and all. Use the material wealth, knowledge and spiritual wisdom that you

SONG OF EIGHTEEN 'ITIES

possess as a divine trust, entrusted to you by God, to be distributed among His children.

(17) **Generosity**: In whatever you give, be liberal. Have a large heart. Be not stingy. Take delight in other people's joys, in making other people happy. Generosity is a sister-virtue of charity. Generosity is the fulfilment of charity, magnanimity and nobility.

(18) **Purity**: Be pure at heart. Eradicate lust, anger, greed and other evil tendencies. Be pure in your thoughts; let no evil thought enter the mind. Think of God always; think of the well-being of all. Be pure in your words; never utter a vulgar, harsh or unkind word. Be pure in body also; keep it clean, keep your dress and your surroundings clean. Observe the rules of physical, mental, moral and spiritual hygiene.

These eighteen 'Ities will pave the way for you to march into the kingdom of God. They will open out the gates of immortality for you. You will achieve great success in this life on earth also. A man who possesses these qualities in a very large measure is a saint, indeed, who will be respected, adored and worshipped by one and all. May you all become Jivanmuktas and the very embodiments of these virtues!

PART II
How to Eradicate Vices

AFFECTATION

DAMBHA

Affectation is a striving after or an attempt to assume, what is not natural or real. It is pretence.

Affectation is to make a show or pretence of, to assume, to counterfeit, or pretend to.

Affectation is a studied or ostentatious pretence. It is artificial, false or shallow display. It is artificiality of manner or behaviour.

Affectation is an attempt to assume or exhibit what is not natural or real. It is false pretence, artificial appearance or show.

Affectation proceeds either from vanity or hypocrisy. Vanity puts on false characters to gain applause. Hypocrisy conceals vices under the appearance of their opposite virtues, in order to avoid censure.

Affectation proceeds from the supposition of possessing something better than what the rest of the world possesses.

Affectation is a trick or stratagem played by vanity. It is a perpetual disguise of the real character by false appearances.

Affectation is a badge of ignorance or stupidity.

A man of affectation knows his defects and attempts to conceal them by artificial excellence. He is easily found out by others. He is an object of disgust for his neighbours.

Be natural. Be yourself. Do not imitate. Ape no greatness. Give up all affectation. What is natural is best.

Cultivate simplicity, humility, nobility, integrity, magnanimity, etc.

A man is not humble, but he puts on a show or affectation of humility.

Affectation is petty hypocrisy.

Pretence commonly signifies the offering of something for what it is not.

Hypocrisy is the pretence of moral excellence, either as a cover for actual wrong or for the sake of the credit and advantage attaching to virtue.

Sanctimoniousness is the assumption of saintly manner without a saintly character.

Cant is hypocrisy in utterance.

Sanctimoniousness is hypocrisy in appearance as in looks, tones, etc.

Affectation is in matters of intellect, taste, etc., much what hypocrisy is in morals and religion.

Sham is a trick or device that puts one to shame or that shamefully disappoints expectation or falsifies appearances.

AHAMKARA

EGOISM

I

Ahamkara or egoism is the self-arrogating principle in man. It is a Vritti or modification that arises in the mind. Patanjali Maharshi calls this by the name 'Asmita.' The same mind assumes the form of egoism when man self-arrogates to himself. Ahamkara manifests first and then comes "Mamata."

This baneful egoism generates actions, desires and pains. It is the source for all evils. It is illusory. It deludes people. Though it is nothing, it is everything for the worldly people. It is associated with mineness. It is born of Avidya or ignorance. It springs from false conceit. Vanity fosters it. It is the greatest enemy. If one renounces this dire Ahamkara he will be happy. The secret of renunciation is renunciation of egoism. Ahamkara has its seat in the mind. It is under the influence of egoism that man commits evils and wrong actions. It is deep rooted. Anxieties and troubles proceed from egoism. Ahamkara destroys our virtues and peace of mind. It spreads the snare of affection to entrap us. He who is free from egoism is very happy and peaceful. Desires multiply and expand on account of egoism. Our inveterate enemy of egoism has spread about us the enchantments of our wives, friends, children etc., whose spells it is hard to break. There is no enemy greater than egoism.

He who neither desires nor dislikes anything and who preserves the serenity of mind at all times is not affected by the feeling of egoism. There are three kinds of egoism in the world. Of these two kinds of egoism are beneficial and of superior nature but the third is of a vile kind and is to be abandoned by all.

The first is the supreme and undivided ego which is eternal and which pervades through the world. It is the supreme soul, besides which there is nothing in nature. Meditate on the formula 'Aham Brahma Asmi—I am Brahman.' Identify yourself with Brahman. It is Sattvic Ahamkara. The knowledge which makes us perceive our own Self to be more subtle than the tail-end of paddy or to be as minute as the hundredth part of a hair and to be ever existent is the second kind of Ahamkara. These two kinds of egoism are found in Jivanmuktas or liberated sages. They lead to the liberation of men. They will not cause bondage. Hence they are of beneficial and superior nature. The third kind of Ahamkara is the knowledge which identifies the 'I' with the body composed of the hands, feet, etc., which takes the body for the soul or the Self. This is the worst or basest form of egoism. This is found in all worldly persons. This is the cause for the growth of the poisonous tree of rebirths. Those who possess this kind of egoism can never come to their right senses. Countless persons have been deluded by this form of Ahamkara. They have lost their intelligence, power of discrimination and power of enquiry. This kind of egoism produces baneful results. People come under the influence of all evils of life. Those who are slaves of this form of Ahamkara are troubled by various desires which induce them to do wrong actions. It debases them to the state of beasts. This kind of Ahamkara should be destroyed by the other two kinds of Ahamkara. The more you thin out this egoism, the more you will get knowledge of Brahman or the light of the soul.

Again there are three kinds of Ahamkara, viz., Sattvic egoism, Rajasic egoism and Tamasic egoism. Sattvic egoism will not bind a man to Samsara. It will help the aspirant to attain the final emancipation. If you try to assert 'Aham Brahma Asmi: I am Brahman'—this is Sattvic egoism. Even in a Jivanmukta there is a slight trace of Sattvic egoism. He does actions through this Sattvic egoism. 'I am a king, I know everything. I am very intelligent'—this is Rajasic egoism. 'I am a fool. I do not know anything'—this is Tamasic egoism.

The literal meaning or Vachyartha of 'Aham' Pada is Aham Vritti that arises in the mind, the little 'I' which identifies itself with the physical body. The indicative meaning or Lakshyartha of 'Aham' Pada is Atman or Brahman, the big or infinite 'I.' Mere illusion is the cause of egoism. Knowledge is the cause of egoism. Knowledge is produced through the illusory objects such as the body, tree, river, mountains, cow, horse, etc. If there are no objects, cow, horse, etc., we will have no knowledge of objects at all. Then egoism, the seed of Manas, will be absorbed.

The idea of 'I' which is the nest containing all frailties is the seed of the tree of mind. The sprout which at first germinates from the seed of Ahamkara is Buddhi or intellect. From this sprout, the ramifying branches called Samkalpa take their origin. Through such a differentiation, the mind, Chitta, and Buddhi are but the different names or qualities of the same Ahamkara. The branches of Vasanas will naturally produce innumerable crops of Karmas, but if with the sword of Jnana you sever them from the heart's core, they will be destroyed. Cut the branches of the tree of mind and eventually destroy the tree at its root completely. Cutting the branches is only a secondary thing, the primary one being the eradication of the tree at its root. If you, through virtuous actions, destroy the idea of 'I' at the root of the tree (mind) then it will not grow up. Atma Jnana or knowledge of the Self is the fire which destroys the conception of Ahamkara, the seed of the tree.

There is another classification of egoism, viz., gross (Sthula) and subtle (Sukshma). When you identify yourself with the gross physical body, it is gross egoism. When you identify yourself with the mind and Karana Sarira (seed-body), it is subtle egoism. If you destroy pride, selfishness, desires and identification with the body, the gross egoism will perish but the subtle egoism will remain. You must annihilate the subtle egoism also. Subtle egoism is more dangerous and more difficult of eradication. 'I am a rich man, I am a king, I am a Brahmin,'—this is gross egoism. 'I am a great Yogi, I am a Jnani, I am a good Karma Yogi, I am a moral man, I am a good Sadhaka or Sadhu'—this is subtle egoism. There is another classification of Ahamkara viz., Samanya Ahamkara (ordinary egoism) and Visesha Ahamkara (special egoism). Ordinary egoism is present in animals. Visesha Ahamkara is present in human beings.

You say, "This body is mine." The vultures, jackals and fishes also say, "this body is mine." If you peel off the layers of the onion one by one, the onion dwindles into an airy nothing. So is the 'I.' This body, mind, Prana, senses, etc., are all combinations of the five elements and Tanmatras. They are all modifications of the Prakriti only. Where is the 'I' then? This physical body belongs to Virat, astral body to Hiranyagarbha and causal body to Isvara. Where is the 'I' then? 'I' is an illusory nothing fabricated by the juggler mind. Nothing can be said to exist. That which is produced through Karmas is not itself the cause. The knowledge or consciousness that we have of it is itself illusory. Therefore, Ahamkara and other effects which are produced through the delusion of knowledge are also non-existent. The real 'I' is the Sat-Chit-Ananda Brahman only.

Just as the motion of the train or the boat is apparently transferred to the trees, so also 'I' is transferred, through the jugglery of Maya, to the body, mind, Prana and senses. When you say, 'I' am stout, 'I' am lean, the 'I' is transferred to the body and you identify yourself with the body; when you say, 'I' am hungry, 'I' am thirsty, the 'I' is transferred to the Prana, you identify yourself with the Prana; when you say, 'I' am angry, 'I' am lustful, the 'I' is transferred to the mind. If you identify yourself with the Supreme Self, all false identifications will vanish.

If you kill the commander of an army, you can very easily subdue the soldiers. Even so, if you kill the commander-egoism in the Adhyatmic battlefield, you can very easily subdue the soldiers, viz., lust, anger, pride, jealousy, greed, delusion, hypocrisy, who fight for their master—egoism.

Try to attain Brahman by means of the first two kinds of superior egoism. If you are firmly established in that supreme immaculate state wherein even these two kinds of superior egoism are abandoned one by one, then such a state is the imperishable abode of Brahman. Do not identify the 'I' with the physical body. Identify yourself with the Supreme Self or Para Brahman.

You might have reduced or thinned out your egoism to a very great extent but if you are still susceptible to censure and praise, know that the subtle egoism is still lurking in you.

An aspirant who treads the path of devotion destroys his egoism through self-surrender or Atma Nivedana to the Lord. He says, "I am Thine, my Lord. All is Thine. Thy will be done." He feels that he is an instrument in the hands of the Lord. He dedicates all his actions and the fruits of his actions to the Lord. He feels that there is nothing but the Lord, that everything is done by the Lord, that even an atom cannot move without Him and that all live, move and have their very being in Him alone.

A Karma Yogin destroys his egoism through self-sacrifice. A Jnana Yogin kills his egoism through self-denial or self-abnegation, through Vichara and the practice of "Neti-Neti—I am not this body, I am not the Prana, I am not the senses", and through identification with the Supreme Self by meditating on the formula 'I am the all-pervading Self or Brahman.'

May you rest in the big Infinite 'I', the pure Sat-Chit-Ananda Brahman and enjoy Eternal Bliss by annihilating this little illusory 'I', the product of Maya, through self-sacrifice or self-surrender.

II

A certain Brahmin went to a landlord to get a house for feeding Sadhus on a Bhandara. The landlord gave him a house. He utilised it for the purpose. He did not vacate the house on the next day, but remained there for some months. The landlord asked the Brahmin when he would vacate the house. The Brahmin said he would keep the house for some months more, as he wanted to celebrate his son's marriage. The landlord granted permission. The greedy Brahmin did not vacate even after two years. The landlord again asked the Brahmin when he would vacate it. The Brahmin said that he lost his mother and he would keep the house till the anniversary was over. The landlord patiently allowed. Three years passed. Now the covetous Brahmin thought that he could claim the house as his own, as he had lived in the house for a pretty long time and as the neighbours also knew well that he was the proper resident and owner. When the landlord asked now the Brahmin about the house, the Brahmin said that the house belonged to him, and refused to vacate it. The matter went to the chief court. The poor Brahmin was not able to produce proper records, though he managed to bring false witnesses. He had to give back the house to the landlord.

Similarly, you are provided with the house, the physical body, to inhabit for some years, during which period you are expected to realise Sat-Chit-Ananda and vacate the body during Videha-kaivalyam. Instead of doing this, owing to Ahamkara you are behaving like the covetous Brahmin. Destroy Ahamkara and rest in Brahman.

ANGER

KRODHA

Anger is a negative Vritti or whirlpool in the mindlake. It is born of ignorance.

It is a strong emotion, excited by a real or fancied injury and involving a desire for retaliation.

Anger is the natural passion or emotion of displeasure and antagonism aroused by injury or insult, real or imagined, and directed against the cause thereof. Anger arises from an idea of evil having been inflicted or threatened.

Anger is often accompanied by a desire to take vengeance, or to obtain satisfaction from the offending party.

It begins in folly and ends in repentance.

The fire you kindle for your enemy, burns yourself.

When anger arises, think of the consequences. It will soon subside.

You think of objects of senses. Attachment to these objects develops. From attachment desire is born. From desire anger comes forth. From anger proceeds delusion; from delusion confused memory; from confused memory the destruction of reason; from destruction of reason you perish.

Raga or attachment is a long-standing associate of anger.

Control anger through patience, enquiry, self-restraint, love and meditation. This is manly and divine. This is wise and glorious.

To become angry for trifling things is mean, childish and brutal.

When you are angry, count twenty before you speak. If you are very angry, count one hundred.

An angry man is again angry with himself when he comes to his senses.

When anger is on the throne, reason takes to its heels.

Be always ready to forgive the faults of others. Kill the spirit of revenge. Return good for evil.

Anger begins from folly or weakness. It ends with remorse and repentance. Act not in a furious passion.

He who is influenced by anger is like one intoxicated with a strong liquor.

Fury, indignation, choler, ire, temper, irritation, rage, resentment, wrath are synonymous with anger.

Displeasure is the mildest and most general word. 'Temper' is used in the sense of anger. This is colloquial. We say: "Mr. Johnson is a man of hot temper, a fiery temper."

Anger is sharp, sudden and brief. Resentment is persistent. It is the bitter brooding over injuries. Exasperation, a roughening, is a hot superficial intensity of anger, demanding instant expression.

Rage drives one beyond the bounds of prudence or discretion. Fury is stronger and sweeps one away into uncontrollable violence.

Anger is personal and usually selfish, aroused by real or supposed wrong to oneself. Indignation is impersonal and unselfish displeasure at unworthy acts. Pure indignation is not followed by regret and needs no repentance. It is also more self-controlled than anger. Anger is commonly a sin. Indignation is often a duty. We speak of "righteous indignation."

Wrath is deep and vengeful displeasure. It simply expresses the culmination of righteous indignation without malice in a pure being.

Anger is a stronger term than resentment, but not so strong as "indignation" which is awakened by what is flagitious in character or conduct; nor as wrath, fury, rage in which anger is wrought up to a still higher point in the order of these words. Anger is a sudden sentiment of displeasure; resentment is a continued anger; wrath is a heightened sentiment of anger.

CONTROL OF ANGER

Control anger by practice of Kshama, love, Dhairya, patience, and Nirabhimanata (absence of egoism).

When anger is controlled, it will be transmuted into an energy by which you can move the whole world.

Anger is a modification of passion. If you can control lust, you have already controlled anger.

Drink a little water when you become angry. It will cool the brain and calm the excited, irritated nerves.

Repeat 'OM Santi' ten times.

Count twenty. By the time you finish counting twenty, anger will have subsided.

Try to nip anger when it tries to emerge out from the subconscious mind to the surface of the conscious mind. Watch the small impulse or wave of irritability carefully. Then it will be more easy. Take all precautions. Do not allow it to burst out and assume a wild form.

If you find it extremely difficult to control it, leave the place at once and take a brisk walk for half an hour.

Pray to God. Do Japa. Meditate on God. You will gain immense strength.

Be careful in the selection of your company. Have congenial company. Move with Sannyasins, Bhaktas and Mahatmas. Read the Gita and the Yoga Vasishtha. Do not waste your semen. Take Sattvic food, milk, fruit, etc. Give up hot curries and chutnies, meat, alcohol and smoking. Tobacco makes your heart irritable (tobacco-heart). It produces nicotine poison.

ANXIETY

VYAKULATA

Anxiety is uneasiness regarding something doubtful.

Anxiety is uneasiness or distress of mind regarding some uncertain event which may involve danger or misfortune.

Anxiety is strained or solicitous desire, as for some object or purpose, or eagerness, as one's anxiety to please all.

It is a condition of restlessness and mental agitation with a distressful feeling of tightness and oppression in the region of the heart.

Anxiety is the rust of life. It destroys its brightness and weakens its power.

Anxiety is the poison of human life. Do not anticipate trouble or worry about what may never happen. Sufficient to each day are the duties to be done and the trials to be endured.

Full faith in God puts an end to anxiety. A childlike and abiding trust in God is its best preventive and remedy.

The cares of tomorrow weigh a man down. Do not torment yourself with imaginary dangers or trials or reverses. Be always happy and cheerful. Trust in God and do the right. Leave the rest to God.

God looks after everybody. He feeds even the frog that lives between the strata of rocks. Be not, therefore, anxious, and say

'What will be my fate next year? What shall I eat tomorrow? What shall I do for my clothing and blanket? How can I arrange for the education of my son or the marriage of my daughter?' God knows that you have need for all these things. He will do everything for you.

Do not make yourself wretched by imagining catastrophes unforeseen in the distant future. Do not anticipate misfortune.

Be always busy. Keep yourself ever occupied. Anxiety will take to its heels.

He who worships God, who sings His glory, who recites His Name is raised above anxiety for earthly wants.

You anticipate calamities, dangers and troubles. But they never come. Why do you unnecessarily worry yourself and waste your time, energy and strength?

Be of good cheer. Never bother about trouble till trouble actually troubles you.

Anxiety is mental. It is in regard to the unknown, or what may happen. It refers to some future event, always suggesting hopeful possibility.

Worry is a more petty, restless and manifest anxiety. Anxiety may be quiet and silent. Worry is communicated to all around.

Solicitude is a milder anxiety.

Perplexity often involves anxiety, but may be quite free from it. A student may be perplexed regarding a translation, yet, if he has time enough, not at all anxious regarding it.

Assurance, calmness, carelessness, confidence, ease, light-heartedness, satisfaction, tranquillity are the opposites of anxiety.

ARROGANCE

DARPA

Arrogance is undue assumption of importance. It is unreasonable or excessive assumption or assertion as of superiority. It is overbearing pride.

An arrogant man is unduly or excessively proud, as of wealth, status, learning, etc. He shows pride in spirit or conduct. He is unwarrantably assuming, overbearing and haughty.

It is that species of pride which consists in exorbitant claims of rank, dignity, estimation or power, or which exalts the worth or importance of the person to an undue degree. It is pride with contempt for others.

An arrogant man is abject and base. His head is swollen, like the swelling of dropsy.

Haughtiness thinks highly of itself and poorly of others.

Arrogance claims much for itself and concedes little to others.

Pride is an absorbing sense of one's own greatness.

Haughtiness feels one's own superiority to others.

Disdain sees contemptuously the inferiority of others to oneself.

Presumption claims place of privilege above one's right.

Pride deems nothing too high.

In the presence of superiors, overweening pride manifests itself in presumption or insolence.

Pride is too self-satisfied to care for praise.

Vanity intensely craves admiration and applause.

Superciliousness, as if by the uplifted eyebrow, as its etymology suggests, silently manifests mingled haughtiness and disdain.

Insolence is open and rude expression of contempt and hostility, generally from an inferior to superior, as from a servant to a master or mistress.

Assumption quickly takes for granted superiority and privilege which others would be slow to concede.

PLAY OF ARROGANCE

Ya Devi Sarva Bhuteshu Darpa Rupena Samsthita;
Namastasyai, Namastasyai, Namastasyai, Namo Namah.

Salutations, Salutations to that Devi, who dwells in the form of arrogance in all human beings.

The Sanskrit word for arrogance is "Darpa." Arrogance is undue assumption of importance. Arrogance is claiming proudly and unduly. It is a mixture of Rajasic-Tamasic egoism, insolence, rudeness, over-bearing nature and impertinence or imprudence. It is a modification of egoism. It is Ahamkara itself. It is born of ignorance. Maya keeps up her Lila or play through the arrogance of the deluded souls.

A man behaves insolently with an elderly man, treats him with contempt, sneers at him and speaks disrespectful words. This is arrogance.

Another man throws a book or a note-book in front of a person in anger and utters vulgar words. This is arrogance.

Another person says to another man in anger, "Don't you know who I am? I will break your jaw. I will break your skull. I will break your teeth. I will drink your blood." This is arrogance.

Another man says, "I cannot be dictated by anybody. I have my own ways. Nobody can question me. I cannot dance before him. Why should I go to him? Why should I follow his instructions? Is he more learned than me? Who is he, after all? Who are you to order me? Who are you to question me?" This is arrogance.

Generally a thoughtless man who is not practising introspection and self-analysis says, "I have no arrogance at all. I am humble, gentle and kind." But when the test comes, he hopelessly and miserably fails a thousand and one times. Such is the force or strength of arrogance.

A Sadhaka is very good. He is very intelligent. He is a learned man. He delivers lectures. He meditates silently in a solitary room for hours together. And yet he is not free from arrogance. When a man goes against his sweet will or wish, when a man speaks ill of him and criticises him, when he is not respected, he becomes arrogant and behaves very rudely.

Arrogance assumes various forms. One man may be arrogant on account of his great physical strength. He may say, "I will neck you out now. Get thee gone." Another man may be arrogant on account of his wealth, position and power. Another man may be arrogant on account of his secular learning. Another man may be arrogant owing to his scriptural erudition. Another man may be arrogant owing to his psychic Siddhis, moral virtues, spiritual progress, Sannyasihood, Mahantship, etc.

A man may renounce his wife, children, property, position, wealth, etc. He may renounce the world and live in a cave in the Himalayas for several years, practising Yoga and yet he finds it difficult to renounce arrogance. When he becomes impulsive he is overpowered by arrogance. He does not know what he is exactly doing. He repents afterwards. Impulse is a motive force to make one arrogant.

Watch your thoughts, words and actions very carefully. Know the power of words and use them cautiously. Respect all. Speak sweet and measured words. Be kind. Cultivate patience, love, humility. Enquire. Observe Mouna or the vow of silence. Again and again think, "This world is unreal. What will I gain by being arrogant?" Think of the immense benefits of the opposite virtue, HUMILITY.

You may fail one hundred times. But again stand up and strengthen your resolve: "I have failed yesterday. I will be humble, kind and patient today." Gradually your will-force will develop and you will conquer arrogance, the enemy of peace, devotion and wisdom.

With all your care and vigilance arrogance will hiss and raise its hood several times daily. Raise the rod of Viveka, discrimination and sword of humility and chop its head. Arrogance is a myriad-headed monster, or Asura like the Raktabeeja who fought the Devi. He will again develop more heads. Continue the battle with more vigour, force and strength. Use combined methods, prayer, meditation, enquiry, Brahmabhyasa, self-restraint, Japa, Kirtan, Pranayama. Take recourse to the Yoga of synthesis. He will be burnt in toto and reduced to ashes.

If an arrogant man remains in the cave or in the room, there is no scope for him to eradicate this Vritti. It will lurk in his mind and harass him. An aspirant must mix with persons of different mentality and temperament and watch his thoughts, when he is ill-treated, disrespected and persecuted. If he is calm and serene and humble even under worst trying conditions know that he has eradicated this terrible foe.

The more the learning, the more the arrogance. The bigger the position, the greater the arrogance. The more the wealth, the more the arrogance.

May you all be free from this evil trait! May you all conquer this demon through humility, patience, kindness and love, and enjoy eternal bliss and immortality!

AVARICE

LOBHA

Avarice is an eager desire for wealth. It is extreme covetousness or greed.

Avarice is passion for getting and keeping riches.

Avarice is insatiable. It produces extreme discontentment and restlessness. It is an enemy of peace, wisdom and devotion.

Avarice increases with the increasing pile of gold or bank balance.

Of all the vices, avarice is most apt to taint and corrupt the heart.

An avaricious man is immoderately desirous of accumulating wealth. He is eager to accumulate and hoard. He is greedy of gain. He is ever grasping.

Avaricious and covetous refer especially to acquisition; miserly, niggardly, parsimonious and penurious, to expenditure. The avaricious man desires both to get and to keep, the covetous man to get something away from its possessor. One may be made avaricious by the pressure of great expenditure.

The rapacious have the robber-instinct and put it in practice in some form, as far as they dare. The avaricious and rapacious are ready to reach out for gain.

Greedy is used not only of money, but often of other things, as food, etc. The greedy child wishes to enjoy everything himself; the stingy child to keep others from getting it.

Avarice sheds a blasting influence over the finest affections and sweetest comforts of mankind.

The covetous eagerly desire wealth, even at the expense of others; the avaricious hoard it; the penurious, parsimonious and miserly save it by disgraceful self-denial and the niggardly, by meanness in their dealings with others.

Miserly and niggardly persons seek to gain by mean and petty savings; the miserly by stinting themselves, the niggardly by stinting others.

Parsimonious and penurious may apply to one's outlay either for himself or for others; in the latter use they are somewhat less harsh and reproachful terms than niggardly.

Bountiful, generous, liberal, munificent, are the opposites of avaricious nature.

SONG OF AVIDITY

(Just as the Song of Eighteen 'Ities places before you a set of positive virtues that yo u should cultivate, this Song of Avidity places before you a set of evil traits that you should guard yourself against. It also shows you the method of overcoming them.)

Avidity, cupidity, stupidity,
Audacity, turbidity, unstability,
Angularity, eccentricity, irritability,
These are the obstacles to Samadhi.
These are the impurities of the mind.
Avidity is covetousness or greed.
Cupidity is lust or passion.
Stupidity is delusion or infatuation.
Audacity is arrogance or impertinence.
Turbidity is confusion of mind.
Unstability is wandering of the mind.
Angularity is a form of vanity.
Eccentricity is slavery to whims and fancies.
Irritability is anger in all its forms.
Remove these impurities through the opposite virtues.
Avidity through practice of generosity;
Cupidity through practice of purity;
Unstability through Trataka and Pranayama,
              Upasana and Japa;
Angularity through practice of humility;
Eccentricity through practice of right conduct;
Irritability through practice of patience, forbearance.
You will enter into Samadhi and attain Kaivalya.

BACKBITING

This is a dirty, abominable habit of petty-minded people. Almost all are victims of this dire malady. This has become an ingrained habit of narrow-hearted, mischievous people. This is a Tamo-Guna Vritti. The Lila of this world is kept up by this evil habit of man. It is Maya's strong weapon to spread restlessness throughout the world. If you see four men sitting in a group, think that some backbiting is surely going on there. If you behold that four Sadhus are talking, you can at once infer without any shadow of doubt that they are backbiting against some person or other. A Sadhu who is engaged in contemplation will always be alone. The Sadhu will be talking: "The food of that Kshetra is very bad. That Swamiji is a very bad man." Backbiting is more prevalent amongst the so-called Sadhus than amongst householders. Even educated Sannyasins and householders are not free from this dreadful disease.

The root cause of backbiting is ignorance or jealousy. The backbiter wants to pull down or destroy the man who is in a prosperous condition by false vilification, slander, calumny, false accusation, etc. There is no other work for a backbiter except scandalmongering. He lives on backbiting. He takes pleasure in backbiting, mischief-making. That is his Svabhava. Backbiters are a menace to society. They are the worst criminals. They need capital punishment. Double-dealing, crookedness, diplomacy, chicanery, quibbling, tricks, artifices are the retinues of backbiting. A backbiter can never have a calm, peaceful mind. His mind is always planning or scheming in wrong directions. An aspirant should be absolutely free from this dreadful vice. He should walk alone, live alone, eat alone and meditate alone. If a man who has not removed jealousy, backbiting, hatred, pride, selfishness says: "I am meditating for six hours daily", it is all nonsense. There is no hope of getting a meditative mood even for six minutes unless a man removes all these evil Vrittis and purifies his mind first by selfless service for six years.

BOASTING

ATMASTUTI

Boasting is ostentatious display or bragging. It is an expression of pride.

To boast is to talk vaingloriously, to speak proudly, to magnify or exalt one's own self.

Boast not of what you can or would do. Actions speak louder than words. Doing is the only practical achievement.

Humility is natural to wisdom. Boasting is natural to ignorance.

The boaster may not know a great deal, but it is certain that he does not know as much as he thinks he knows.

The sun has no need to boast of his brilliance, nor the moon of her effulgence. Honest and courageous people have very little to say about their honesty or their courage.

An empty vessel alone makes much sound. So is a boaster. He talks loudly of himself. His neighbours do not like this. They know his real worth. They laugh at him.

Where boasting ends, then dignity begins.

Usually the greatest boasters are the smallest workers. The deep rivers pay a larger tribute to the ocean than shallow brooks and yet empty themselves with less noise.

He is only a beggar who can count his worth.

A braggart should fear this; he will be found an ass soon.

You wound your modesty and make foul the clearness of your deservings when you yourself publish and advertise them.

BRIBERY

The habit of taking bribes is very common. If you ask anybody working in any office: "What is your salary, Mr. Jayadev?" He will say: "Well, my salary is only Rs. 50/- but my income is about Rs. 75/-." This income is nothing but bribe. People are ignorant. Even the so-called educated people have no idea of the law of action and reaction, Samskaras and their force. If you take bribe, you will be punished for this wrong action and the Samskara of taking bribes will force you to take bribes even in the next birth. You will be a dishonest man even in the next birth. Your thoughts and actions are registered in the subconscious mind. You carry your dishonesty from birth to birth and undergo enormous sufferings. Reduce your wants and live honestly within your means. You will have a clean conscience. You will be ever free from anxieties and worries. You will have a peaceful death. I suppose you now understand the gravity of the law. Become an honest man and be true from this very second you read these lines. Never, never join those offices which are amenable to corruption and temptations. You will be corrupted. The educational line is very good. There are very few chances of taking bribes or committing sins. You can lead a quiet life. There are plenty of holidays for study of religious and philosophical literature and for doing practical Sadhana. You can easily evolve rapidly in the spiritual line.

CARES, WORRIES AND ANXIETIES

CHINTA, PIDA, AUTSUKYA

Cares, worries and anxieties are the products of Avidya or nescience. When the mind rests in Brahman during sleep, when the mind is disconnected from the body by chloroform, anaesthesia, there is no pain; there are no cares, worries and anxieties. From this it follows that cares, worries and anxieties are all pure mental creation. They do not at all exist in the blissful Self. If nescience, which is the root cause, is annihilated, these cares and worries die of themselves. Therefore you will have to treat the cause and remove the original cause by getting knowledge of the Self or Atman.

The Sanskrit word for anxiety is Chinta. Cares, worries and anxieties are one and the same. Only sounds are different, like water and aqua, pani and jal. They co-exist. A man says: "I have to take care of my children and old parents; I have to take care of my wife, house and lands; I have to take care of my cows; I have to take care of my body." Identification or Abhimana is the chief factor that brings cares and worries. This Abhimana is brought about by ignorance. When the little ignorant Jiva mistakes this impure perishable body for the pure imperishable Self, all these evils crop up. All originate from this body only. Body is your first enemy. You will have to treat this as a dog and have no Abhimana. Whenever hunger and thirst oppress you, give some food and drink, just as you look after your cows and bulls. This is all. Be a Udaseena. Be indifferent.

Looking at the face in the mirror fifty times daily, application of soap, powder and scented oils, wearing ties, collars and fashionable apparel, intensifies Deha-Abhimana and augments cares. The identification of the Self with this body is extended with those who are connected with this body, such as, wife, son, house, father, mother, sister, etc., and cares increase a hundredfold. You will have to take care of all these people. You will have to take care of the toys of your son also, because the toys are connected with your son. There is absolutely no end for these cares and worries. Man creates for himself all these cares. No one is to blame. Just as the silk-worm and the spider create a web for their own destruction, out of their own saliva, so also, man creates these cares and worries for his own destruction out of his own ignorance. The clouds arise from the ocean by evaporation of the heat of the sun and then obstruct the sun itself which gives heat for the rising of the cloud. So also, cares and worries are created by man for his annihilation. How can these cares and worries have real existence in the Atman which is an embodiment of bliss and peace? Destroy Abhimana of the body. All connection and cares will die by themselves, this very second. Do this now and feel the bliss. There is no use of hearing the method for preparing a custard pudding. Eat the pudding and rejoice. This is what I expect from you without delay.

A businessman worries himself: "How can I pay my debts? There is trade depression now. The business is dull." The college student worries himself: "I have appeared for the M.Sc. examination. I don't know whether I will pass or not. Then I don't know what I will do in order to earn a livelihood. There is keen competition everywhere nowadays. There is no scope of employment in any office. Even M.Sc.'s and graduates get only Rs. 50/- in sugar factories. For that post also there are no vacancies. My father has sold all his property for my education. Now he is starving. I am thinking of opening a hair-dressing saloon or a shop for manufacturing shoes. I now realise the dignity of labour. I shall now follow the teachings of Mahatma Gandhi and his path. The cinema is no doubt paying now. But I have not got the gift of an actor, not even a good voice. I am the only prop of my parents." The husband worries himself: "My wife had serious abortion on two occasions. She is now in the family way. It is six months now. I have no money to pay the doctor. I have not saved a single pie. I don't know what to do." The Raja says: "My tenants have not paid their taxes this year. They say that crops have failed. My treasury is empty. I have spent away about two lakhs for my trip to the continent. I donated five lakhs to the Earthquake fund." He also cries. Thus you see no one is free from cares and worries in this world. But a Yogi, a Jnani or a Bhakta is absolutely free from all these.

The hairs of a man turn grey within a couple of hours if he worries himself much. Worries have got a corroding effect on the brain tissues, nerves and cells. Worries impair digestion, bring exhaustion and sap the vitality and vigour of man. Worries make a man anaemic and bloodless. The mental energy is dissipated by cares and worries. Worries, when combined with fear and anger, kill a man in a second. In fact worries shorten the life of man. Many diseases take their origin in worries. Worries weaken the will. A man of worries cannot turn out any good work with attention. He is careless and listless. He cannot apply himself steadily to any work. He is a living dead man. He is a burden to his family and to mother earth.

Some people have developed a worrying habit. You cannot find any bit of cheerfulness on their faces. They always have "castor-oil faces" or "quinine-faces." Have you carefully noticed the face of a man when he takes a dose of quinine or castor oil? They are gloomy and depressed. Such people should not come out of their rooms. They pollute the world atmosphere and the thought-world and affect other people. Gloomy is an epidemic disease. All those who come in contact with gloomy people are immediately affected. A gloomy man should cover his face when he comes out.

The mind that worries much, takes a merry-go-round inside. I think you know what I mean by merry-go-round? A worrying habit is formed in the mind. The worrying thoughts recur again and again and the mind moves in a circle.

Never worry yourself over any matter. Be always cheerful. Think of the opposite which is cheerfulness. Use your reason and commonsense always. Be sagacious and prudent. You can avert dangers and failures. You can overcome any shortcomings. If you are careful and also vigilant, if you are honest and straightforward, if you discharge your daily Sandhya, meditation, prayer, and other duties of Varnashrama, and if you speak truth and practise celibacy, nothing can harm you. Even Brahma, the creator, will be afraid of you. Everything will go on smoothly. You will have an unruffled life. Even difficulties will roll on smoothly without affecting you a bit. Why then should there be room for cares and worries. Have always a balanced mind. Always smile and laugh. Develop this habit. Even if any difficulty manifests, keep a cool mind. Remember the formula: "EVEN THIS WILL PASS AWAY." Reflect and assert: "Why should I unnecessarily worry myself? I have gained power now. I know the ways to pull on in this world now. I am not afraid of anything. I have a strong will now. I meditate on Atman. Nothing can upset me now. I am invincible. I can move the world. I am a dynamic personality. I know how to adjust myself to my environments and surroundings. I can influence people. I know the art of suggestion and auto-suggestion. I will never worry myself about anything. I am always peaceful and strong. I derive bliss from within. I always say now: 'Mr. Worry, good-bye unto you.' I am a different man now. I am made of a sterner stuff. Worries are now afraid to show their faces to me. I can also remove the worries of millions of other people."

O little man of little faith! See how the birds are care-free and happy. Become as care-free as the bird or a Paramahamsa Sannyasin. Have faith in your inner Self. Rely on your Self. Stand up and assert the divine majesty of your Self. Thou art not this perishable body. Thou art the All-pervading blissful Self. Even if you have nothing to eat, even if you have nothing to wear, never budge an inch from this position. Blessed is he who is care-free and who is resting in his own Svarupa, always smiling and laughing and radiating joy unto others.

CARELESSNESS AND FORGETFULNESS

ASAVADHANA, VISMRITI

Carelessness and forgetfulness are two other evil qualities that stand in the way of success of man. A careless man cannot do any work in a neat and proper manner. These are qualities born of Tamas. Application and tenacity are unknown to a careless and forgetful man. There is lack of attention in him. He loses his key, shoes, umbrella and fountain pen daily. He cannot produce papers and records to the office at the proper moment. He blinks. Follow the lessons in memory-culture and you can have a good memory within a short time. You will have to develop a strong desire to remove these qualities and develop their opposites. This is important. Then alone the will and the subconscious mind will do the work for you. Keep your money in the inside pocket. Keep your spectacles in the side pocket. Always count your belongings whenever you travel in railway trains. Keep accounts regularly.

COVETOUSNESS

LALASA

Covetousness is greed or avariciousness. Inordinate desire of wealth is covetousness.

All virtue, all honesty and peace run away from a man of covetousness.

A covetous man is always poor and discontented. A covetous man is a fool. He is a miserable wretch. He lives in perpetual slavery, fear, suspicion, sorrow, discontentment. He never enjoys life.

A covetous man heaps up riches not to enjoy, but to have them. He starves himself in the midst of plenty. His sons squander his money quickly.

Covetousness is the first vice in corrupt nature which moves and the last which dies.

A covetous man acquires money by unjust or unlawful means. He leads a miserable life. His lot is pitiable and lamentable!

COWARDICE

KATARYA

Cowardice is want of courage. It is timidity.

A coward is a faint-hearted person. He is afraid of danger. He fawns upon those who are above him. He falters. He yields to fear. He dreads pain or harm unduly.

A coward is a poltroon. He is a pusillanimous man. He is a dastard.

A coward dies many times before his death. A coward can never attain God-realisation.

Cowardice is the one deadly sin. Cowardice is loss of fame.

A lie is contemptible, chiefly because it is cowardly.

CROOKED-MINDEDNESS

KAUTILYA

Crooked-minded people also are to be found in abundance in the world. Crooked-mindedness is a Tamo-Guna Vritti. Such people are always crooked in talking and arguing. They indulge in quibbling and wrangling. They are always fond of vain talks. They will assert emphatically that only their statement is correct and the statements of others are false and absurd. They cannot keep quiet even for a single minute. Their arguments are very peculiar. They will not argue with any person in a respectable manner. They will take to vituperation and fall out in the end. Cultivation of nobility, politeness and straight-forwardness will eradicate this evil quality.

DEPRESSION

VISHADA

Depression is a failing in or sinking. It is dejection, cheerlessness.

Depression causes pessimism. It stultifies all effort; it kills initiative, produces despair and sickness of mind and body.

Depression is falling of the spirits. It is low spirits or dejection. It is a lowering of vital powers. It is a state of sadness. It is want of courage or animation as depression of the mind.

Hope, courage and work can overcome all depression and fear, and convert your mountains of trouble into molehills. Things are never so bad as you believed them to be.

Stand up and gird up your loins. Pray. Do Japa. Do Kirtan, Meditate on the All-Blissful Atman. Cultivate cheerfulness. Depression will take to its heels.

Depression is a negative state. It cannot last for a long time. Be cheerful. Positive always overcomes the negative.

Chant OM. Do Pranayama. Study my article "Thy Real Nature." Hear the record "Thy Real Nature." You will be filled with new strength, joy and cheer.

Thy real nature is Satchidananda. Realise this and roam about happily.

Aspirants get moods of depression occasionally. These moods may be due to indigestion, cloudy condition, influence of lower astral entities, and revival of old Samakaras from within. Treat the cause. Remove the cause. Do not allow depression to overpower you. Immediately take a brisk, long walk. Run in the open air. Sing divine songs. Chant OM loudly for one hour. Walk along the sea-side or river-side. Play on the harmonium if you know the art. Do some Kumbhakas and Sitali Pranayama. Drink a small cup of orange juice or hot tea or coffee. Read some of the elevating portions of Avadhoota Gita and Upanishads.

DIFFIDENCE

AVISHVASA

Diffidence is want of confidence, want of self-reliance.

A diffident man lacks faith in his own self. He is distrustful of his own self.

Diffidence is want of confidence in oneself. It is lack of trust in one's own power, correctness, wisdom, judgment or ability. It is timidity, self-distrust, shyness.

Diffidence checks resolution and obstructs performance of actions. It sinks you down.

Cultivate confidence and self-reliance. Think less of what others may think of you. This will help you to overcome diffidence and aid you to self-possession, confidence and self-reliance.

We say: "Ram, fearing the critics, wrote with diffidence." "Krishna failed through diffidence alone." Many people are always diffident. They have no self-confidence. They have energy, capacity and faculty. But they have no confidence in their own powers and faculties and in getting success. This is a kind of weakness that brings failures in all attempts. A man appears on the pulpit to deliver a lecture. He is a capable man. He is well-read. But he is diffident. He thinks foolishly that he would not be able to produce an impressive speech. The moment this kind of negative thought comes to his mind, he becomes nervous, he staggers and gets down the platform. This failure is due to lack of self-confidence. You may have little capacity and yet you must have full confidence that you will succeed in your venture. There are people who have very little substance and capacity and yet they can thrill the audience. This is due to their self-confidence. Confidence is a kind of power. It develops will.

Always think: "I will succeed. I am fully confident of my success." Never give room for negative quality, diffidence, to enter your mind. Confidence is half success. You must fully know your real worth. A man of confidence is always successful in all his attempts and ventures.

DILLY-DALLYING

(Aimless Wandering)

VRITHA PARIBHRAMANA

Some aspirants have got a habit of wandering aimlessly. They cannot stick to one place even for a week. The wandering habit must be checked. They want to see new places, new faces and want to talk with new people. A rolling stone gathers no moss. A Sadhaka should stick to one place at least for a period of twelve years (one Tapas period). If his health is delicate, he can stay for six months in one place during summer and rainy season and in another place for six months during winter. During winter he can stay either at Rajpur (Dehradun) or Rishikesh. During summer he can go to Badrinath or Uttarkashi. Sadhana suffers if one wanders constantly. Those who want to do rigorous Tapas or Sadhana and study must stay in one place. Too much walking produces weakness and fatigue.

DISHONESTY

DHURTATA

Dishonesty is another evil quality. Almost all have got some form of dishonesty or another. Honest people are very rare. Dishonesty is the hand-maid of greed or avarice. Wherever there is dishonesty, there are double-dealing, diplomacy, cheating, fraud, chicanery, etc. These are the retinues of dishonesty. Greed is the chief officer of passion. For the gratification of lust, all dishonest practices are indulged in. If lust and greed are eradicated the man becomes honest. A dishonest man cannot thrive in any kind of business. Sooner or later, his dishonesty will be found out. He will be hated by all men in society. He will fail in all his ventures. He will not hesitate a bit to take bribes and tell lies. To cover up an untruth he will tell ten lies. To establish the ten lies, he will tell fifty lies. He will not be able to speak even truth with force. He has a rotten Antahkarana. Develop honesty by eradicating dishonesty. Be content with your lot. Never crave for more. Lead a simple life. Let your thoughts be lofty. Fear God. Speak the truth. Love all. See your own self in all. Then you will not be dishonest in your dealings with others. You will be prepared to sacrifice even the very little that you possess. You will develop a large heart and a magnanimous nature. That is what is exactly wanted of you if you want to succeed in life and in God-realisation.

ENVY

IRSHYA

Envy is grief and burning of heart at the sight of another's success and prosperity.

Envy is spite, hatred, ill-will; envy is an evil eye.

Envy is uneasiness, mortification or discontent at the sight of another's superiority or success, accompanied with some degree of hatred or malignity and often or usually with a desire or an effort to deprecate the person envied.

Envy is the daughter of pride and the author of murder and revenge.

Envy is like a fire. It consumes a man quickly.

If you rejoice in the happiness of another, you increase your own happiness.

One is envious of that which is another's and to which he himself has no right or claim.

He is jealous of intrusion upon that which is his own or to which he maintains a right or claim.

Envy is a venom which consumes the flesh and dries up the marrow of bones.

Deformed persons, eunuchs, old men and bastards are envious. Fellows in office, relatives, envy their equals when they are raised to a better status.

Contentment, friendliness, satisfaction, well-disposed nature are the opposites of envy.

Crush this envy, dire enemy of peace, devotion and wisdom through the practice of nobility, magnanimity and contentment.

EVIL COMPANY
DUHSANGA

The effects of evil company are highly disastrous. The aspirant should shun all sorts of evil company. The mind is filled with bad ideas by contact with evil companions. The little faith in God and scriptures also vanishes. A man is known by the company he keeps. Birds of the same feather flock together. These are all proverbs or wise maxims. They are quite true. Just as a nursery is to be well-fenced in the beginning for protection against cows etc., so also a neophyte should protect himself very carefully from foreign evil influences. Otherwise he is ruined totally. The company of those who speak lies, who commit adultery, theft, cheating, double dealing, who indulge in idle-talks, backbiting, talebearing, who have no faith in God and in the scriptures etc., should be strictly avoided. The company of women and of those who associate with women is dangerous.

Bad surroundings, obscene pictures, obscene songs, novels that deal with love, cinemas, theatres, the sight of pairing of animals, words which give rise to bad ideas in the mind, in short anything that causes evil thoughts in the mind constitutes evil company. Aspirants generally complain: "We are doing Sadhana for the last fifteen years. We have not made any solid spiritual progress." The obvious answer is that they have not totally shunned evil company. Newspapers deal with all sorts of worldly topics. Aspirants should entirely give up reading of newspapers. Reading of newspapers kindles worldly Samskaras, causes sensational excitement in the mind, makes the mind out-going, produces an impression that the world is a solid reality and makes one forget the Truth that underlies these names and forms.

FANATICISM

Fanaticism is wild and excessive religious enthusiasm. It is extravagant or frenzied zeal.

Nothing has brought more prejudice to religion or brought more disparagement upon truth than fanaticism or the boisterous or unreasonable zeal.

Be not so bigoted to any custom as to worship it at the expense of truth.

Earnestness is good, but fanaticism overdoes and is consequently reactionary.

Fanaticism is the offspring of false zeal and superstition. It is the father of intolerance and persecution.

Fanaticism is the false fire of an overheated mind.

The blind fanaticism of one man causes more evil than the combined efforts of one hundred rogues.

Bigotry is narrow; fanaticism is fierce; superstition is ignorant. Bigotry is obstinate and unreasonable attachment to a cause or creed.

Fanaticism and bigotry usually include intolerance which is unwillingness to tolerate beliefs or opinions contrary to one's own.

Superstition is ignorant and irrational religious belief.

Credulity is not distinctly religious, but is a general readiness to believe without sufficient evidence, with a proneness to accept the marvellous. Credulity is weak; intolerance is severe.

Bigotry has not the capacity to reason fairly; fanaticism has not the patience; superstition has not the knowledge and mental discipline; intolerance has not the disposition.

Bigotry, fanaticism, and superstition are perversions of the religious sentiment. Credulity and intolerance often accompany scepticism or atheism.

Cynicism, indifference, latitudinarianism are the opposite of fanaticism.

FASHION: A TERRIBLE CURSE

This subject is not foreign to Karma Yoga. He who wears simple dress, who is free from this terrible scourge of fashion only can do Karma Yoga. One should be fully aware of the disastrous effects of fashion. Hence I have introduced this article here.

People are dying of fashion. Gents and ladies have become absolute slaves of fashion. If there is a slight error in the cutting of a gown or uniform, there are damage suits in courts in London and Paris against tailors. Even Bombay and Delhi have become Paris nowadays. You can see the multifarious fashions in the evening. Fashion consists in half-nudity. They will call this as scientific, hygienic ventilation of the exposed parts. Half the chest, half-arms, half-legs, must be exposed. This is fashion. They have full control over their hairs. This is their Siddhi or psychic power. They can cut it and dress it in any way they like in a hair-dressing saloon. Fashion increases and excites passion.

Even a poor lady at Bombay pays five rupees for making a single ordinary frock. She never thinks a bit how her husband will be able to manage all these things. Poor husband! a slave of passion! a miserable soul! borrows here and there something, takes bribes in various ways, and pleases his wife anyhow with an outward smile and an inward burning resentment. He kills his conscience, destroys his intellect and walks self-deluded in this world, and gets carbuncles and pyorrhoea as a result of his bad actions. He cries when he is in trouble; "I am a great sinner. I cannot bear this pain. I have done many bad actions in my previous birth. O Lord! forgive me, save me." But he never tries a bit to improve his lot in this birth.

The whole world can be clothed out of the cuttings of the vain fashionable people. Money is wasted enormously in fashion. Man wants after all very little on this earth, a pair of ordinary clothes, four breads and a tumbler of cold water. If this money that is wasted in fashion is utilised in virtuous actions, in charity and service of society, man will be transmuted into Divinity. He will be in the enjoyment of eternal peace and bliss. What do you see now, instead, in fashionable people? Restlessness, anxiety, worry, fear, depression and pallor of face. They may be dressed in silken gowns or dinner suits in up-to-date fashion and style with stiff double collar, ties and bows. But you see in their faces cheerlessness and ugliness. The canker of worry, greed, passion and hatred has eaten the very core of their hearts.

If you ask a Baron of England to remove his boots and hat when he is about to enter a Hindu temple, he feels he has lost all personality. Look at the vanity of an egoistic man! A small piece of leather, a card-board covered with a cloth make up a mighty Baron; minus these he dwindles into an airy nothing. There is no spirit or strength in him. The pulse fails at the wrist. He cannot talk now with the same force. The world is full of people with a small heart and little understanding. They imagine that turbans and fashionable long-coats, hats and boots constitute a big man. A really big man is one who is simple and free from egoism and Raga-Dvesha (likes and dislikes).

Why do ladies and gents put on fashionable dress? They want to appear as big people in the eyes of others. They think they will get respect and honour by putting on fashionable dress. The wife wants to appear beautiful in the eyes of her husband. She wants to attract him. The husband puts on fashionable dress to attract his wife. The sister of ill-fame wants to get more customers by putting on fashionable dress. This is all delusion. Can a fashionable dress give real beauty? This is all artificial decoration, temporary false glittering, decaying false beauty! If you possess good virtues such as mercy, sympathy, love, devotion and forbearance, you will be respected and really honoured. This will give everlasting beauty even though one is clad in rags.

Fashion is a terrible curse. It is a dreadful enemy of peace. It infuses evil thoughts, lust, greed and devilish tendencies. It fills the mind with worldly taints. It begets poverty. Fashion has made you beggar of beggars. Annihilate this desire for fashion to the very root. Wear simple clothing. Have sublime thinking. Do not keep company with fashionable people. Remember those saints who led a simple life and those living persons of to-day who are very simple. Simplicity will cause piety. It will infuse divine thoughts. You will be free from worry and unnecessary thoughts. You can devote more time to divine contemplation and spiritual pursuits.

A Sattvic man or lady is really beautiful. He or she does not require any artificial decoration with gold pins, with nose screws or with any ornament or fashionable dress. Millions of people are attracted unconsciously towards them even when they are in very poor dress.

How simple was Mahatma Gandhi in his dress! He had a loin cloth only. How simple was Ramana Maharshi? He had a Kaupeen only. A loin cloth and a Kaupeen were thier personal effects. They did not want suit-cases or trunks to carry their dresses. They were as free as a bird. Avadhutas like Krishnashram of Gangotri, Brahmendra Sarasvati of Senda-mangalam, Salem, South India, have not even a Kaupeen. They are absolutely nude. They are now in the same state as they were when they were born.

This body is like a big wound or ulcer with various filthy discharges. It has to be bandaged simply with any piece of cloth. Silken, laced borders, frills etc., are not necessary. It is the height of folly to decorate this filthy perishable compound of flesh and bone with artistic borders. Have you realised your folishness now? Stand up. Give up fashion now. Take a vow. Give me a definite promise that you will use simple clothing from this very second.

You came naked. You will go naked. Your silken waist-thread and upper-cloth even will be snatched for the use of your grandchildren, when you are on the death-bed. Why, then, do you make these ceaseless selfish efforts for earning money and preparing fashionable dress? Realise your folly. Learn to discriminate. Get wisdom of the Self and rest in everlasting peace.

O fashionable man! O fashionable woman! O ye slayers of the inner Atman! Why do you waste your time, energy and life in vanity, in running after fashionable dresses? This is highly preposterous. The beauty of beauties, the undecaying source of beauty, the ever-lasting beauty is ever shining in the chambers of your hearts. The whole beauty of this world is a mere shadow or reflection of that fountain-head of beauty. Purify your heart. Control your mind and the senses. Sit quietly in a room and meditate on this Beauty of beauties—your Immortal Friend, Atman, or the highest Self. Realise this Self. Then and then alone you are really beautiful. Then and then alone you are really happy. Then and then alone you are really rich. Then and then alone you are really a big man.

FAULT-FINDING

This is a detestable old habit of man. It clings to him tenaciously. The mind of the aspirant who always tries to poke his nose into the affairs of other men is always out-going. How can he think of God, when his mind is ever engaged in finding the faults of others?

If you spend even a fraction of the time that you waste, in finding your own faults, you would have become a great saint by this time. Why do you care for the faults of others? Purify yourself first. Improve yourself first. Reform yourself first. Wash the impurities of your own mind. He who applies himself diligently to his spiritual practices cannot find even a single second to look into the affairs of others.

If the fault-finding nature dies, there will be no occasion for criticising others. Much time is wasted in backbiting, tale-bearing, scandalmongering, etc. Time is most precious. We do not know when will Lord Yama take away our lives. Every second must be utilised in Divine contemplation. Let the world have its own ways. Mind your own affairs. Clean your mental factory.

That man who does not interfere with others is the most peaceful man in the world.

Fault-finding is the art of pointing out faults. It is making of frivolous objections. It is carping criticism.

Do not be quick to tell people of their faults. Look for your own faults.

To find fault is easy; to do better may be difficult.

Everyone is eagle-eyed to see another's faults!

Endeavour to be always patient of faults and imperfections of others, because you have many faults and imperfections which require forbearance. If you are not able to make yourself that which you wish, how can you expect to mould another in conformity to your will?

Fault-finding nature only indicates narrowness of mind and ill nature.

Never speak of the faults if you do not think thereby to effect some useful purpose.

Develop the good-finding nature in others. Every man has his own virtues and good points which can be appreciated. The fault-finding nature will perish.

A fault-finder is dishonoured and condemned by the society.

Why do you poke your nose into other people's affairs, when you yourself have a thousand and one faults? Correct your faults first. Others will take care of their own faults. Mind your business. Do not interfere with other people. You can enjoy peace.

A Rajasic man sees only the defects in others. He cannot see their virtues. He even superimposes vices on others when they have not got these evil traits. But a Sattvic man sees only the virtues in others.

A sage beholds only the Atman in all beings. He never looks either into defects or virtues.

FEAR

Fear is a great human curse. It is a negative thought. It is your worst enemy. It assumes various forms, viz., fear of disease, fear of death, fear of public criticism, fear of losing your property or money, etc.

Fear blights many lives, makes people unhappy and unsuccessful. Think you are immortal, fearless Atman (Amrita, Abhaya). Slowly the fear will vanish. Develop the positive virtue, namely, courage. Fear will slowly disappear.

The power of imagination in the mind intensifies fear. Attachment to the body (Moha, Dehadhyasa) is the cause of all fear. He who can throw off the physical sheath (Annamaya Kosha) either by Yoga or Jnana will be free from fear.

He who has conquered fear has conquered everything, has gained mastery over the mind.

Some people can bravely face the shell or the shot in the battlefield. But they are afraid of public criticism and public opinion. Some can face a tiger fearlessly in the forest. But they are afraid of the surgeon's knife. You should get rid of fear of all sorts.

The one idea that you are the Immortal Self (Atman) can destroy efficiently fears of every description. This is the only potent tonic, the one sure panacea for this dire disease of fear.

Fear is a very great obstacle in the path of God-realisation. A timid aspirant is absolutely unfit for the spiritual path. He cannot dream of Self-realisation even in one thousand births. One must risk the life, if he wants to attain immortality.

The spiritual wealth cannot be gained without self-sacrifice, self-denial or self-abnegation. A fearless dacoit who has no Deha-Adhyasa is fit for God-realisation. Only his current will have to be changed.

Fear is not an imaginary non-entity. It assumes solid forms and troubles the aspirant in various ways. If one conquers fear, he is on the road to success. He has almost reached the goal.

Tantrika Sadhana makes the student fearless. This is the one great advantage in the line. He has to make practices in the burial ground, by sitting over the dead body at mid-night. This kind of Sadhana emboldens the student.

Fear assumes various forms. There are fear of death, fear of disease, scorpion-phobia, fear of solitude, fear of company, fear of losing something, fear of public criticism in the form of "What will people say of me?" Some are not afraid of tiger in the forests. They are not afraid of gun-shots in the battlefield. But they are awfully afraid of public criticism. Fear of public criticism stands in the way of the aspirant in his spiritual progress. He should stick to his own principles, and his own convictions, even though he is persecuted and even though he is at the point of being blown up at the mouth of a machine gun. Then only he will grow and realise.

All aspirants suffer from this dire malady, fear. Fear of all sorts should be totally eradicated by Atma-Chintana, Vichara and devotion and cultivation of the opposite quality, courage. Positive overcomes negative. Courage overpowers fear and timidity.

Fear is a painful emotion excited by danger. It is apprehension of danger or pain. Fear is an emotion excited by threatening evil or impending pain, accompanied by a desire to avoid or escape it and to provide for one's security.

Fear is born of ignorance. It is a negative Vritti or wave in the mind. It has no real form or existence. It is a product of imagination.

Constant fear saps your vitality, shakes confidence and destroys your ability. It makes you powerless. It is an enemy of your success. Therefore, shun fear and be courageous always.

From fear proceeds misfortune. The fears of a coward expose him to dangers. Terrify not yourself with vain fears. Be bold, friend.

Fear is a kind of bell which rings in the mind to make it quick and alert for the avoidance of danger.

Fear is the beginning of all evil. Therefore, conquer fear through meditation on the fearless Brahman or cultivate the opposite virtue, courage.

Poverty and failure are due to thoughts of fear.

If you are afraid of something, look at it in the face. Fear will vanish.

What paralysis is to the physical body, so is fear to the mind. It paralyses the mind and makes you powerless.

Fear is the most destructive emotion. It breaks down the nervous system and undermines your health. It creates worry and renders happiness and peace of mind impossible.

Wherever there is attachment to objects, there are fear and anger. Anger and worry are the long-standing associates of fear.

Fear assumes various forms. There are fear of disease, fear of death, fear of loss of property, fear of enemy, fear of public criticism, fear of scorpion, fear of cobra, and fear of wild animals.

Fear in all its different phases is the greatest enemy of man. It has destroyed the happiness and efficiency of man. It has made more men cowards, more people failures.

Fear of God is the beginning of wisdom. This is virtuous fear, the effect of faith.

There is vicious fear, the effect of doubt.

Half of your fear is baseless and imaginary.

Fear kills effort and stultifies endeavour.

Alarm, apprehension, awe, consternation, dismay, dread, fright, horror, misgiving, terror, timidity, trepidation are synonymous with fear.

Boldness, assurance, bravery, confidence, courage, fearlessness, fortitude, trust are the opposites of fear.

FICKLENESS

Fickleness is unsteadiness of the mind. It is inconsistency or irresoluteness.

A fickle mind oscillates and changes every second. It is never steady. It ever wanders.

A fickle-minded man now promises and breaks his promises the next second. You cannot rely on him.

A fickle memory is bad, a fickle course of conduct is worse; but a fickle heart and purpose is the worst of all.

A fickle-minded man is unduly changeable in feeling, judgment or purpose. He is wavering, inconsistent and capricious.

A fickle-minded man is like the restless sea or the restless monkey.

A fickle-minded man is irresolute, shifting, vacillating and whimsical.

A fickle-minded man always fails in any attempt. Success is unknown to him. He weeps and regrets. A fickle-minded man has a wavering disposition. He is unsteady in opinion or purpose. Fickleness of mind is a great obstacle in meditation. Light Sattvic diet and practice of Pranayama will remove this state of mind. Do not overload the stomach. Walk briskly in your compound hither and thither for half an hour. As soon as you have made a firm resolve, you must carry it out promptly at any cost. This will remove fickleness of mind and develop your will power.

Constancy, decision, determination, firmness, fixedness, immutability, resoluteness, steadfastness, steadiness are the opposites of fickleness.

Fickleness is due to too much Rajas or passion. Annihilate Rajas by increasing Sattva or purity or harmony. Take Sattvic food. Practise Japa, Kirtan, concentration, Trataka or gazing, Pranayama. Study sacred scriptures. Fickleness will take to its heels. Steadiness alone will prevail.

FILM-GOING

CHALANACHITRA-DARSANAM

Drinking, meat-eating, hearing vulgar music, company of prostitutes, attendance at nautch parties, theatres and cinemas, excite passion and throw the victim into the fire of hell. The Cinema has become a curse even in India. An officer spends half of his salary on cinemas and runs into debts. All have developed a bad habit for some kind of sight-seeing. They cannot remain without it. The eyes want to see some kind of lights and sensational pictures. The Cinema is a very good paying business nowadays. Various sorts of half-nude pictures and obscene sights are shown on the screen. College boys and young girls are unduly thrown into a state of mental excitement. Various sorts of evils are propagated. The Cinema is an enemy of devotion. It is havocking the world. It does immense harm to the people. It is a great drain on the resources of man. It is a great temptation. All bad films should be thoroughly investigated and censored. Films should be passed by a religious body before they are brought on the screen. Only films which contain religious stories that are calculated to develop the moral and philosophical aspects of man may be allowed to come on the screen.

It is gratifying to note that highly educated men and women of India take part in the cinema. But college education will not do. If they want to impress the people and to do real spiritual good to the world, they should lead a life of Tapas, meditation and Brahmacharya.

Cinemas produce an evil habit in man. He cannot remain even for a day without attending a show. His eyes want to see some half-nude pictures and some kind of colours, his ears want a little music. Young girls and boys become passionate when they see the actors in the film kissing and embracing. Those who want to develop themselves in the spiritual line should entirely shun cinemas. Spiritual people only can bring out impressive stories with good morals that can elevate the minds of the spectators.

FORGETFULNESS

Forgetfulness is losing or putting away from the memory.

Forgetfulness is the quality of being apt to let anything slip from the mind.

Forgetfulness is loss of remembrance or recollection; oblivion.

We speak of sweet forgetfulness of human care.

Forgetfulness is careless omission; inattention is forgetfulness of duty.

There is a noble forgetfulness—that which does not remember injuries.

Learn the art of forgetting; you often remember what you would not and cannot forget what you would.

Forgetfulness is a blessing of God. If you remember constantly certain unhappy things, you will die quickly.

People who have bad memory are forgetful. They are inattentive. They neglect to do certain things. This must be got rid of by cultivating good retentive memory.

Forget not good deeds done by others and help given to you by others in times of your distress. Be grateful to them.

Forgetfulness is a personal quality, as in "He was noted for his forgetfulness." Obliviousness, the stronger word, is a state into which a person or thing has fallen or passed completely, as "His obliviousness of his duties."

Prayer, practice of Pranayama, meditation, practice of exercises in memory as indicated in "Sure Ways for Success in Life and God-realisation," application of Brahmi-Amla oil, taking of Brahmi Ghee or Brahmi Powder with milk, will increase your memory power.

GLOOM AND DESPAIR

Just as clouds screen and obstruct the sun the cloud of gloom and despair will stand on your way of practice. Even then you must not leave the practice of Japa, concentration and meditation. These small clouds of gloom and despair will pass off soon. Give the suggestion to the mind: "EVEN THIS WILL PASS AWAY."

GAMBLING

DYUTA

Gambling is another dreadful curse. It is a great friend of Satan or anti-God. It is Maya's great weapon. It has broken the hearts of many. It tantalises, tempts and deludes. A little gain in the first betting itches the nerves of the gamblers and forces them to bet a large sum. Eventually they lose everything and return home with black or weeping faces. Man becomes a bankrupt by gambling. He weeps bitterly. Yet he will not leave it. Maya havocks through wrong habits, wrong thinking, wrong Samskaras and through bad company, gambling, cinema, drinking, smoking and meat-eating. Reason and discrimination fail. Intellect becomes perverted. Enormous money is wasted uselessly in gambling, drinking etc. No virtue will dwell in the heart of a man who gambles. Gambling is a net spread by Maya to entrap the bewildered souls. There is no evil greater than gambling. All vices cling to a gambler. No real gain will come to a gambler. He is always drowned in sorrow. He drags a cheerless life from day to day. Cards-play and horse-races are modifications of gambling only.

O Man! It is very difficult to get a human birth. Life is meant for God-realisation. Perennial joy, eternal bliss are in God. Do not waste this precious life in drinking, gambling, smoking and meat-eating. What will you say to the God of Death at the time of your death? No one will help you. You will carry your own thoughts and actions. Give up gambling, meat-eating, drinking, cinema, smoking from this very second. Give me a definite promise now. I am your friend and well-wisher. Wake up now. Open your eyes. Become a virtuous man. Do good actions. Sing Hari's Name. God's Name is a potent antidote for all evil habits. Study religious books. Seek the company of sages and devotees. All evil habits will be eradicated. Serve. Love. Give. Purify. Concentrate. Meditate. Realise this very second. Time is the most precious thing in the world. Ignorant people waste their whole time in playing cards and gambling. What a horrible state of affairs. Highly deplorable! How powerful is Avidya or Ignorance! People are lamentably sunk in the mire of darkness! Pitiable specimens of humanity! Slayers of Atman! May Lord Krishnaswami, Antaryami, the Indweller of your heart, give you strength to overcome all these evil habits! May His blessing be upon you all!

GREED

LOBHA

First comes Kama. Then comes anger. Then comes greed. Then comes Moha. Kama is very powerful. So prominence is given to it. There is intimate connection between Kama and Krodha. Similarly there is close relationship between greed and Moha. A greedy man has got great Moha for his money. His mind is always on the money-box and the bunch of keys he has tied to his waist-cord. Money is his very blood and life. He lives to collect money. He is a gate-keeper only for his money. The enjoyer is his prodigal son. He sucks the blood of poor people by taking enormous interest (25%, 50% and even 100% at times). Cruel-hearted people! They pretend to show that they are of charitable disposition by doing acts such as opening of Kshetras, buildings, etc.

Such acts cannot neutralise their abominable sins and merciless acts. Many poor families are ruined by these people. They do not think that the bungalows and palaces in which they live are built out of the blood of these people. Greed has destroyed their intellect and made them absolutely blind. They have eyes but they see not. Greed always makes the mind restless. A man of one lakh of rupees plans to get 10 lakhs. A millionaire schemes to become a multimillionaire. Greed is insatiable. There is no end for it. Greed assumes various subtle forms. A man thirsts for name and fame and applause. This is greed. A sub-judge thirsts for becoming a High Court judge; a third class magistrate thirsts for becoming a first class magistrate with full powers. This is also greed. This is another form of greed. A Sadhu thirsts for opening several Ashrams in different centres. This is also greed. A greedy man is absolutely unfit for spiritual path. Destroy greed of all sorts by Vichara, integrity, disinterestedness and enjoy peace.

HATRED

DVESHA

Hatred is another evil quality. This world is full of hatred. There is no real love. The son dislikes his father and tries to poison him to take possession of the legacy soon. The wife poisons the husband to marry another young man of wealth and position. Brothers fight in courts. Guru Nanak and Kabir have tried best to unite the two great communities in our land but failed very miserably in their attempts. Vedanta alone can unite them. How can a man who beholds the same Self in all, hate or dislike another man? The principles of Vedanta should be taught in all schools and colleges. This is an imperative necessity. The sooner this is done the better. From the very early boyhood healthy ideas should be sown in the minds of young boys. All boys should be trained in the service of humanity. The necessity of universal love should be very clearly emphasised. Then alone there can be a possibility of developing pure love and eradicating hatred. You all should try from now onwards to remove hatred sincerely and earnestly. Conquer hatred by love, jealousy by love and intolerance by love and you will succeed in life.

Hatred is the deadliest foe of an aspirant. It is an inveterate enemy. It is an old-standing associate of the Jiva. Ghrina, contempt, prejudice, sneering, taunting, teasing, ridiculing, mocking, frowning, showing wry faces are all forms of hatred. Hatred bubbles out again and again. It is insatiable like lust or greed. It may temporarily subside for sometime, and may again burst out with redoubled force. If the father dislikes a man his sons and daughters also begin to hate that man without any rhyme or reason whatsoever, although that man has not done them any wrong or injustice. Such is the force of hatred. If anyone even remembers the figure of a man who has done him some serious injury some forty years ago, at once hatred creeps into his mind immediately and his face shows clear signs of enmity and hatred.

Hatred develops by repetition of hatred-Vritti. Hatred ceases not by hatred but ceases by love only. Hatred needs prolonged and intense treatment as its branches ramify in various directions in the sub-conscious mind. It lurks in different corners. Constant selfless service combined with meditation for a period of twelve years is necessary. An Englishman hates an Irishman and an Irishman hates an Englishman. A Catholic hates a Protestant and a Protestant hates a Catholic. This is religious hatred. There is communal hatred. One man hates another man at first sight without any reason. This is Svabhavic. Pure love is unknown in this world amongst worldly people. Selfishness, jealousy, greed and lust are retinues of hatred. In Kali-Yuga the force of hatred is augmented.

A son hates his father and sues him in the court. The wife divorces her husband. This has come to stay even in India. In course of time divorce courts also will be established in India. Where is the Pativrata Dharma of Hindu ladies? Has it disappeared from the soil of India? In India marriage is a sacrament. It is a sacred act. It is not a mere contract as in the West. The husband holds the hands of his wife, both look at Arundhati star and take a pledge before the holy fire. The husband says, "I shall be as chaste as Rama and promise to live with you peacefully, procreating healthy, intelligent offspring. I shall love you till I die. I will never look at the face of another lady. I will be true to you. I shall never separate myself from you." The wife in return says, "I shall be unto you like Radha unto Krishna, like Sita unto Rama. I shall serve thee till the end of my life in sincerity. Thou art my very life—Thou art my Prana Vallabha—I shall realise God by serving thee as God." Look at the horrible state of present day affairs! Absolute freedom should not be given to Hindu ladies. Manu says: "Hindu ladies should always be kept under control." This deplorable state of affairs is due to so-called modern civilisation and modern education. Pativrata Dharma has gone. Ladies have become independent. They forsake

212 HOW TO ERADICATE VICES

their husbands and do whatever they like. Culture does not consist in husband and wife walking on Mount Road and Marina Beach holding their hands or placing their hands on the shoulders. This is not real freedom. This is vile imitation. This is unfit for Hindu ladies and destroys the feminine grace and modesty which are their characteristics and which adorn them.

Pure unselfish love should be cultivated. One should have fear in God. Solomon says: "Fear of the Lord is the beginning of wisdom." Service with Atma Bhava can remove hatred completely and bring in Advaitic realisation of oneness of life. Ghrina, prejudice, contempt etc., will completely vanish by selfless service. Vedanta in daily life when put into actual practice can eradicate all sorts of hatred. There is one Self hidden in all beings. Then why do you hate others? Why do you frown at others? Why do you treat others with contempt? Why do you divide and separate? Realise the unity of life and consciousness. Feel Atman everywhere. Rejoice and radiate love and peace everywhere.

HOW TO ERADICATE HATRED?

Adveshta Sarvabhutanam Maitrah Karuna Evacha
Nirmamo Nirahamkarah, Samaduhkha Sukhah Kshami.

Gita, Chap. XII. 13.

A Bhagavata or devotee who has attained God-realisation has no hatred to any being. He is friendly and compassionate. He is without attachment and egoism. He is balanced in pleasure and pain and is forgiving.

Hatred can be removed by the cultivation of virtues such as friendliness, compassion, forgiveness and eradication of egoism and mine-ness. Positive overcomes negative.

An egoistic man is easily upset by trifling things. As his heart is filled by vanity and pride, a little disrespect or harsh word or mild rebuke or censure throws him out of his balance. He hates others out of his wounded vanity. Hence removal of pride and egoism will pave a long way towards eradication of hatred.

Hatred is born of egoism. Eradication of egoism by the root will itself lead to the annihilation of hatred.

If you are attached to a thing you will hate that man who tries to take away from you the thing to which you are attached. If you are endowed with the quality of forgiveness you will excuse that man who tries to harm you or who has done you any harm, and you will entertain no hatred for anybody.

Cultivation of divine virtues like compassion, love, forgiveness, etc., will thin out or attenuate hatred. Vision of God or God-realisation or the knowledge of the Supreme Being can completely eradicate or burn hatred.

May you all be free from hatred and become Bhagavatas with God-vision and Daivi Sampat!

RELIGIOUS HYPOCRISY

DHARMIKA-CHALA

There are as many fashions in Sadhus as there are in worldly persons.

Just as hypocrisy prevails in the worldly persons, so also hypocrisy manifests in aspirants, Sadhus and Sannyasins who have not completely purified the lower nature. They pretend to be what they are not in reality. They pose for big Mahatmas and Siddha-purushas when they do not know even the alpha-beta of Yoga or spirituality. They put on serious Sunday faces. This is a dangerous Vritti. They cheat others. They boast too much of themselves. They do mischief wherever they go. They practise hypocrisy to get respect, honour, good food and clothing and to cheat credulous simpletons. There is no greater crime than trading in religion. This is a capital sin. Householders can be excused. There cannot be any excuse for aspirants and Sadhus who are treading the path of spirituality and who have renounced everything for God-realisation. Religious hypocrisy is more dangerous than the hypocrisy of worldly persons. A long drastic course of treatment is needed for its eradication. A religious hypocrite is very far from God. He cannot dream of God-realisation. Thick Tilaks, elaborate painting of the fore-head, wearing of too many Tulasi and Rudraksha Malas on neck, arms, forearms, ears are some of the external signs of religious hypocrisy.

IDLENESS

ALASYA

An idle man is a burden to himself. He wastes his life.

He is sickly, anaemic. He has no application. He has no resolution. He has no purpose in life. He has no determination.

His mind is clouded. His thoughts are confused. He drags a dreary, cheerless existence.

He has ruined his life. He puts his head down in shame and repentance.

IMPURE AND IMMODERATE FOOD
ASUDDHA-AHARA

Mind is formed out of the subtlest portion of food. If the food is impure, the mind also becomes impure. This is the dictum of sages and psychologists. Food plays an important part in the evolution of mind. Meat, fish, eggs, stale, unwholesome food, onions, garlic, etc., should be avoided by spiritual practitioners as they excite passions and anger. The food should be simple, bland, light, wholesome and nutritious. Liquors and narcotics should be strictly abandoned. Chillies, condiments, spiced dishes, pungent articles, hot things that are sour, sweetmeats etc. must be rejected.

In the Gita you will find: "The foods that augment vitality, energy, vigour, health, joy and cheerfulness, delicious, bland, substantial and agreeable, are dear to the pure. The passionate desire foods that are burning, and which produce pain, grief and sickness. That which is stale and flat, putrid and corrupt, leavings also and unclean, is the food dear to the dark"—Ch. XVIII 8, 9, 10. Aspirants should not overload the stomach. Ninety percent of diseases take their origin in immoderations in diet. People have developed a strong habit of eating more food than what is actually necessary from their very boyhood. Hindu mothers stuff the stomachs of their children with too much food. This is not the way of caressing and loving children. Overloading produces drowsiness and sleep immediately. If there is no hunger, you must not take any food. The night meals should be very light for Sadhakas. Half a seer of milk, with one or two plantains is quite sufficient. Overloading is the chief factor in bringing night-pollution. Sannyasins and aspirants should take their Bhiksha from the hands of those householders who earn their livelihood by honest means.

INCONSTANCY

ASTHIRATA

Inconstancy is fickle-mindedness. The mind is subject to frequent change.

Inconstancy is instability of affection or temper. It is the quality or state of not being uniform. A man of inconstancy is unstable. He is vacillating. He has a character or constitution which renders change natural or preferable. He is inconstant in friendship or love like an inconstant flame. He changes his views and opinions. He is not firm in resolution. He is unsettled in his thoughts, speech and action.

Clocks will go as they are set, but man, irregular man, is never constant, never certain. His mind ever vacillates, oscillates, and fluctuates, on account of Rajas or passion.

Inconstancy makes you imperfect, fills you with faults and makes you run through sins.

The man of inconstancy has no peace of mind. He is never at ease. His life is unequal. Today he loves you, tomorrow he detests you. This morning he is joyful and laughs; this evening he weeps and is sorrowful.

Cultivate resolution, firmness and steadiness and conquer inconstancy, the cause for unhappiness and misfortune.

Be firm, be steady, be resolute, you will attain success in all your undertakings. You will have neither anxiety nor disappointment.

INDOLENCE

AALASYA

Indolence is the sleep or inertia of the mind.

Indolence is indisposition to exertion, arising from a love of ease or aversion to work, or the resultant inaction. It is habitual idleness.

An indolent man is indisposed to activity. He is dull and lethargic and lazy and slothful.

Indolence is the waste of what might be a happy and useful life.

Indolence is born of Tamas or darkness or inertia. It is an enemy of evolution, progress, success, peace, devotion and wisdom.

Indolence and stupidity are first cousins.

Indolence is a sort of suicide.

A man of indolence can be compared to a buffalo. He is a burden on this earth.

Indolence is the dry rot of even a good mind and good character.

Dullness, torpor, inactivity, sluggishness are synonymous with indolence.

INDECISION

ANISCHAYA

Indecision is want of decision or resolution.

Indecision is want of settled purpose or resolution. It is failure or inability to form a judgement or decide on a course of action. It is indetermination or irresolution.

A man of indecision is not able to decide or come to a final definite conclusion. He has a wavering mind.

Indecision is want of decision, want of settled purpose or of firmness in the determination of the will as an indecisive state of mind.

A man of indecision is unsettled. There is always hesitation for him.

Half the worries of the day spring from indecision. Determine on a plan, work on a policy. March forward.

The lot of man of indecision is indeed pitiable. He is ever unhappy. He always fails in all his undertakings. He is like a feather or cottonwool in the air which is blown about hither and thither by every breeze.

Some people are not able to decide anything definitely in certain important matters. They have not got an independent power of judgement. They will simply prolong the matter. They will not come to a definite positive decision. The opportunity will slip away. It will be too late to gather honey in winter. You must think deeply over a matter for some time and should be able to come to a definite decision. At once you must apply your will. You must immediately try to put the matter into execution. Then only you will succeed. Too much thinking will upset the matter. In important matters you can consult some of your elders who have got plenty of experience in the line and who are your real well-wishers. Remember the wise saying: "Cut the Gordian knot."

INERTIA
TAMAS

A microscopic minority only are fit for wholetime meditation. People like Sadasiva Brahman and Sri Sankara only can spend whole time in meditation. Many Sadhus who take to Nivritti Marga have become completely Tamasic. Tamas is mistaken for Sattva. This is a great blunder. One can evolve beautifully by doing Karma Yoga in the world if he knows how to spend his time profitably. A householder should seek the advice of Sannyasins and Mahatmas from time to time, draw a daily routine and adhere to it strictly amidst worldly activities. Rajas can be converted into Sattva. Intense Rajas takes a Sattvic turn. It is impossible to convert Tamas all on a sudden into Sattva. Tamas should be first turned into Rajas. Young Sadhus who take to Nivritti Marga do not stick to routine. They do not hear the words of elders. They do not obey the orders of the Guru. They want absolute independence from the very beginning. They lead a happy-go-lucky life. There is no one to check. They have their own ways. They do not know how to regulate the energy and how to chalk out a daily programme.

They aimlessly wander about from place to place. They become Tamasic within six months. They sit for half an hour in some Asana and imagine that they are having Samadhi. They think they are realised souls. If an aspirant who has taken Nivritti Marga finds that he is not evolving, he is not improving in meditation, he is going into Tamasic state, he should at once take up some kind of service for some years and work vigorously. He should combine work along with meditation. This is wisdom. This is prudence. This is sagacity. Then he should go in for seclusion. One should use his commonsense all throughout his Sadhana. It is very difficult to go out of Tamasic state. A Sadhaka should be very cautious. When Tamas tries to overtake him, he should immediately do some brisk work. He can run in the open air, draw water from wells etc. He should drive it off by some intelligent means or other.

SENSE OF INFERIORITY

HEENA BHAVA

Many a man worries himself too much that he is inferior to others. The idea of superiority and inferiority is purely mental creation. The inferior man can become a superior man if he exerts, struggles and develops virtues. The superior man may become inferior if he loses his property and falls into evil ways. Never think that you are inferior or superior to anybody. If you think that you are superior to others, you will begin to treat them with down-right contempt. The idea of superiority and inferiority is the product of ignorance. Develop equal vision. Live in the true spirit of the Gita. Hear what the Gita says: "Sages look equally on a Brahmin adorned with learning and humility, a cow, an elephant, and even a dog, and an outcaste." Namdev ran after a dog with a cup of ghee to soften and moisten the bread. He said: "O dog, you are a form of Vittala. This dry bread will hurt your throat. Pray, allow me to apply this ghee to this bread." Ekanath gave the Ganga water (which he carried from Gangotri on his shoulder for Abhisheka at Rameswaram) to an ass which was very thirsty and lying on the roadside. Where is superiority or inferiority when you behold the one Self in all and everywhere? Says William Hazlitt, the reputed essayist: "The sense of inferiority in others without an indirect appeal to self-love is a painful feeling and not an exalting one." Change your angle of vision or mental attitude and rest in peace.

INTOLERANCE

ASAHANAM

Then comes another undesirable negative quality, intolerance. There is religious intolerance. There is intolerance of all sorts. Intolerance is nothing short of petty-mindedness. It is unreasonable dislike for little things. The Sikh can drink alcohol. There is no harm in this. But he becomes intolerant when he sees anybody smoking. A Deccani Brahmin can do anything which is an infringement of the moral code but he becomes intolerant when he sees a Kashmiri Pandit taking meat. A South Indian Brahmin can take anything in a restaurant but he is intolerant when he sees a Bengali taking fish. All restlessness and fighting in this world of man takes its origin in intolerance. An Englishman is intolerant towards an Irishman or a German. A Hindu is intolerant towards a Muslim and vice versa. An Arya Samajist is intolerant towards Sanatanist and vice versa. This is due to perfect ignorance. How can a sage who sees the one Atman in all beings be intolerant? All these small petty differences are pure mental creations. Expand! Expand!! Expand!!! Embrace all. Include all. Love all. Serve all. Behold the Lord in all. See God in everything. See the Lord in every face. Feel the Indwelling Presence everywhere. Change the angle of vision. Be liberal and catholic in your views. Destroy all barriers that separate man from man. Drink the eternal Atmic Bliss. Become perfectly tolerant. Excuse the baby souls who are struggling in the path of life's journey and who are committing mistakes. Forget and forgive their mistakes. You will succeed in life. You will realise God quickly. There is no other way.

IRRESOLUTION

ANIRDHARA

Irresolution is lack of firmness in purpose, or want of resolution or decision.

Irresolution is the cause of failures and unhappiness. It is a great vice.

A man of irresolution lacks determination of character. He is ever vacillating, wavering and hesitating. He is given to doubt. He is without firmness of mind. He is without decision. He has a fluctuation of mind as in doubt or between hope and fear.

Indecision denotes lack of intellectual conviction. Irresolution denotes defect of volition, weakness of will.

A thoughtful man may be undecided as to the course to take in perplexing circumstances, but when decided, he may act with promptness. An irresolute man lacks the nerve to act. Indecision commonly denotes a temporary state or condition, irresoluteness a trait of character.

JEALOUSY

Jealousy is another canker that consumes man. It is nothing but petty-mindedness. Even educated people and Sannyasins are not free from this terrible scourge. All restlessness and fighting between one community and another, one man and another, one nation and another, are due to this evil quality. The heart of a jealous man burns actually when he sees his neighbour in more prosperous condition. The same is the case with nations and communities. Jealousy can be eradicated by developing the opposite quality, viz., nobility or magnanimity; just as pride is removed by developing frankness and simplicity; and anger is overcome by developing Kshama and a spirit of service.

Jealousy is also a great obstacle. Even Sadhus who have renounced everything, who live with one Kaupeen only in the caves of Gangotri and Uttarkashi in the Himalayas are not free from this evil Vritti. Sadhus' hearts burn when they see some other Sadhu in a flourishing condition, when they notice that the neighbouring Sadhu is respected and honoured by the public. They try to vilify this neighbour and adopt methods for his destruction or elimination. What a sad sight! What a deplorable spectacle! Horrible to think! Dreadful to imagine! When the heart burns, how can you expect peace of mind? Even highly educated people are very mean and petty-minded. Jealousy is a worst enemy of peace and Jnana. It is the strongest weapon of Maya. Aspirants should be always on the alert. They should not become slaves of name and fame and jealousy. If there is jealousy he is a small, little being only. He is far from God. One should rejoice at the welfare of others. One should develop Mudita (complacency) when he sees others in prosperous conditions. He should feel Atma-Bhava in all beings. Jealousy assumes various forms such as Irshya, Asuya, Matsarya etc. All forms of jealousy must be totally eradicated. Just as milk again and again bubbles out during the process of ebullition, so also jealousy bursts out again and again. It must be entirely rooted out.

The Sanskrit term for jealousy is Irshya. Irshya, Matsarya, Asuya are all synonymous terms. But there is a subtle difference. Jealousy is a particular kind of emotion or Vritti that arises in a Rajasic mind wherein the victim looks upon with a grudging eye on the prosperity or success or higher virtuous qualities of his neighbour or any other person. His heart burns when another man is more prosperous than himself. Hatred and anger are hidden in jealousy. Ill-will is the modification of jealousy. A man filled with jealousy hates another man if he is in a better position than himself. He gets grief at the sight of another's success. He tries his level best to pull down the prosperous man, to undermine him by various foul means, by backbiting, tale-bearing or vilification. He tries to injure the man also. He attempts to annihilate him. He creates dissensions and party-spirit amongst his friends. These are the external, physical manifestations of a man of jealousy.

A man of Irshya thinks that he should not get any kind of sorrow and that all others should be afflicted with grief. A man of Asuya gets agitated when another man enjoys like himself. A man of Matsarya cannot bear the sight of a man more prosperous and wealthy than himself. This is the subtle difference between Irshya, Asuya and Matsarya.

Jealousy is the root of all evils. It is very deeply rooted. Maya havocks through this particular Vritti. The restlessness of the world, Asanti, is due to jealousy. The whole play or Lila of Maya is kept up by this one emotion. Anger, hatred, malice exist side by side with jealousy. They are the old-standing associates or comrades of jealousy. If jealousy dies, hatred and anger die by themselves without any further treatment. Many murders are committed on account of sex-jealousy, money-jealousy.

No one can enjoy an iota of real happiness if his mind is filled with jealousy. Kings, Barons, Lords and Earls cannot have any happiness so long as they are slaves of this emotion. What can money do? It can only augment the uneasiness of the mind. "Uneasy lies the head that wears the crown."

There are six ways of eradicating this emotion:

1. Rajayogic method.
2. Vedantic method.
3. Bhakta's method.
4. Karma Yogin's method.
5. Method of Vichara of Vivekins.
6. Theosophist's method.

A Raja Yogi destroys the Vritti by "*Yogah Chitta Vritti Nirodhah.*" He destroys all Sankalpas of jealousy by introspection, careful watch and meditation. He adopts another method of "Pratipaksha Bhavana" by cultivating the opposite virtues of jealousy, viz., nobility or magnanimity, "Udarata." Jealousy is the result of petty-mindedness. If nobility is supplanted, jealousy will die of itself.

JILLY-JALLYING

ATIBHASHANAM

Too much talking is jilly-jallying. If a man talks too much he suffers from diarrhoea of the tongue. Quiet people cannot sit even for a second in the company of these loquacious or garrulous people. They will talk five hundred words per second. There is an electric talking-dynamo in their tongues. They are restless people. If you lock these people for a day in a solitary room, they will die. Much energy is wasted by too much talking. The energy spent in talking must be conserved for divine contemplation. The Vak-indriya distracts the mind considerably. A talkative man cannot dream of having peace even for a short time. An aspirant should talk only a few words when necessary and that too on spiritual matters only. A talkative man is unfit for the spiritual path. Practise Mouna daily for two hours and especially during meals. On Sundays observe full Mouna for 24 hours. Do lot of Japa and meditation during Mouna. The Mouna that is observed during meditation cannot be taken as vow of silence. Then sleep also should be taken as Mouna. Mouna should be observed by house-holders at such a time when there are opportunities for talking and when visitors come to meet. Now only the impulse of speech can be checked. Ladies are very talkative. They create troubles in the house by idle-talks and gossiping. You should speak measured words only. Too much talking is Rajasic nature. Great peace comes by observance of Mouna. By gradual practice, prolong the period of Mouna to six months and then to two years

MANORAJYA

Manorajya is building castles in the air. This is a trick of the mind. Look at this wonder! The aspirant is meditating in an isolated cave in the Himalayas. He plans in the cave: "After finishing my meditation, I must move about in San Francisco and New York and deliver lectures there. I must start a centre of spiritual activity in Columbia. I must do something new in the world. I must do something which no one has done upto this time." This is ambition. This is egoistic imagination. This is a great obstacle. This is a powerful Vighna. This will not allow the mind to rest even for a second. Again and again there will be resurrection of some scheme, speculation, plan or the other.

The aspirant will be thinking that he is having deep meditation, but if he closely watches his mind through introspection and self-analysis, it will be a pure case of building castles in the air. One Manorajya will subside and another will crop up in the twinkling of an eye. It will be a small Sankalpa or ripple in the mind-lake. But it will gain tremendous force within a few minutes by repeated thinking. The power of imagination is tremendous. Maya havocks through the power of imagination. Imagination fattens the mind. Imagination is like musk or Siddha-Makaradhvaja. It renovates and vivifies a dying mind. The power of imagination will not allow the mind to keep quiet even for a second. Just as swarms of locusts or flies come forth in a continuous stream, so also currents of Manorajya will stream forth incessantly. Vichara, discrimination, prayer, Japa, meditation, Satsanga, fasting, Pranayama, practice of thoughtlessness will obviate this obstacle. Pranayama checks the velocity of the mind and calms the bubbling mind. A young ambitious man is unfit to remain in a solitary cave. He who has done selfless service in the world for some years and who has practised meditation for several years in the plains in solitary rooms can live in a cave. Such a man only can really enjoy the solitude of the Himalayan retreats.

MEAN-MINDEDNESS
KSHOUDRAM

This world abounds in mean-minded people of every sort. Ninety nine per cent of people are mean-minded in some way or other. This is due to Tamo-Guna. The heart of a mean-minded man burns when he sees others in prosperous condition. It burns when he hears of the success and attainments or virtuous qualities of others. He vilifies them and aims at their downfall. He does scandal-mongering and backbiting. He is extremely jealous and envious. Mean-mindedness is a form of jealousy. One may be an intellectual giant. He may be a very great poet. His books might have been prescribed as texts for the students of M.A. in the University. But he may be a very mean-minded man without any scruples or principles. The whole society may admire his talents as a poet or as a scholar and at the same time may hate him as he is very mean. As a real man he is nothing.

A mean-minded man will not hesitate to poison his brother to usurp his property. He will not hesitate to put false signature, utter deliberate lies, defraud a man, commit adultery and rob a man of his wealth. He is ready to do any kind of mean act to amass wealth. He has not got a clean conscience. He is very calculative. Miserliness goes hand in hand with mean-mindedness. He will be pained to part even with a paisa. Charity is unknown to him. He may be a great man in society but he will be fighting on the railway platform shamelessly with a porter for two paise. He may spend kerosene-oil worth about two annas to find out a missing paisa in his daily account. He will eat sweetmeats, fruits, etc., but his heart will burn if his servant also eats the same articles. He will ask his servant to eat gram and black sugar. He will make great differences in serving tea or anything to others. He will keep the best things for himself and distribute the rotten stuff to others. He will not give even a single morsel of food to save a dying man. He has a heart as hard as flint.

Rich people are meaner than poor people. A mean-minded man fights with others for trifling things. He is of a quarrelsome nature. He is proud, egoistic and irritable. He is of highly suspicious nature. He is ever gloomy and depressed. The accumulated money of mean-minded people is generally squandered away by their profligate sons. A large portion of such money goes to pay the doctor's bills and lawyer's fees. They do not enjoy life. They are simply care-takers of their money.

The remedy for this dire disease is the cultivation of the opposite virtue which is nobility or magnanimity. Charitable nature, cosmic love and the spirit of service should be developed. Satsanga is highly beneficial. Regular meditation on the virtue of nobility is necessary. Sit very quietly in a solitary room at night and close your eyes. Introspect and find out what sort of mean actions you did during the course of the day. Record these in your daily spiritual diary. Watch also the mean Vrittis that arise from the mind-lake and nip them in their very bud.

MEAT-EATING

MAMSA-BHAKSHANAM

Meat is not at all necessary for the keeping up of health. Meat-eating is highly deleterious to health. It brings a host of ailments such as tapeworm, albuminuria and other diseases of the kidneys. After all man wants very little on this earth. A few breads, a little dal will quite suffice to keep up his health, vigour and vitality. Killing of animals for food is a great sin. Instead of killing the egoism and the idea of "Mine-ness," ignorant people kill innocent animals under the pretext of sacrifice to Goddess but it is really to satisfy their tongues and palates. Horrible! Most inhuman! Ahimsa is the greatest of all virtues. *"Ahimsa Paramo Dharmah."* Ahimsa is the first virtue that a spiritual aspirant should possess. We should have reverence for life. Lord Jesus says: "Blessed are the merciful, for they shall obtain mercy." Lord Jesus and Mahavir shouted at the top of their voice: "Regard every living being as thyself, harm no one." The law of Karma is inexorable, unrelenting and immutable. The pain you inflict upon another will rebound upon you and the happiness you radiate to another will come back to you, adding to your happiness.

Dr. J. Oldfield, senior physician, Lady Margaret Hospital, writes: "Today, there is the chemical fact in the hand of all, which none can gainsay that the products of the vegetable kingdom contain all that is necessary for the fullest sustenance of human life." Flesh is unnatural food, and therefore tends to create functional disturbances. As it is taken in modern civilisation, it is infected with such terrible diseases (readily communicable to man) as cancer, consumption, fever, intestinal worms, etc., to an enormous extent. There is little need for wonder that flesh-eating is one of the most serious causes of the diseases that carry off ninety-nine out of every hundred people that are born.

Meat-eating and alcoholism are closely allied. The craving for liquor dies a natural death when the meat diet is withdrawn. The question of birth-control becomes very difficult in the case of those who take meat diet. To them mind control is absolutely impossible. Mark how the meat-eating tiger is ferocious, and the cow and the elephant, which live on grass are mild and peaceful! Meat has a direct evil influence on the compartments of the brain. The first step in the spiritual advancement is the giving up of meat diet. The divine light will not descend if the stomach is loaded with meat diet. In large meat-eating countries cancer mortality is very high. Vegetarians keep up sound health till old age. Even in the West in the hospitals, doctors are now putting patients on a vegetable diet. They convalesce very quickly.

Pythagoras, the Grecian sage, preached: "Not to kill nor injure any creature." He condemned meat diet as sinful food. Just hear what he says: "Beware, O mortals, of defiling your bodies with sinful food! There are cereals, there are fruits, bending their branches down by their weight, and luxurious grapes on the vines. There are sweet vegetables and herbs which the flame can render palatable and mellow. Nor are you denied milk, nor honey, fragrant of the aroma of the thyme flower. The bountiful earth offers you an abundance of pure food and provides for meals obtainable without slaughter and bloodshed."

If you want to stop taking mutton, fish, etc., just see with your own eyes the pitiable, struggling condition at the time of killing the sheep. Now mercy and sympathy will arise in your heart. Then you will determine to give up flesh-eating. If you will fail in this attempt just change your environments and live in a vegetarian hotel where you cannot get mutton and fish and move in that society where there is only vegetable diet. Always think of the evils of flesh-eating and the benefits of a vegetable diet. If this also cannot give you sufficient strength to stop this habit, go to slaughter-house and butcher's shop and personally see the disgusting rotten muscles, intestines, kidneys and other nasty parts of the animal which emit bad smell. This will surely induce Vairagya in you and a strong disgust and hatred for meat-eating.

MISERLINESS

KRIPANATA

My experience after close study is that miserliness is ingrained in many persons. That is why they do not make any progress in the spiritual line despite their earnestness, sincerity and other qualifications and continued practice of Yoga. A miser is very far from God. He who expects Samadhi and Darshan of God by practising Asanas and Kumbhaka, and little Japa keeping up extreme miserliness and unsympathetic hard heart, cheats himself. He is a downright hypocrite indeed.

Miserliness is a great curse. It is an enemy of peace and a friend of selfishness. Miserly persons are quite unfit for the spiritual path. Generous-hearted persons are very rare. Many have achieved power, popularity, peace and happiness only through a generous heart. Miserly persons can never dream to have these and get success in life. Their very company is very dangerous for spiritually-minded persons. They poison the whole atmosphere on account of their corrupted, contracted hearts.

You should have a very large heart. You should throw money like stones to poor people. Then only you can develop Advaitic feeling, Samadhi and Cosmic love. The majority of householders are absolutely selfish in these days. Money is their blood. You will find cheerlessness and ugliness in their faces. Worry, greed, passion, jealousy, hatred, depression and all other evil qualities stick to the man who has the miserly nature in him and they consume the very core of his heart. It is a pity even judges and zamindars fight with porters on the railway platforms for the sake of an anna.

One may be able to stand on his head for three hours. One may be able to stop the breath for ten minutes. But this is nothing if he has no generous heart. See the fun here: Madrasis take their food on plantain leaves. Some of the ladies are very miserly. They will open the bundle of leaves and take out the decaying ones for the day's use and keep the good ones for the next day. By the time they open the bundle the following day, these good ones also will be rotting. In this manner, they will be using daily rotten leaves only. They cannot enjoy fresh leaves on any day. Such is their niggardliness. A fruit-seller also will be daily eating the rotten fruits only. He will never eat good ones. He preserves the good ones to get money from the people. If they are sold, then he will eat the rotten ones. Same is the case with the Panshopwalas. Misers have no happiness here and hereafter. They are watchmen only for their money. Many misers will not use new clothes. They will be wearing torn clothes. By the time they open the trunk, all new clothes will be eaten away by moths. Such miserly people will not part with anything of their own and in the name of generosity, they will give away in charity the property of others.

If a miserly man keeps Rs. 50,000 he will not enjoy the money but crave for a lakh more. A millionaire will be craving to become a multi-millionaire. It is horrible to find that rich persons are so miserly and hard-hearted that they do not live to share with their friends some of the rich delicacies. They will keep nice cakes in the almirah under lock and key and eat them in the night when others have gone to bed. Such persons will not give even a pie in charity. They will be eating nice food, but they will never have a heart to give a small portion even to a poor man who has been starving since three days. Such is the nature of their heart. They will take nice fresh cow's milk and offer only diluted milk to their guests. They will take fresh rich articles of food and offer the useless preparations to their servants, after keeping them for three days. They will wait for three days for getting good opportunity to use the old preparations of food and then throw them to their servants with a painful heart. They do not like to part with these decaying things also. You will find such heart-rending instances in almost all the houses of rich persons. To hide their inborn miserly nature, they will talk high philosophy on economy. They will never admit their actions are due to miserly nature, but will try to prove that it is economical.

Some officers retire from service and live on the banks of the Ganga, Narmada and Yamuna. They do a little Japa and meditation and study the Yoga Vasishtha and the Upanishads, and imagine they are Jivanmuktas. They entertain still intense Moha for their children. They remit their pension money to their sons and grandchildren. They are the embodiments of miserliness. They are hopeless, self-deluded souls! A miser cannot dream of Self-realisation even in thousand births. Lord Jesus says: "It is easier for a camel to go through the eye of a needle than for a rich man to enter the kingdom of God."

If one can destroy this miserly nature a greater portion of Sadhana is over. He has achieved something substantial. Sins can be destroyed by charity. Lord Jesus says: "Charity covereth multitude of sins." In the Gita you will find: "*Yajno danam tapaschaiva pavanani manishinam*—Yajna, charity and austerity are purifying to the wise."

Doing abundant, spontaneous and unrestrained charity to relieve the pains of the suffering humanity is an effective means to destroy this evil nature. Develop therefore this Udaravritti. Then only you can become a King of kings. Never think of your wife, children and dependents only. Whenever you come across poor people, wherever there is suffering, give money like water. If you give, the whole wealth of the world is yours. Money will come to you. This is the immutable, inexorable, unrelenting law of nature. Therefore give, give. See God everywhere. Share with all. The best portion must be given to

others. Destroy the ingrained miserliness. Your heart will expand. You will have broad outlook on life. You will have a new
wide vision. You can feel the help from the Indweller of your heart.
You can experience an indescribable thrill of Divine ecstasy and
Spiritual Bliss. This will give tremendous inner strength. Your root-
ing in the spiritual path will be firm. You will become a modern
Buddha!

NAME AND FAME

One can renounce even wife, son, property, but it is difficult to
renounce name and fame. Pratishtha is established name and
fame. This is a great obstacle in the path of God-realisation.
This brings downfall in the end. This does not allow the aspirant
to march forward in the spiritual path. He becomes a slave of
respect and honour. As soon as the aspirant gets some purity
and ethical progress, ignorant people flock to him and pay
homage and salutations. The aspirant gets puffed up with
pride. He thinks he is a great Mahatma now. He becomes eventually a slave of his admirers. He cannot notice his slow downfall. The moment he mixes up freely with householders, he
loses what little he had gained during eight or ten years. He
cannot influence the public now. The admirers also leave him
because they do not find any solace or influence in his company.

The people imagine that the Mahatma has got Siddhis and
they can get children through his grace, wealth and roots for removal of diseases. They always approach a Sadhu with various motives. The aspirant through bad association loses his
Vairagya and Viveka. Attachment and desires crop up now in
his mind. Therefore an aspirant should hide himself always.
Nobody should know what sort of Sadhana he is doing. He
should never attempt to exhibit any Siddhi. He should be very
humble. He should pass for quite an ordinary man. He should
not accept any rich present from householders. He will be
affected by the bad thoughts of those who offer presents. He
should never think that he is superior to anybody. He should not
treat others with contempt. He should always treat others with
respect. Then only respect will come by itself! He should treat
respect, honour, name and fame as dung or poison. He should
wear disrespect and dishonour as a golden-necklace. Then
only he will reach the goal safely.

NOVEL-READING

Novel-reading is another evil habit. Those who are in the habit of reading novels that deal with passion and love cannot remain even for a single second without novel reading. They always want their nerves to be tickled with sensational feelings. Novel reading fills the mind with base, lustful thoughts and excites passion. It is a great enemy of peace. Many people have started libraries for distribution of novels on a small subscription of four annas per mensum. They have not at all realised how much harm they are doing to the country. It is better they chalk out another avocation to eke their livelihood. They spoil the minds of young men by the distribution of these worthless novels which excite their passion. The whole atmosphere is polluted. Severe punishment is awaiting them in the Yama Loka. Newspaper reading is also an evil habit. People cannot leave their papers while they are taking their food also. They always like to hear some sensational news. They feel quite dull when they do not read the papers. They are quite unfit for a life of meditation and seclusion. Place them in solitude for three days. They will feel like fish out of water. The reading of newspapers makes the mind always outgoing, brings in revival of worldly Samskaras and makes a man forget God.

OBSTINACY

HATHA

Obstinacy is foolish stubbornness, born of Tamas or darkness. It is pig-headedness.

Obstinacy is stubborn adherence to purpose, opinion or course of action, arising from conceit or the desire to have one's own way and generally unreasonable.

It is the quality of being unyielding or difficult to control or subdue.

A man of stubbornness is unyielding to argument or entreaty. He has no regard for the wishes and views of others.

The man of obstinacy is bluntly and unyielding.

Obstinacy is the vice of the ignorant who vainly persevere in their own understanding.

Obstinacy is the strength of the foolish, weak and the stupid.

Firmness founded upon principle, upon duty, truth, right, order and law is the obstinacy of the Yogi and the sage.

Obstinacy is certainly a great vice. It is the cause of great mischief.

Firmness or adherence to truth and duty is sometimes mistaken for obstinacy by those who have no knowledge of its nature.

A child (Bala-Hatha), a Yogi (Yogi-Hatha), a woman (Sthree-Hatha), and Raja (Raja-Hatha) are reputed for their obstinacy.

The headstrong person is not to be stopped in his own course of action, while the obstinate and stubborn is not to be driven to another's way.

The headstrong act; the obstinate and the stubborn may simply refuse to stir.

The most amiable person may be obstinate on some one point; the stubborn person is for the most part habitually so. We speak of obstinate determination, stubborn resistance.

Obstinacy is a habit of the mind. Stubborn and headstrong are species of the obstinate. The former lies altogether in the perversion of the will; the latter in the perversion of the judgement.

Be not under the dominion of your own will. Hold not to all your determinations, but to those which are right.

OSTENTATION

DAMBHA

Ostentation is the art of making a display to draw attention or admiration. It is boasting.

Ostentation is display or show dictated by vanity and intended to invite applause or flattery. It is an ambitious showing forth of whatever is thought adapted to win admiration or praise.

Ostentation is the signal-flag of hypocrisy. It is the master sin of the devil and the father of lies.

As in a pair of bellows there is a forced breath without life, so in those who are puffed up with the wind of ostentation, there are empty words without action.

Ostentation may be without words as the ostentation of wealth in fine residences, rich clothing, costly equipage or the like. When in words, ostentation is rather in manner than in direct statement, as the ostentation of learning.

Boasting is indirect statement and is louder and more vulgar than ostentation. There may be great display or show with little substance. Ostentation suggests something substantial to be shown.

Pomp is some material demonstration of wealth and power, as in grand and stately ceremonies, rich furnishings, processions, etc., considered as worthy of the person or occasion in whose behalf it is manifested. Pomp is the noble side of that which as ostentation is considered as arrogant and vain.

OVER-CREDULOUSNESS
ANDHAVISVASA

Some people are over-credulous. This is also bad. They are very easily cheated by others. You must know his nature, qualities, his antecedents and his behaviour. You must try and test him on several occasions. When you are fully satisfied, then you can place your entire confidence in him. He may be a deep man. He may put on a false appearance and turn out to be quite reverse after some time. You will have to watch him very closely and move with him shoulder to shoulder and hear all about him from several other persons with whom he has moved. Man cannot hide his nature for a very long time. His face is the advertisement board that registers all his inner thoughts and, in short, all that take place in the inner factory. After close examination and test only, one should place his confidence and trust in another man.

PASSION
RAGA

Any strong desire is passion.

Passion is an intense or overpowering feeling, such that the mind is as if passively swayed by it. Any intense or inordinate, continuous affection or impulse as, the passions of love, pride, jealousy, avarice etc., specifically, ardent affection for one of the opposite sex, is passion. Amorous feeling is passion. A fit of intense and furious anger is also passion.

Passion is an emotion by which the intellect is swayed. The object of strong desire is passion. We say: "Music became a passion with Ram.".

Passion is an enemy of peace, devotion and wisdom. If you do not have victory over passion, it will annihilate your happiness, health and peace.

He who is ruled by passion is the worst of slaves.

Passion is like a convulsive fit. It is a momentary excitement. It weakens you after enjoyment.

Passion is like an unruly horse. Govern it through prudence, dispassion and discrimination and grow wiser and better. Deliver yourself from passions and you will be free.

Destroy your ruling passion, your master passion first. Then all other passions can be easily annihilated.

A dictator or king rules the people, but passion rules the dictator or the king. A sage or a Yogi alone is a master of the passion. He alone is ever happy, blissful and peaceful.

Your headstrong passion shuts the door of the illimitable kingdom of Bliss. Slay this passion and enter the domain of Bliss.

The strongest of animal passions is that with which you cling to life mundane.

Have passion for God-realisation. This will kill all worldly passions.

CONQUEST OF PASSION
RAGAJAYA

In a broad sense, passion means any strong desire. There is passion for service of the country in patriots. There is passion in first class aspirants for God-realisation. In some people there is a strong passion for novel-reading. There is passion for reading religious books. But generally in common parlance, passion means lust or strong sexual appetite. This is a physical craving for sexual or carnal gratification. When any sexual act is repeated very often, the desire becomes very keen and strong. The sexual instinct or the reproductive instinct in a man involuntarily prompts him for sexual acts for the preservation of his species.

Passion is a Vritti or modification that arises from the mind-lake when the Rajo-Guna predominates. It is an effect or product of Avidya. It is a negative Vikara in the mind. Atman is ever pure. Atman is Vimala or Nirmala or Nirvikara. It is Nitya-Suddha. Avidya Sakti has taken the form of passion for keeping up the Lila of the Lord. You will find in 'Chandi-Path' or 'Durga-Sapta-Sati': "*Ya Devi sarva bhuteshu kamarupena samsthita, namastasyai namastasyai namastasyai namo namah*—I bow to that Devi who has taken the form of passion in all these beings."

Passion is in a seed state in young boys and girls. It does not give them any trouble. Just as the tree is latent in the seed, so also, passion is in a seed state in the minds of children. In old men and women passion gets suppressed. It cannot do any havoc. It is only in young men and women who have reached adolescence that this passion becomes troublesome. Men and women become slaves of passion. They become helpless.

Rajasic food such as meat, fish, eggs etc., Rajasic dress and Rajasic way of living—scents, novel-reading, cinemas, talk on sensual things, bad company, liquors, intoxicants of all description, tobacco, etc.—excite passion. It is very difficult to understand, even by the so-called educated persons, the fact that there is super-sensual happiness in the Atman which is independent of sensual objects. They experience the Atmic bliss daily during deep sleep. They rest in their own Self daily at night. They crave for it. They cannot remain without it. They prepare nice bedding and pillows to enjoy the bliss of the Atman where the Indriyas do not play, where the mind gets rest and the two currents of attraction and repulsion do not operate. They say every morning: "I had a sound sleep last night. I enjoyed it. I did not know anything. There was no disturbance. I went to bed at eight and got up only at seven in the morning." Yet man forgets everything. Such is the force of Maya or Avidya. Mysterious is Maya! It hurls down a man into abyss of darkness. Man again starts his sensual life from the morning. There is no end.

Some ignorant people say: "It is not right to check passion. We must not go against nature. Why God has created young beautiful women? There must be some sense in His creation. We should enjoy them and procreate as many as possible. We should keep up the progeny of the line. If all people become

Sannyasins and go to forests what will become of this world? It will come to an end. If we check passion we will get disease. We must get plenty of children. There is happiness in the house when we have abundant children. The happiness of married life cannot be described in words. It is the be-all and end-all of life. I do not like Vairagya, Tyaga (renunciation), Sannyasa and Nivritti." This is their crude philosophy. They are the direct descendants of Charvaka and Virochana. They are life members of Epicurean school of thought. Gluttonism is their goal of life. They have a very large following. They are friends of Satan. Admirable is their philosophy!

When they lose their property, wife and children, when they suffer from an incurable disease, they will say: "O God, relieve me from this horrible disease. Forgive me of my sins. I am a great sinner."

Passion should be checked at all costs. Not a single disease comes by checking passion. On the contrary, you will get immense power, joy and peace. There are also effective methods to control passion. One should reach the Atman beyond nature by going against nature. Just as fish swims up-stream in a river, so also you will have to move against the worldly currents of evil forces. Then alone you can have Self-realisation. Passion is an evil force and it should be checked if you want to enjoy undecaying Atmic bliss. Sexual pleasure is no pleasure at all. It is attended with dangers, pain, fear, exertion and disgust. If you know the science of the Atman or Yoga you can very easily control the dire malady which is passion. God wants you to enjoy the bliss of the Atman which can be had by renouncing all these pleasures of this world. These beautiful women and wealth are the instruments of Maya to delude you and entrap you into the nets. If you wish to remain always as a worldly man with low thoughts, debasing desires, you can by all means do so. You are at perfect liberty. You can marry three hundred and fifty wives and procreate as many children. No body can check you. But you will soon find that this world cannot give you the satisfaction you want, because, all objects are conditioned in time, space and causation. There are death, disease, old age, cares, worries and anxieties, fear, loss, disappointment, failure, abuse, heat, cold, snake-bites, scorpion-stings, earthquakes, accidents etc. You cannot at all find rest of mind even for a single second. As your mind is filled with passion, and impurity, your understanding is clouded and your intellect is perverted now. You are not able to understand the illusory nature of the universe and the everlasting bliss of the Atman.

Passion can be effectively checked. There are patent methods. After checking passion, you will enjoy real bliss from within—from the Atman. All men cannot become Sannyasins. They have various ties and attachments. They are passionate and cannot therefore leave the world. They are pinned to their wives, children and property. Your proposition is wholly wrong. It is Asambhava (impossible). Have you ever heard in the annals of world history that this world had become vacant as all men were Sannyasins? Then why do you bring in this absurd proposition. This is an ingenious trick of your mind to support your foolish arguments and satanic philosophy which has passion and sexual gratification as its important tenets. Do not talk like this in future. This exposes your foolishness and passionate-nature. Do not bother yourself about this world. Mind your own business. God is All-powerful. Even if this world is completely evacuated when all people retire to forests, God will immediately create crores of people by mere willing within the twinkling of an eye. This is not your look-out. Find out methods to eradicate your passion.

The population of the world is increasing by leaps and bounds. People are not religious even a bit. Passion is reigning supreme in all parts of the world. The minds of people are filled with sexual thoughts. The world is all fashion, restaurants, hotels, dinners, dances and cinemas. Their life ends in eating, drinking and procreating. That is all. The food production is inadequate to meet the demands of the people. There is likelihood of severe famine and pestilence. Mother of the world sweeps away the extra population when the supply or production of food cannot meet adequately their demands. People are trying to have birth-control methods, or check pessaries, French letters, rubber goods, injection and application of protargol jellies. These are foolish attempts. Further the seminal energy is wasted. There is conservation and transmutation of this energy into Ojas by the practice of celibacy. People are wasting their money in these useless contraceptives. The whole world is under a tremendous sexual intoxication. The so-called educated persons are no exceptions to this rule. All are deluded and move in the world with perverted intellects. Poor miserable specimens of humanity! My sympathies are with them. May God elevate them from this quagmire and open their eyes towards spiritual realms. Self-restraint and celibacy are the only effective natural methods of birth control.

Early marriages form a menace to the society. It is indeed an evil. Bengal and Madras are filled with young widows. Many young men in whom there is a spiritual awakening write to me in pitiable words: "Dear Swamiji, my heart throbs for higher spiritual things. My parents forced me, much against my will, to marry. I had to please my old parents. They threatened me in various ways. I now weep. What shall I do now?" Young boys, who have no idea of this world and this life, are married when they are eight or ten years of age. We see children begetting children. There are child-mothers. A boy of about eighteen has three children. What a horrible state of affairs! There is no longevity. All are short-lived. Frequent child-bearing destroys the health of women and brings in a host of other ailments.

A clerk who gets a salary of Rs. 50/- has six children at the age of 30. Every two years there is an addition. He never thinks, "How shall I maintain such a big family? How shall I educate my sons and daughters? How shall I arrange for the marriage of my daughter?" At the heat of sexual excitement, he repeats the same ignoble act again and again. He has not got a bit of self-control. He is an absolute slave to passion. Like rabbits, he procreates and brings forth numberless children to swell up the number of beggars in the world. Even animals have got self-control. Lions visit their partners only once in all their lives or once in a year. It is only man with his boasted intellect that breaks the rules of health and has become a criminal in this direction. He will have to pay a heavy penalty in the near future for violating the laws of nature.

You have adopted various habits from the West in matters relating to dress and fashion. You have become a creature of vile imitation. They, in the West, do not marry unless they are able to maintain a family decently. They have got more self-restraint. They first secure a decent station in the life, earn money, save something and then only think of marriage. If they have not got sufficient money they remain bachelors throughout their lives. They do not want to bring forth beggars into this world just in the same manner as you do. He who has understood the magnitude of human suffering in this world will never dare bring forth even a single child from the womb of a woman.

When a man with a poor salary has to maintain a big family, he is forced to take bribes. He loses his sense and power of understanding and is prepared to do any kind of mean act to collect money. The idea of God is forgotten. He is swayed by passion. He becomes a slave to his wife. He bears, with a shrug of his shoulders, her taunts and scolding when he is unable to supply her demands. He has no knowledge of the theory of Karma, Samskaras and the working of the inner mental factory. The evil habits of taking bribes, cheating others and telling lies, are imbedded in the sub-conscious mind and is transferred to every physical body in its future births. He brings his own wrong Samskaras and starts the same life of cheating and telling lies in the following births. Will a man who knows this immutable law of Samskaras ever do wrong deeds? A man by his wrong actions spoils his mind and becomes a thief or a cheat in the coming births also. He brings in his old thoughts and feelings which are by nature devilish. One should be very careful in his thoughts, feelings and actions. He should always watch his thoughts and actions and entertain divine thoughts, sublime feelings and do noble actions. Action and reaction are equal and opposite. One should understand and remember this law. Then he will not do any wrong action.

Throughout the Gita the one ringing note that arrests the imagination and mind of the readers is that the man who has calmed his passion-nature is the most happy man in this world. It is also very very easy to control passion which is your deadliest enemy if only you take this subject very seriously and apply yourself to spiritual Sadhana whole-heartedly with a single-minded devotion and concentration. Nothing is impossible under the Sun. Dietetic adjustment is of paramount importance. Take Sattvic food, such as, milk, fruits, green dal, barley, etc. Give up pungent foods such as, curries, chutneys, chillies, etc. Take simple diet. Do Vichara. Chant 'OM.' Meditate on the Atman. Enquire "Who am I"? Remember that there is no Vasana in the Atman. Passion belongs to the mind only. Sleep separately. Get up at 4 A.M., and do the Japa of Maha Mantra or 'Om Namah Sivaya' or 'Om Namo Narayanaya' according to your taste, temperament and capacity. Do meditation on the Divine attributes such as Omnipotence,

Omniscience Omnipresence, etc. Study one chapter of the Gita daily. Make it a point not to tell lies even at the cost of death itself. Fast on Ekadasi days or whenever your passion troubles you. Give up novel-reading and cinema-going. Spend every minute profitably. Practise Pranayama also. Study my book "*Science of Pranayama*." Do not look at women with passionate intents. Look at your toes when you walk along the streets and meditate on the form of your deity. Repeat always your Guru Mantra even while walking, eating and working in the office. Try to see God in everything. Keep the daily diary regularly and send it to me for review at the end of every month. Write down your Guru Mantra daily in a clean note book for an hour and send the notebook to me.

You will be able to control passion if only you strictly adhere to the above instructions to the very letter. You can laugh at me if you do not succeed. Blessed is the man who has controlled his passion for he will soon have God-realisation. Glory unto such a soul!

Practise Sirshasana, Sarvangasana and Siddhasana simultaneously, with Pranayama. These are all highly useful in the conquest of passion. Do not overload your stomach at night. Night meals should be very light. Half a seer of milk or some fruits will constitute a good regimen or menu at night. Have the motto: "PLAIN LIVING AND HIGH THINKING" engraved in letters of gold in the forefront of your conscience.

Study select works of Sankara such as, Bhaja Govindam, Maniratna Mala or Prasnottari, Viveka-Chudamani, etc. Read with care "Vairagya Sataka" of Bhartrihari. They are all very elevating and inspiring. Practise always Atma Vichara. Have Satsanga. Attend Kathas, Sankirtan and philosophical discourses. Do not be too familiar with anybody. Familiarity breeds contempt. Do not multiply friends. Do not court friendship with women. Do not also be very familiar with them. Familiarity with women will eventually end in your destruction. Never forget this point. Friends are your real foes.

Avoid looking at women with lustful intents. Entertain Atma Bhava or the Bhava of mother, sister or Devi. You may fail many times. Again and again try to realise this Bhava. Whenever the mind runs towards attractive women with lustful thoughts have a definite clear-cut photo in the mind of the flesh, bone, urine and faecal matter of which women are composed. This will induce Vairagya in the mind. You will not commit again the sin of unchaste look at a woman. It takes some time no doubt. Ladies can also practise the foregoing method and can keep a mental picture just the same way as is described there.

Inflict self-punishment if the mind runs towards women with lustful ideas. Give up night meals. Do twenty Malas of Japa more. Hate lust but not women. Always wear a Kaupeen (Langoti).

Gradually give up salt and tamarind. Salt excites passion and emotion. Salt excites and strengthens the Indriyas. Renunciation of salt brings in a cool condition of the mind and the nerves. It helps meditation. You will suffer a bit in the beginning. Later on you will enjoy a saltless diet. Practise at least for six months. In this way you will be able to realise your own Svarupa very quickly. All that is wanted of you is sincere and earnest effort. May Sri Krishna give you courage and strength to tread the path of spirituality and attain the goal of life.

PESSIMISM

NIRASAVADA

Pessimism is the doctrine that on the whole the world is bad rather than good. It is a temper of mind that looks too much on the dark side of things. It is a depressing view of life. It is the opposite of optimism, which looks on the bright side of life and things here.

Pessimism is a disposition to take a gloomy or despairing view of life. It is a habit of anticipating failure or misfortune. It is a tendency to look on the dark side.

It is the doctrine that the world and human life, or some essential and permanent conditions and limitations of either or both, are essentially evil; in its extreme form, that this is the worst possible world compatible with its continuance in existence.

A pessimist is one who believes that everything is tending to the worst. He who looks too much on the dark side of things is a pessimist.

Pessimism is the great destroyer. It is despair and death. No matter if property, health or even reputation is lost, there is always life if you maintain faith in yourself and look up.

Do not be sure the worst will happen; it rarely does.

The Vedantic and Buddhist view is that life is illusory and burdensome.

Hume's view is that good and evil are so mixed that a beneficent First Cause cannot certainly be predicated.

Schopenhauer's view is that it is the worst possible under the conditions essential to its existence at all, and that life should be a denial and suppression of will.

Pessimism is an undesirable negative quality. This is a temper of mind that looks too much on the darker side of things. It is the doctrine that the whole world is bad rather than good. It is a depressing view of life. Buddhists preach pessimism. Vedantins, though they talk that the world is unreal, are wonderful optimists. They talk of Vairagya to create a taste in the mind of people for the immortal blissful life in Brahman and a distaste for the worthless materialistic life of this world. The opposite of pessimism is optimism. It always looks on the bright side of the picture. A pessimist is ever gloomy and depressed, lazy and lethargic. Cheerfulness is unknown to him. He infects others. Pessimism is an epidemic and infectious disease. A pessimist cannot succeed in this world. Become a powerful optimist and rejoice in the all-pervading Atman. Try to be very cheerful under any condition of life. You will have to practise this.

PIG-HEADEDNESS

HATHA

Pig-headedness is Tamasic obstinacy or stubbornness. This is born of Tamo Guna or darkness. The pig-headed man sticks tenaciously to his own foolish ideas. I gave instructions to a young aspirant. "Do not climb the hill with a plate in each hand and with shoes on, you will slip and break your bones." I gave him an example of a European lady who died instantaneously near Badri Hills from a fall from the summit of a mountain when she was making a vigorous attempt to get Himalayan herbs. I further cited to him another example of a professor of Geology, an M.Sc., of the Lucknow University, who also died of a fall from the mountain in Lakshman-Jhula (Rishikesh), when he was attempting to find out the nature of the rock. The young aspirant did not listen to my words. He was very obstinate. Despite my clear instructions, he climbed the Tehri hills with his shoes on and plates in his hands. This is a clear case of pig-headedness. Pig-headed students cannot make any definite progress in the spiritual path. You should eradicate this evil modification of mind. You should be ever eager to get good instructions from any source, from any sage. You should be ever ready to grasp the truth, no matter from whatever corner it comes.

PILFERING HABIT

ALPACHOURYA

Steya or the pilfering habit is very dangerous. It may develop into a serious crime under suitable conditions and favourable circumstances. If the aspirant is not established in perfect Asteya or non-stealing, he cannot hope to get an iota of progress in the spiritual path. He may retain his breath for five hours, he may do Trataka on the mid-day sun, he may get himself buried underneath the ground for three months or he may show many other dexterous Yogic feats. These are of no value if he has the pilfering habit. He may be respected and adored for a week or a month. People will treat him with contempt when he starts pilfering.

Do not be deceived by external appearances. Just hear this remarkable incidence. A Pundit of vast erudition was a guest of high personage. The Pundit could recite by-heart the whole of the Vedas and the Upanishads and he had done great Tapasya. He was very abstemious in his diet and took only a very small quantity of food. He would never waste unnecessarily a single minute of the day and was always absorbed in the study of religious books, Puja, Japa and meditation. His host held him in very high esteem. This learned Pundit stole one day some articles from his host's house. They were not valuable at all. In the beginning he totally denied the theft. Later on he admitted it and apologised. Would anybody take such a learned Pundit of severe austerities for a petty thief? The subtle Vritti of pilfering was hidden in the Pundit's mind, he had not destroyed it through self-analysis and drastic purificatory Sadhana. He had only controlled his tongue to a small extent and crammed some sacred books.

PREJUDICE

AVICHARAPURVA-PAKSHAPATA

Prejudice is judgment or opinion formed beforehand or without due examination of the facts or reasons that are essential to a just and impartial determination. It is unreasonable presupposition for or against anything. It is bias.

The destructive qualities of prejudice can be removed by goodwill.

Prejudice shuts out the truth and often leads to ruinous error.

Prejudice is a mist which dims your vision and obscures the good and glorious objects.

Prejudiced persons never speak well, but also never think well of those whom they dislike.

Prejudice is the child of ignorance. It is a great obstacle to progress.

When the judgment is weak, the prejudice is strong.

A prejudice is grounded often on feeling, fancy, associations, etc. A prejudice is always unfavourable.

Prejudice is unreasonable dislike for something or some person. Prejudice makes the brain callous. The brain cannot vibrate properly to grasp the things in their true light. One cannot endure honest differences of opinion. This is intolerance. Religious intolerance and prejudice are great obstacles in the path of God-realisation. Some orthodox Sanskrit Pundits strongly think that only Sanskrit-knowing people will have God-realisation. They think that English-knowing Sannyasins are barbarians and they cannot have Self-realisation. Look at the thick foolishness of these bigoted Pundits! Incorrigible, petty-minded, narrow-hearted, crooked sectarians! If one has prejudice against Bible or Koran, he cannot grasp the truths that are included there. His brain becomes hard, stony and callous. A man can realise by studying and following the principles that are laid down in Koran, Bible or Zend Avesta or the Pali books of Lord Buddha.

Aspirants should try to remove prejudice of all sorts. Then only they can see truth everywhere. Truth is not the sole monopoly of the Sanskrit Pundits of Benares or the Vairagis of Ayodhya. Truth, Rama, Krishna, Jesus are the common property of all. Our Bengalee brothers think that Ramakrishna Paramahamsa and Vivekananda belong to the Bengalees only. There is a general complaint that the Bengalees and Bengalee Sannyasins are clannish and provincial. It is high time now for them to remove this undesirable spirit in them. This is a great taint. They are famous for their intelligence. Those Sannyasins who have gone abroad to the Continent and those who are educated in the West are exceptions. They are catholic.

Sectarians and bigoted people confine themselves to a small circumscribed circle or area. They have no large heart. They cannot see the good points in others on account of their jaundiced vision. They think that their principles and doctrines only are good. They treat others with contempt. They think that their Sampradaya only is superior to others, and that their Acharya only is a man of God-realisation. They always fight with others. There is no harm in praising one's own Guru and sticking to his principles and teachings. But one should pay equal regard to the teachings of other prophets and other saints. Then only the feeling of universal love and universal brotherhood will manifest. This will eventually lead to the realisation of God or Atman in all beings. Prejudice, intolerance, bigotry, sectarianism should be thoroughly eradicated. Prejudice and intolerance are forms of hatred.

MORAL AND SPIRITUAL PRIDE
NAITIKA GARVA, ADHYATMIKA GARVA

As soon as an aspirant gets some spiritual experiences or Siddhis he is puffed up with vanity and pride. He thinks too much of himself. He separates himself from others. He treats others with contempt. He cannot mix with others. If anyone has some moral qualifications such as spirit of service or self-sacrifice, or Brahmacharya, he will say: "I am Akhanda Brahmachari for the last twelve years. Who is pure like myself? I lived on leaves and gram for four years. I have done service in an Ashram for ten years. No one can serve like myself." Just as worldly people are puffed up with the pride of wealth, so also Sadhus and aspirants are puffed up with their moral qualifications. This kind of pride is also a serious obstacle in the path of God-realisation. It must be eradicated thoroughly. As long as a man boasts himself, so long he is the same little Jiva only. He cannot have Divinity.

PROCRASTINATION
VILAMBANAM

Procrastination is putting off till a future time, through indolence or lack of resolution. It is dilatoriness. It is postponing or delaying. It is culpable delay.

Procrastination is the thief of time. It is the destroyer of initiative. It closes the door to advancement.

That "tomorrow" will never come. Tomorrow is too late for anything. He who sees help and salvation in tomorrows shall continually fail and fall today. That lazy tomorrow will be like today.

The foolish man says: "I will rise early tomorrow. I will pray and meditate tomorrow. I will carry out my intentions tomorrow." But the wise man rises early today, starts prayer and meditation today, carries out his intentions today and attains strength, peace, and success today.

What you can do this morning never postpone till the evening. Never put off till tomorrow that which you can do today.

Tomorrow is a period found in the fools' calendar alone.

Be wise today. Delay not till tomorrow. Tomorrow's sun may never rise.

'By and by' is a dangerous thing. You can arrive at the house of 'never' by the avenues of 'by and by.'

PRODIGALITY
ATIVYAYA

Prodigality is extravagance. It is spending without necessity.

A prodigal wastes his money. He throws away his money without necessity.

A prodigal squanders his fortune in bagnios, gambling and drinking and digs his own grave.

He falls into poverty, misery and abject disgrace. He becomes a victim to various vices.

He is intemperate, luxurious and ultimately starves. He cannot get even the necessities of life. He drags a cheerless existence. He leads a life of dissipation.

It is said that the prodigal of twenty makes the miser of seventy.

Spend money in charitable purposes. Be extremely liberal, but not extravagant. Waste not money.

REVENGE

PRATIKARA, PRATIDROHA

Revenge is injury inflicted in return. It is a malicious injury in return for an injury received. It is passion for retaliation.

To revenge is to inflict punishment, or injury, whether positive or negative in retaliation for an injury in a vindictive, malicious or spiteful manner.

Revenge is vindictive nature. It is a desire to inflict injury in return.

If anyone injures you, ignore it, forgive it. It is finished. You will have peace of mind.

Revenge is a common passion. The religion of love emphatically condemns it. Nothing so debases man as revenge.

Revenge is no valour. To bear an insult and an injury is indeed valour, strength and conquest.

Revenge returns back and hits your own heart with a heavy blow. It recoils on your own self. Revenge is a self-tormentor. Therefore, revenge not. Forget and forgive.

The spirit of revenge is the very spirit of the devil.

If any man injures you out of malicious nature, it is like the thorn which pricks and scratches. Mind it not. Be noble. Love him. He is weak and ignorant. He knows not really what he is exactly doing.

The indulgence of revenge tends to make man more savage and cruel.

Sweet is revenge, especially to women.

Revenge boils your blood and produces various diseases. It burns your heart and disturbs your peace. Therefore, revenge not.

Retaliation and revenge are personal and often bitter. Retaliation may be partial. Revenge is meant to be complete and may be excessive.

Vengeance, which once meant an indignant vindication of justice, now signifies the most furious and unsparing revenge. Revenge emphasises more the personal injury in return for which it is inflicted: vengeance is the ill-desert of those upon whom it is inflicted. A requital is an even return, such as to quit one of obligation, for what has been received and may be good or bad. Avenging and retribution give a solemn sense of exact justice, avenging being more personal in its infliction whether by God or man, and retribution to the personal visitation of righteous law.

Compassion, excuse, forgiveness, grace, mercy, pardon, pity, reconciliation are opposites of revenge.

RUDENESS

DHRISHTATA

Rudeness is roughness, harshness, wildness.

Rudeness is uncivil nature. It is brutal nature. It is ferocious nature. It is barbarous nature.

It is born of ignorance. It is the child of Tamo-Guna.

It is due to lack of culture, good breeding, good manners, good education.

Whoever one is, and wherever one is, one is always in the wrong if one is rude.

Rudeness is characterised by abrupt or rough discourtesy, as of manner or speech.

A rude man is offensively blunt or uncivil. He is impolite. He is impudent. He is impetuous. He is insolent. He is boisterous.

We say: "Mr. John is a rude fellow. He uses rude language."

Rudeness is characterised by lack of polish, refinement, or delicacy, as from lack of training or acquaintance with polite or civilised usage.

A rude man is a raw, crude man. He is without grace, finish, or cultivation. He is clownish. He is lacking good taste, chasteness, grace or elegance.

Rudeness is characterised by violence, harshness or cruelty.

Cultivate politeness, courtesy, good manners, elegance, civil nature, gentleness, softness, sweetness. Rudeness will take to its heels.

Be gentle. Be sweet. Be soft. Be polite. Be courteous. You will win friends. You will be liked by all. You will be honoured and respected.

SELF-ASSERTION

AHAMPRATYAYA, AHAMTA, ATMASLAGHANAM

Self-assertive nature is a great obstacle in the spiritual path. This is an evil quality born of Rajas. This is accompanied by vanity and arrogance. The aspirant who is a slave of the self-assertive nature wants to cut an important figure. He poses to be a great Yogi with many Siddhis. He says, "I am much advanced in Yoga. I can influence many people. No one is equal to me in the field of Yoga. I possess tremendous psychic powers." He expects others to pay respect to him and do prostration. He gets easily annoyed with people if they do not honour him and do not make prostrations. He tries to keep up his position and prestige. The self-assertive aspirant does not pay any attention to the instructions of his Guru. He has his own ways. He pretends to be obedient to his Guru. At every step his little ego asserts itself. He is disobedient and breaks discipline. He creates party-spirit, revolt, chaos and disorder. He forms parties. He criticises Mahatmas, Sannyasins, Yogis and Bhaktas. He has no faith in the scriptures and the words of sages. He insults his own Guru even. He conceals facts and tells deliberate lies to keep up his position or to cover up his wrong actions. He tells several lies to cover up one lie. He twists and tortures real facts.

SELF-CONCEIT

SVABHIMANA

Self-conceit is an over-high opinion of one's own self, one's own merits, abilities, acquirements, etc. Self-conceit is vanity.

A fool thinks he knows everything. He will not learn anything.

A man of self-conceit is not able to discover his mistakes, defects and weaknesses. His intellect is veiled and clouded.

His intellect is turbid. His intellect is in a state of intoxication. Conceit is more intoxicating than alcohol, opium or cannabis indica.

A man of self-conceit will always speak of himself.

Self-conceit and affectation are twins. They are merely different shades of the same feeling.

A man of self-conceit will not stoop to be vain. He is very busy in wriggling to catch fair words from others.

The more you speak of yourself, the more you are likely to utter falsehood.

Self-conceit is the tongue of egoism and vanity. A man of self-conceit always bores all persons.

If you want men to speak well of you, never speak well of yourself.

A man of self-conceit talks so much about himself that he gives no time for others to speak.

You can never expect justice from a man of self-conceit.

A man of self-conceit is a slave of praise. He is a slave to everyone who flatters him. He is everybody's fool.

Self-conceit is the foundation of the most ridiculous and contemptible vice.

Kill this ignoble self-conceit ruthlessly, through humility, meekness, and enjoy peace.

SELF-JUSTIFICATION

ATMAPRATIPADANAM

This is a very dangerous habit for an aspirant. It is an old-standing habit. Self-assertion, self-sufficiency, obstinacy, dissimulation, speaking falsehood are the constant retinue or attendants of self-justification. He who has developed this can never improve himself as he will never admit his faults. He will always try his level best to justify himself in various ways. He will not hesitate to tell several lies to support his false statements. He will tell one lie to cover another lie and he will speak lies *ad infinitum*. The aspirant should always admit his faults, mistakes, weaknesses, etc., then and there. Then only he can improve quickly.

SELFISHNESS

SVARTHAPARATA

Selfishness is the state or quality of being selfish.

A selfish man chiefly or wholly regards one's own self. He is void of regard for others. He acts from the consideration of what will give him the greatest pleasure.

He who clings to self is his own enemy. He is surrounded by enemies. He who abandons self is his own saviour. He is surrounded by friends.

O man! Fear the atom bomb far less than human selfishness.

Selfishness is the basis of all the world's troubles. It is at the root of all evils. It is the bane of happiness. It is a detestable vice. It destroys spirituality. It is the dire enemy of peace.

Selfishness is that evil quality of wholly regarding one's own self without regard for others.

Selfishness is an undue or exclusive care for one's own comfort or pleasure regardless of the happiness and often of the rights of others. It limits endeavour to a narrow circle of intensely personal aims, destroys all tender sympathies and is ultimately fatal not only to the welfare but to the happiness of him who cherishes it.

Selfishness is a detestable vice. It is the basis of all the worldly troubles and wars. It is at the root and source of all national and moral evils.

Destroy selfishness, the bane of happiness, through the practice of cosmic love, disinterestedness and selflessness.

Selfishness destroys your spiritual nature.

A selfish man lives only to benefit himself.

Selfishness is the root of all sins.

Selfishness is leprosy. Selfishness is cancer.

Selfishness is only generosity with narrow walls. A selfish man maintains a wife in luxury and makes his children rich.

Selfishness is the root and source of all natural and moral evils. Selfishness itself is the master evil of the world.

Sensual pleasure is the chief aim of a selfish man. Selfishness works through the senses. A selfish man gives a full play to his senses.

Selfishness is undue regard for one's own interest, gratification, advantage or the like, regardless of others and exhibited as disposition, character or conduct, distinguished from a reasonable self-regard or self-love.

A selfish man is influenced by personal motives or desires to the disregard of the rights, comforts or wishes of others.

Self-love is due care for one's own happiness and well-being, which is perfectly compatible with justice, generosity and benevolence towards others.

Selfishness is an undue or exclusive care for one's own comfort or pleasure, regardless of the happiness and often of the rights of others.

Self-love is necessary for high endeavour, and even for self-preservation. Selfishness limits endeavour to a narrow circle of intensely personal aims, destroys all tender sympathies, and is ultimately fatal not only to the welfare but to the happiness of him who cherishes it.

Selfishness is the cause of war. Selfishness, lust and greed co-exist.

According to the selfish theory of morals man is incapable of acting from other than a selfish motive.

Destroy selfishness through selflessness, nobility and magnanimity, and become a selfless Karma-Yogin.

SELF-SUFFICIENCY

ALAMBUDDHI

Self-sufficiency is another evil Vritti in the mind-lake. This also is born of a mixture of Rajas and Tamas. It acts as a stumbling block in the spiritual path. The student who is a victim to this evil trait thinks foolishly that he knows everything. He is quite contented with his little knowledge and achievements. He stops his Sadhana. He never attempts for further acquisition of knowledge. He never endeavours to attain the highest knowledge of Bhuma (Highest Self). He does not know that there is a vast realm of knowledge beyond. He is like the toad in the well which has no knowledge of the ocean, which thinks that the well is the only illimitable expanse of water.

A self-sufficient man foolishly thinks and imagines, "I know everything. There is nothing more to be known by me." Maya spreads a thick veil in his mind. The self-sufficient man has a turbid mind, clouded understanding and a perverted intellect.

Self-sufficiency is a strong weapon of Maya with which she deludes people and puts a strong break on the Sadhana of an aspirant. She does not allow him to proceed further or look beyond the veil, as he is carried away by false contentment through self-sufficiency.

The self-sufficient scientist who has knowledge of electrons and laws of the physical aspect of nature thinks that there is nothing beyond this. The moralist who has developed some ethical virtues thinks that there is nothing beyond this. The self-sufficient Yogic student who experiences Anahata sounds and flashes of lights thinks that there is nothing beyond this. The self-sufficient Sannyasi who knows the Gita and the Upanishads by heart thinks that there is nothing beyond this. The self-sufficient Yogi or Vedantin who gets experiences of the lower Samadhi thinks that there is nothing beyond this. All are groping in the dark. They know not what perfection is.

Maya tests the student at every step, at every stage, and appears before the student in various forms and colours, like an Asura or a chameleon. It is very difficult to detect Her presence. But he who has obtained the grace of the Mother will experience no difficulty in his onward march. She Herself lifts him up and carries him in Her hands to the destination to introduce him to Her Lord—Lord Siva—and to get him established in unshaken Nirvikalpa Samadhi.

The aspirant should always think, "What I know is very little. It is only a handful of knowledge. What is still to be learnt by me is oceanful." Then alone he will have intense aspiration or yearning for further knowledge.

SHILLY-SHALLYING

VIKSHEPA

Vikshepa is tossing or oscillation of mind. This is an old habit of the mind. All Sadhakas generally complain of this trouble. The mind never stays at a fixed point for a long time. It jumps hither and thither like a monkey. It is always restless. This is due to the force of Rajas. Whenever Sri Jaya Dayal Goyandka came to me for an interview he used to put always two questions: "Swamiji, what is the remedy to control sleep? How to remove

Vikshepa? Give me an easy and effective method." My answer was: "Take light diet at night. Do Sirshasana and Pranayama. Sleep can be conquered. Trataka, Upasana and Pranayama will remove Vikshepa." It is better to have a combined method. This will be more effective. Patanjali Maharshi prescribes Pranayama for destroying Rajas which induces Vikshepa and for getting one-pointed mind.

In the Gita Lord Krishna prescribes a Sadhana for removing Vikshepa. "As often as the wavering and unsteady mind goeth forth, so often rein it in, let him bring it under the control of the Self. Abandoning without reserve all desires born of the imagination, by the mind curbing in the aggregate of the senses on every side, little by little let him gain tranquillity by means of Reason controlled by steadiness; having made the mind abide in the Self, let him not think of anything"—Chapter VI: 24, 25, 26. Trataka is an effective method for destroying Vikshepa. Practise this for half an hour on a picture of Lord Krishna or on a black point on the wall. First do this for two minutes and gradually increase this period. Close the eyes when tears come. Look steadily at the object without winking. Do not strain the eyes. Look gently. There are students who can do Trataka for 2 or 3 hours. For full description read my book: *"Kundalini Yoga."*

SHYNESS

LAJJA

Shyness is a great hindrance in the path of success in life. This is a form of timidity of low fear. Almost all boys have got this weakness. This is a feminine quality which is the Svabhava of women. Shyness manifests when one is in the wrong path. Every woman knows that the goal of life is God-realisation and yet she indulges in sexual pleasures. This wrong action makes her shy when she appears before any man. A shy boy or man cannot express his thoughts boldly before any person. He cannot look directly at the eyes of another man. He will talk something and look at the ground. He cannot approach freely any stranger. A shy man cannot get on well in any kind of business or office. Modesty is not shyness. Modesty is decency or chastity. This comes out of politeness and polish of character. Some *zenana* ladies are very shy in the beginning in talking to men when they come outside after the death of their husbands.

Gradually they become bold and shyness vanishes. Those who are shy should try to talk with others boldly. They should look directly at the eyes of others. Shyness is a great weakness. It should be eradicated quickly by cultivating courage.

SLANG TERMS AND ABUSES

APASABDA, NINDA

The vast majority of persons have got the evil habit of using slang terms and abuses every second, during their conversation. When they become excited and angry they pour forth a continuous shower of all sorts of foul words. It cannot be described. There are people who use such words as *Sala*, every second. It will come out like the words: 'you see' in some people. '*Sala*' means brother-in-law (in Hindi). If you call anybody by the term '*Sala*' he will become very furious. People have got a vulgar habit and use these slang terms. A man of refined taste, culture and polish can never utter any such words. English people very often use the words; "Damn fool: The son of a bitch," etc. The English military people use the word 'Damn' every second. They cannot talk without a *damn* in a sentence. This also is a very bad habit. See the children in the streets. They fight, quarrel and use obscene words. When any Englishman comes to India or to any new country, he first tries to learn some obscene words. Look at human nature! He does not want to learn the names of God. When the cart-driver twists the tail of the bull, when the *Tongawala* whips the horse, there come the words: "*Sala, Badmash, Suwar Ka Batcha*, the son of a pig," and so on.

Parents should check their children when they utter any bad words. They themselves should not use any bad words. They themselves become the Gurus for these children. Children simply imitate. Children have got a strong power of imitation. Practise to use the words such as: "Hare Rama, Hare Krishna, Hae Prabhu" always, even when you talk. Bring these words every second. Train your children also. This itself will form a kind of Japa or remembrance of God. Train your mind. Check also people who often use vulgar words through bad habit. This is the most important duty of the parents. Any healthy habit sown in the minds of children becomes firmly rooted.

SLEEPING IN DAY TIME
DIVASVAPA

Sleeping in day time is another evil habit. It shortens life. Time is wasted considerably. It brings in laziness and lethargy. It develops gastritis, dyspepsia and a host of other ailments. It should be entirely given up, if you want to grow quickly. Snatch every second and utilise it properly. Life is fleeting, time is short, death is waiting. How happy is the man who is thoroughly destitute of a single evil habit. He can attain great success in life and apply himself diligently to Yogic Sadhana.

SMOKING HABIT
DHUMRAPANAM

He who smokes is unfit for the practice of Karma Yoga. He becomes dull when he cannot get a whiff of smoke. He cannot work in the absence of cigarettes. He wastes his money that can be very well utilised in the service of others. A Karma-yogi should be strictly free from the evil habit of smoking.

Smoking is an evil habit. Smokers bring a little bit of philosophy and medical opinion in support of their principles. They say: "Smoking keeps bowels free. I get a good motion in the morning. It is very exhilarating to the lungs, brain and the heart. When I sit for meditation after a smoke, I get nice meditation. Why should I give it up?" Very sound philosophy! They bring in ingenious arguments to support their evil habit. They cannot get rid of this evil habit. They are heavy smokers who can finish a tin of cigarettes within five minutes. This habit starts from early boyhood. A little boy gets a curiosity smoking. He stealthily removes a cigarette from his elder brother's pocket and tries a first smoke. He gets little tickling of nerves and hence he continues stealing daily. After some time he arrives at a stage when he finds it extremely hard to manage with a few cigarettes. He begins to steal money to get a tin of cigarettes independently. The father, brothers and sisters are all heavy smokers. They are the Gurus for these little boys for initiation in smoking. What a nasty state of affairs! Horrible indeed is the sight!

The parents are wholly and solely responsible for the evil conduct of their sons and daughters. Any intoxicant breeds in a bad habit soon and the man finds it difficult to give up the habit.

He falls a prey to smoking. Maya havocks through habits. This is the secret of her workings. You will not get an iota of benefit from smoking. Pray, give up this wrong, foolish imagination. Money is simply wasted. Smoking brings irritable heart, "tobacco heart" and amblyopia and other deadly diseases of the eyes and nicotine poisoning of the system. Various nervous diseases and impotency also develop.

Short-sightedness, palpitation of the heart, irregular action of the heart, angina pectoris (a painful disease of heart), gastric catarrh, throat troubles, inflammation of the wind pipe or trachea, tremors, muscular weakness etc., have been traced to smoking and the consequent nicotine poisoning. There is cumulative effect of nicotine from protracted smoking. The nicotine accumulates in the system by the addition of slow doses and produces deleterious effects on the constitution, various systems and different organs.

The correction of any evil habit is very simple. An advocate was a terrible smoker for a period of fifteen years. With one strong and powerful will he abandoned it entirely. Feel strongly first that you have got an evil habit and feel strongly also that you should give up that evil habit immediately. Think strongly of the advantages of sobriety and temperance. Then you have already attained success. Will strongly: "I will give up this intolerable habit this very second." You will succeed. Giving up any bad habit at once is better. The habit of slowly giving up by gradual reduction generally does not turn out to be productive of good results. Beware of recurrences. Turn your face resolutely when a little temptation tries to reappear. Keep the mind fully occupied in your work. Be always busy. Entertain a strong desire: "I must become a great man presently." All these habits will take to their heels. Feel strongly: "I must become a spiritual man." All these habits will fly away. Use your subconscious mind for the eradication of your habits. It is your intimate bosom friend with whom you should keep companionship at all times. He will make matters all right. Establish new and healthy habits. Develop your will also. Give up bad company and always enjoy Satsanga or the company of learned Sadhus and Mahatmas. Their strong currents will overhaul your evil habits. Prayer, Japa and meditation will also help in the eradication of this evil habit. There is nothing impossible under the sun. Where there is a will there is a way.

SUSPICION

SANKHA

Suspicion is the imagining of something without evidence or on slender evidence. It is mistrust.

Suspicion is conjecture with imperfect or with little or no evidence to support it, that something, especially something wrong exists or is about to happen. It is doubt.

Suspicion clouds the mind. It creates rupture among friends. It loses friends. It is a defect not in the heart, but in the brain.

Suspicion is the mark of a mean spirit and a base soul. A noble man suspects none.

Suspicion checks business, disposes kings to tyranny and irresolution, husbands to jealousy and hatred.

Freedom from suspicion promotes happiness in man. Suspicion is an enemy to happiness.

Ignorance is the mother of suspicion. Attain knowledge. Suspicion will vanish.

Suspicion is the poison of true friendship.

If suspicion enters your mind, love and confidence will go out.

Suspicions among thoughts are like bats among birds. They ever fly by twilight.

Suspicion is an enemy to virtue. A suspicious man will soon be corrupt. He who is corrupt is naturally suspicious.

Too much suspicious nature is very bad. This is the opposite to over-credulousness. Mind always moves in extremes. Husband suspects his wife always. The wife also suspects the husband. There is always tug-of-war and trouble in the house. The proprietor of a shop suspects his servants always. How can business go on smoothly? The world runs on faith. The directors of biggest railway companies in India are in England. They do not know in detail what exactly is going on in India. Yet the railways run smoothly. The directors have full confidence in the Agents, the officials. These people in turn believe the directors. The shareholders of the coffee, tea and rubber estates in India and Ceylon are in America and England and the business goes on well. Business runs on faith. If people are too much suspicious, friction and rupture will be always going on. Allow a margin and try the man. Do not go to extremes. Do not be over-credulous. Do not be over-suspicious. Keep to the golden medium.

TALE-BEARING

PISHUNATA

Tale-bearing is the act of maliciously telling tales or giving information. It is the act of spreading scandal.

A tale-bearer circulates idle and injurious tales with a view to making mischief. He is a scandal-monger, a meddling informer.

Do not go up and down as a tale-bearer among your people. Where there is no tale-bearer, all quarrels stop.

Tale-bearing is despicable. A tale-bearer is condemned by all.

Why do you meddle in the affairs of others unnecessarily? Abandon tale-bearing. Mind your business. You can save time. Spend your time profitably in prayer, Japa, Kirtan, meditation and study of religious books. You will attain eternal peace.

TIMIDITY

KAATARATA

Timidity is another meanness. This is faint-heartedness. This is a form of fear. This is also akin to shyness. A timid man has a chicken-heart. He is unfit for public activities and any kind of adventurous work. He is a toad that lives in a small well. He cannot run out to be a resourceful man in life. He cannot talk boldly to his superiors. He cannot deal boldly with his customers. How then can he expect prosperity? He is also afraid of losing his life, wife, children and property. He is afraid of public opinion. A timid man is more or less like a woman. Timidity must be eradicated by developing courage. Timidity is a curse. It weakens man. It checks his growth. It hinders his success in life.

TREACHERY

VISVASA-GHATA

Treachery is faithlessness.

A treacherer is a traitor.

There is no knife that cuts so sharply and with such poisoned blade as treachery.

Violation of allegiance, confidence or plighted fact is treachery. Traitorous or perfidious conduct is treachery.

A treacherous man is untrustworthy. He gives a specious and misleading impression. He puts on a good or fair appearance, but he is bad in character or nature. He betrays a trusted friend.

He smiles and laughs, but cuts the throat in the end.

You cannot place any confidence on a treacherous man. He is waiting for opportunities to plunder and kill you. He is deceptive.

'Treacherous' respects a man's private relations; 'traitorous' his public relation to his country. He is a treacherous friend and a traitorous subject or citizen.

One may be treacherous to his enemies as well as his friends. One may be traitorous to his country by abstaining to lend that aid which is in his power.

A soldier is traitorous who goes over to the side of the enemy against his country. A man is guilty of treasonable practices who attempts on the life of the ruler or aims at subverting his government.

Kill this treacherousness by practising honesty, reliability and trustworthiness.

VANITY

DAMBHA

Vanity is empty pride or ostentation. It is vain display or idle show.

Vanity is a feeling of shallow pride. It is inordinate self-esteem. It is conceit. It is emptiness.

Vanity is the quality or state of being vain or elated with a high opinion of one's own accomplishments or achievements. It is empty pride inspired by an overwhelming conceit of one's personal attainments or decorations and causing its possessor to be morbidly anxious for the notice, admiration and applause of others.

Vanity is that species of pride which, while it presumes upon a degree of superiority in some particular articles, fondly courts the applause of everyone within its sphere of action, seeking every occasion to display some talents or some supposed excellence.

Vanity exposes a man to scorn and derision and ruins his character. He is ridiculed wherever he goes. Vanity is the foundation of the most ridiculous and contemptible vices of affectation and uttering falsehood.

A man of vanity takes immense delight to speak of himself but he knows not others do not like to hear of him.

A man of vanity is arrogant. He is puffed up with pride. He does not hear the wise counsels of elders. He cares not for the judgment and opinion of others.

He treats others with insolence. He treats his inferiors with contempt and impudence. He puts on showy dress and walks in the public street. He casts round his eyes and courts observation.

He takes immense delight in hearing and speaking of himself throughout the day. He gossips and wastes his time.

Vanity is the mother. Affectation is the darling daughter. Pride and vanity are merely different shades of the same feeling. A man of pride has at least something, but a man of vanity is absolutely empty.

One does not know anything of Yoga. He may know a few Asanas, but he poses as a great Yogi of Nirvikalpa Samadhi. This is one form of vanity.

One does not know anything of Vedanta. He might have learnt a bit of Vicharasagara and Panchadasi; but he poses as a realised Sage. This is another form of vanity.

Even a fool, a porter, a wood-cutter, wishes to have his own admirers. Vanity is so rooted in the heart of every man.

Vanity is attached to the opinion of others while conceit is perfectly satisfied with its opinion of itself.

Everyone cherishes vanity at the bottom of his heart. Even the crow, the pig or the deformed man thinks himself good-looking and beautiful.

This world is a vanity fair. It is a scene of vanity and folly. It is the world of fashion. It is a collection of the most alluring temptations of the world.

A learned Pundit who is versed in the Sastras and who is proud of his knowledge in vain without any spiritual Anubhava is pitiable indeed. He is like a peacock. He is fond of pedantry and arguments. He engages himself in lingual warfare and intellectual gymnastics. He is a *'Dukrin Karane'* of Sri Sankara's Bhaja Govindam song. Surely high sounding Johnsonian words cannot make a man pious.

Even if you know the Gita, the Upanishads and the Brahma Sutras by heart what would all these profit you if you have not got the Grace of the Lord and Anubhava? You will be like the ass which carries a heavy load of sandal-wood on its back. Have you not heard the stories of Bharadwaja and Narada who carried a cart-load of religious books to Indra and Sanat Kumara respectively?

What you have learnt is only a handful. What you have not learnt is an oceanful. False learning makes one proud and self-conceited.

Do not think much of yourself and your learning. This is pure self-conceit.

Vanity is exaggerated pride. A proud man possesses at least something either physical or mental. But a man of vanity (Dambha) or hypocrisy does not possess anything and yet he thinks that he is superior to all.

Some aspirants have got more vanity than worldlings. They are proud of their moral virtues, some sort of Siddhis and their spirituality and Samadhi.

Moral and spiritual pride are more dangerous than the ordinary pride of wealth and power. Also they are more difficult to be eradicated. Aspirants should be ever vigilant and cautious. They should always keep up the spirit of service and humanity.

VILLY VALLYING

DISCUSSING TOO MUCH

Some people in whom the reason has developed have got the habit of entering into unnecessary controversies and discussions. They have got Tarkika Buddhi. They cannot remain quiet even for a second. They will create opportunities for heated debates. Too much discussions end in enmity and hostility. Much energy is wasted in useless discussions. Intellect is a help if it is used in the right direction of Atmic Vichara. Intellect is a hindrance if it is used in unnecessary discussions. Intellect takes the aspirant to the threshold of intuition. Thus far and no further. Reason helps in inferring the existence of God and finding out suitable methods for Self-realisation. Intuition transcends reason but does not contradict reason. Intuition is direct perception of Truth. There is no reasoning here. Reasoning concerns matters of physical plane. Wherever there is why and wherefore there is reasoning. In transcendental matters which are beyond the reach of reason, reason is of no use.

Intellect helps a lot in reflection and ratiocination. But people in whom reasoning has highly developed become sceptical. Their reason becomes perverted also. They lose faith in the Vedas and in the teachings of Mahatmas. They say: "We are rationalists. We cannot believe anything which does not appeal to our reason. We do not believe the Upanishads. We reject anything that does not come within the domain of reason. We have no faith in God and Sat-Gurus." Those so-called rationalists are a type of atheists only. It is very difficult to convince them. They have an impure, perverted reason. Thoughts of God cannot enter their brains. They will not do any kind of spiritual Sadhana. They say: "Show us your Brahman of the Upanishads or Isvara of the Bhaktas." Those who are of doubting nature will perish. Reason is a finite instrument. It cannot explain many mysterious problems of life. Those who are free from the so-called rationalism and scepticism can march in the path of God-realisation.

WORRY

Worry is tearing oneself with anxiety, vexation, trouble, perplexity, etc., as the worry of business, the worry of politics, the cares and worries of life.

Do not anticipate trouble or worry about what may never happen.

Keep yourself always very busy. Be doing something useful. This is the surest antidote for worry.

No one has yet been able to claim any good thing through worry. Then, why worry?

It is not the cares of today, but the cares of tomorrow that weigh you down. When tomorrow's burden is added to the burden of today, then the weight is more than a man can bear.

Worry not over what is past. Forget it.

Do not worry about things which are not likely to happen. "Sufficient unto the day is the evil thereof."

Worry is uneasiness in mind by reason of cares or solicitude. It is a state of perplexing care, anxiety or annoyance. It is distracting or disturbing care or occasion for anxiety. It is vexation, fret.

Worry is harassing turmoil as the worry of business, the worry of politics, the worry of a householder. We generally say: "The cares and worries of life here are formidable."

Worry kills a man. It destroys his joys of life. It is a canker or cancer that slowly eats away a man. It wears you out.

Hard work with a peaceful, harmonious mind will never kill anyone. It builds up the system and prolongs life but worry kills a man. It shortens life.

Do not worry over what is past. Forget it. No one has yet been able to claim any good thing through worry.

Do not worry about things which are likely to happen, so often they don't. Sufficient for the day is the evil thereof.

The surest antidote or penicillin injection for worry is to keep busy. Do always something useful.

Do your best and leave the rest to God. Do not worry. You are indeed blessed now.

DESTROY EVIL VRITTIS

1. Lust (Kama)   Brahmacharya, Mumukshutva.
2. Anger (Krodha)   Love, Kshama (forgiveness), mercy (Daya), Maitri (friendship), Santi, Dhriti (patience), Ahimsa.
3. Pride (Mada)   Humility (Namrata or Vinaya).
4. Greed (Lobha)   Honesty, disinterestedness, generosity, Santosha (contentment), Aparigraha (non-covetousness).
5. Jealousy (Irshya)   Nobility (Udarata), magnanimity, Mudita (complacency).
6. Moha (delusion)   Viveka (discrimination).
7. Dambha (vanity, hypocrisy)   Simplicity.
8. Darpa (arrogance)   Politeness, Hri (modesty).
9. Paisunam, (cunningness, crookedness)   Arjava Straightforwardness.

10. Parushyam   Mardavam (mildness).
    (harshness)
11. Raga (attachment)   Vairagya.
12. Insincerity   Sraddha (faith).
    (Asraddha)
13. Fickleness   Determination, Nischaya
    (Chanchalatvam)   Vritti (Adhyavasya).

LIST OF VICES TO BE ERADICATED

(Take a copy of this and hang it in a prominent place in your house.)

Ambition	Anger
Arrogance	Attachment
Avaricious nature	Avenging nature
Backbiting	Censure and criticism
Conceit	Committing cruel and atrocious deeds
Crooked-mindedness	Deceitful nature
Cruelty	Depression
Desire	Double-dealing
Dullness	Eating more than enough and very often
Egoism	
Envy	Evil thoughts and habits
Godlessness	Harsh words
Hatred	Hypocrisy
Jealousy	Laziness
Lust	Mischief-mongering
Merciless nature	Miserliness
Obstinacy	Pride
Scandal-mongering	Selfishness
Tale-bearing	Telling lies
Unchaste look	

MINOR VICES

Arguing nature	Agitation of mind
Belittling	Bragging
Brooding over nothing	Building castles in the air
Chicanery	Degrading others
Delusion	Despondency
Diplomacy	Drinking habit

Emotions
Fault finding
Gambling
Greed
Humbug
Impertinence
Indolence
Interrupting nature
Killing ants and
    other small insects
Mental Weakness
Mocking at others
Novel-reading
Obscurity
Pedantry
Pettiness
Planning and scheming
Protesting nature
Rashness
Retaliating
Roguery
Self-conceit
Slander
Sleeping during day time
Smoking habit
Stubborn nature
Talking too much
Unnecessary arguments
Unsteady mind
Vanity
Wasting time for nothing
    and in useless company

Enmity
Fighting nature
Gloomy appearance
Haughtiness
Ill-treating the menials
Improper actions
Injustice
Irritability
Looking into others' faults
Maliciousness
Misbehaving
Negligence
Obloquy
Ostentatious nature
Persecution
Pilfering
Procrastinating
Quarrelling nature
Restlessness
Revenging nature
Rudeness
Showing one's skill and
    power before others
Slothful nature
Stagnation
Talking ill of others
To have a honied tongue
    and a gall-heart
Using obscene words
Wandering nature
Worrying habit

TWENTY IMPORTANT
SPIRITUAL INSTRUCTIONS
By
H.H. Sri Swami Sivanandaji Maharaj

1. BRAHMA-MUHURTA: Get up at 4 a.m. daily. This is Brahmamuhurta which is extremely favourable for meditation on God.

2. ASANA: Sit on Padma, Siddha or Sukha Asana for Japa and meditation for half an hour, facing the east or the north. Increase the period gradually to three hours. Do Sirshasana and Sarvangasana for keeping up Brahmacharya and health. Take light physical exercises as walking, etc., regularly. Do twenty Pranayamas.

3. JAPA: Repeat any Mantra as pure Om or Om Namo Narayanaya, Om Namah Sivaya, Om Namo Bhagavate Vasudevaya, Om Saravanabhavaya Namah, Sita Ram, Sri Ram, Hari Om, or Gayatri, according to your taste or inclination, from 108 to 21,600 times daily.

4. DIETETIC DISCIPLINE: Take Sattvic food, Suddha Ahara. Give up chillies, tamarind, garlic, onion, sour articles, oil, mustard, asafoetida. Observe moderation in diet (Mitahara). Do not overload the stomach. Give up those things which the mind likes best for a fortnight in a year. Eat simple food. Milk and fruits help concentration. Take food as medicine to keep the life going. Eating for enjoyment is sin. Give up salt and sugar for a month. You must be able to live on rice, Dhal and bread without any chutni. Do not ask for extra salt for Dhal and sugar for tea, coffee or milk.

5. MEDITATION-ROOM: Have a separate meditation-room under lock and key.

6. CHARITY: Do charity regularly, every month, or even daily according to your means, say six paise per rupee.

7. SVADHYAYA: Study systematically the Gita, the Ramayana, the Bhagavata, Sri Vishnu-Sahasranama, Lalita-Sahasranama, Aditya Hridaya, Upanishads or Yoga Vasishtha, the Bible, Zend Avesta, the Koran, the Tripitakas, the Granth Sahib, etc., from half an hour to one hour daily and have Suddha Vichara.

8. BRAHMACHARYA: Preserve the vital force (Veerya) very, very carefully. Veerya is God in motion or manifestation—Vibhuti. Veerya is all power. Veerya is all money. Veerya is the essence of life, thought and intelligence.